D1563173

Equal to
the Occasion

Eleanore Bushnell and
Don W. Driggs
*The Nevada Constitution: Origin and
Growth* (6th ed., 1984)

Ralph J. Roske
*His Own Counsel: The Life and Times
of Lyman Trumbull* (1979)

Mary Ellen Glass
*Nevada's Turbulent '50s: Decade of
Political and Economic Change*
(1981)

Joseph A. Fry
*Henry S. Sanford: Diplomacy and
Business in Nineteenth-Century
America* (1982)

Jerome E. Edwards
*Pat McCarran: Political Boss of
Nevada* (1982)

Russell R. Elliott
*Servant of Power: A Political
Biography of Senator William M.
Stewart* (1983)

Donald R. Abbe
*Austin and the Reese River Mining
District: Nevada's Forgotten Frontier*
(1985)

Anne B. Howard
*The Long Campaign: A Biography of
Anne Martin* (1985)

Sally Zanjani and Guy Louis Rocha
*The Ignoble Conspiracy: Radicalism
on Trial in Nevada* (1986)

James W. Hulse
*Forty Years in the Wilderness:
Impressions of Nevada, 1940–1980*
(1986)

Jacqueline Baker Barnhart
*The Fair but Frail: Prostitution in San
Francisco, 1849–1900* (1986)

Marion Merriman and Warren Lerude
*American Commander in Spain:
Robert Hale Merriman and the
Abraham Lincoln Brigade* (1986)

A. Costandina Titus
*Bombs in the Backyard: Atomic
Testing and American Politics* (1986)

Wilbur S. Shepperson, ed.
*East of Eden, West of Zion: Essays on
Nevada* (1989)

John Dombrink and
William N. Thompson
*The Last Resort: Success and Failure
in Campaigns for Casinos* (1989)

Kevin J. Mullen
*Let Justice Be Done: Crime and
Politics in Early San Francisco* (1989)

Eugene P. Moehring
*Resort City in the Sunbelt: Las Vegas,
1930–1970* (1989)

Sherilyn Cox Bennion
*Equal to the Occasion:
Women Editors of the
Nineteenth-Century West*

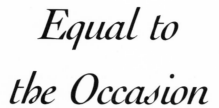

Equal to the Occasion

Women Editors of the

Nineteenth-Century West

 Sherilyn Cox Bennion

University of Nevada Press
Reno and Las Vegas

Nevada Studies in History and Political Science No. 30
Studies Editor: Wilbur S. Shepperson

Library of Congress Cataloging-in-Publication Data
Bennion, Sherilyn Cox, 1935–
Equal to the occasion : women editors of the nineteenth-century West /
Sherilyn Cox Bennion.
   p.   cm. — (Nevada studies in history and political science ; no. 30)
Includes bibliographical references and index.
ISBN 0-87417-163-6 (alk. paper)
1. Women journalists—West (U.S.)—Biography.   2. Editors—West (U.S.)—Biography.
3. Journalism—West (U.S.)—History—19th century.   I. Title.   II. Series.
PN4872.B46   1990
070.4'1'0922—dc20
[B]   90-39025
CIP

University of Nevada Press, Reno, Nevada 89557 USA
Copyright © 1990 University of Nevada Press
Designed by Joanna Hill
Printed in the United States of America

2 4 6 8 9 7 5 3 1

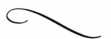

Contents

Preface

Journalism historian Frank Luther Mott, in his history of American magazines, referred to a British writer who said on a visit to the United States that "all papers go from east to west, with the sun, and never in the opposite direction." Mott attributed this phenomenon to the lack of great publishing houses and a settled reading public in the West. Certainly, with a larger population base from which to draw, the eastern publications were more numerous and had higher circulations, which meant that more files survived and historians paid them more attention. On the other hand, easterners sought news of the West, as well. Judging by western papers' claims of far-flung circulations and published letters from eastern readers, western news in eastern papers sometimes came from the western periodicals. News and papers moved both ways.

If western publications generally have suffered from the neglect of historians, researchers have paid even less attention to the western periodicals edited by women. With this work I hope to make a start toward redressing that lack. The book covers the Far West of the nineteenth century—Alaska, Arizona, California, Colorado, Hawaii, Idaho, Montana, Nevada, New Mexico, Oregon, Utah, Washington, and Wyoming—and the period from 1854, when the West's first woman editor began work, to 1900, a convenient cut-off point. Alaska and Montana, with small populations and few towns, had no women editors during that period.

The book's title comes from the introductory quotation to chapter 1. A male editor used the phrase in commending eighteen-year-old Candace

Alice De Witt for improvements she had made in Utah's *Piute Pioneer* upon assuming editorship. Each chapter treats two or three editors of a particular kind of publication, such as weekly newspapers, religious papers, medical and health journals, or literary magazines. Every chapter begins with a section that places the periodicals in the context of their times and moves on to cover what is known about the editors' lives and descriptions of their publications, in chronological order.

Several considerations came into play in selecting the editors to be included. I attempted to cover the geographical area as widely as possible, with both urban and rural representation, and to choose editors from throughout the forty-six years under consideration. I looked for women of different ages, with different backgrounds and life situations, so the variety of their experiences would be apparent. More practically, I had to limit myself to those about whom biographical information could be found. That eliminated many women of whose lives I could glimpse only tantalizing fragments. Finally, I generally chose editors of publications of which examples had survived—if not in the form of complete files, at least in isolated copies. I felt that I needed to see what the editors had produced in order to form as complete an impression of them as possible. Their papers revealed much about their ideas and personalities. California editors dominate, simply because of their numbers, but the proportion they comprise in the book actually is less than the proportion they comprise in the total number of editors.

Deciding on which editors to include was only one of a myriad of choices I faced as I wrote the book, ranging from substantive to stylistic. For example, I chose to include general statements about publication size in the introduction, noting only departures from the norm in the individual descriptions. I retained original spellings in quotations.

Some material in the book appeared earlier in different forms in *American Journalism*, *Brigham Young University Studies*, *Idaho Yesterdays*, *Journalism Quarterly*, *The Pacific Historian*, and the *Utah Historical Quarterly*. The bibliography at the end of the book includes references to these articles.

When a summer research fellowship from the Historical Department of the Church of Jesus Christ of Latter-day Saints took me in the mid-1970s to the church library in Salt Lake City to look at Emmeline B. Wells and the *Woman's Exponent*, I had no idea that I had embarked on a lengthy project that would culminate in this book. I found references in the *Expo-*

nent to other women who edited periodicals in other western states and territories, and I became curious about them. I began to jot down names, and then I applied for and was awarded the Jo Caldwell Meyer Grant by Women in Communications, Inc., which enabled me to spend a summer looking at early magazines for women. The search broadened as more names cropped up, and I began a systematic effort to uncover them. Perhaps I used the word "culminate" inaccurately in referring to this book; a lifetime's worth of research material exists for someone interested in women editors of the West.

Many persons and institutions have helped me reach this point. Libraries, historical societies, and individuals have been uniformly cooperative. Large libraries with extensive collections of materials on women and the West, like the historical societies of Wisconsin and Kansas, have taken time to reply to repeated requests. Mary-Ellen Jones of The Bancroft Library at the University of California, Berkeley, unearthed materials in preparation for my visits and checked citations for me after I returned home and discovered that I had neglected to note a date or page number for a crucial quotation. Karen Gash of the University of Nevada, Reno, helped me find and document the women editors of Nevada. Librarians of small local museums and county historical collections proved equally helpful, searching through old newspapers and giving me names of sources who might be contacted. Larry Odoms of the Oakland Public Library joined me in unraveling the adventures of Sarah Moore Clarke.

Closer to home, Sherry Gordon of the Humboldt State University library explored the outer limits of the possibilities of the interlibrary loan service to find collections willing to lend obscure books and photocopy rare magazine articles. My husband and children have exercised patience as my time for them became limited and my temper short, and my friends and colleagues have prodded me with the question reluctant writers least like to hear, "How's the book coming?" My parents never wavered from their conviction that I could accomplish anything I put my mind to. Staff members at the University of Nevada Press, particularly Editor-in-Chief Nicholas M. Cady and Editor Cynthia Wood, provided both moral support and practical help. Finally, I owe thanks to Professor Emeritus Roland E. Wolseley of Syracuse University, who gave his graduate students an example of industry and integrity that continues to inspire us.

CHAPTER 1

Introduction

With all due respect for ex-editor Brunell of the Piute Pioneer, there has come a great change in that paper since C. A. De Witt (who is a maiden fair, fully equal to the occasion), took hold of the editorial reins. It reminds one of the change a female is competent of making in the appearance of some bachelor's hall after giving it a going over for about ten minutes.[1]
—The Wasatch Wave, *January 1, 1898*

 Candace Alice De Witt, the "maiden fair" referred to above, happened into newspaper editing. Born in Manti, Utah, in 1879, she moved with her family to Marysvale in Piute County, Utah, in 1881 and grew up there. A local schoolteacher, J. F. Brunell, founded the *Piute Pioneer* in 1896, and De Witt assisted him until his death in November 1897. Then, at the age of eighteen, she became editor.

Actually, the *Pioneer* did not require much editing. Typical of many small-town papers, the four-page weekly had preprinted front and back pages which were supplied by a national service. These six-column pages featured small woodcut illustrations and many short articles, jokes, and ads for patent medicines. The articles had titles such as "Temperature in Tunnels," "A Submarine Boat," and "An Oriental Beauty."[2] Legal notices and local ads filled two-thirds of pages 2 and 3. The remaining third was not entirely original, either. Like other nineteenth-century editors, De Witt clipped exchanges from other papers and used them liberally. They might give Utah news, offer poetry or humor, or—like a note that Ulysses S. Grant had predicted easy capture of Havana—comment on the national scene.[3] Piute County material was limited to advertising, legal notices, and a few news notes from Marysvale and nearby Circleville. For example, the issue for March 26, 1898, ran a tongue-in-cheek poetic tribute written from prison by a convicted burglar to his captor, along with the ads and notices.

De Witt kept the editorship for six months, after which she sold the paper but continued her journalistic work. According to an obituary, she assisted her successor by setting type and writing articles "boosting the mining activities of the camp." And as other editors came on board, she would help each to "get a line on the town conditions." After the paper moved, she became its Marysvale correspondent.[4]

In the meantime, De Witt married Roland Blakeslee in 1901 and had three daughters. She also became active in politics, acting as county secretary of the Democratic party for a number of years and as the only woman Democratic county chairman in the state.[5] She served as Marysvale city treasurer under two administrations and as town clerk for fifteen months before her death in 1927.

De Witt was one of almost three hundred women who edited more than 250 publications in the eleven western states of Arizona, California, Colorado, Hawaii, Idaho, Nevada, New Mexico, Oregon, Utah, Washington, and Wyoming between 1854 and 1899. This total includes editors with feminine first names or titles of Miss or Mrs. listed in directories, bibliographies, histories, and contemporary periodicals. Based on counts of female and male editors in directories for 1870, 1880, 1890, and 1900, the proportion of women remained stable at about 1 percent until the end of the century, when it increased to 2 percent.[6]

The first of the western women editors probably was Sarah Moore Clarke, who began publishing *The Contra Costa* in Oakland, California, in September 1854, only eight years after the founding of California's first English-language newspaper. Her weekly paper was intended, according to a California historian, "to do service as a ladies' paper, as well as in the drudgery of a general news organ."[7]

California, most populous of the western states, held a monopoly on women editors throughout the 1850s, but in the 1860s they could be found in four of the thirteen western states and territories. Table 1.1 shows that by the end of the century only Alaska and Montana had no women edi-

TABLE 1.1

Women Editors of the Nineteenth-Century West
According to Period of Activity

State	1850s	1860s	1870s	1880s	1890s	Total
Alaska						
Arizona			1	2	2	5
California	6	9	15	25	74	129
Colorado			3	13	39	55
Hawaii					1	1
Idaho		2		1	2	5
Montana						
Nevada			4	3	4	11
New Mexico					3	3
Oregon		1	2	6	13	22
Utah			3	3	13	19
Washington			1	5	12	18
Wyoming					4	4
Total	6	12	29	58	167	272

Note: Many editors worked during more than one decade, so the totals for all decades add up to more than the total number of individual editors.

tors. California maintained its numerical lead with more than half the total number during the 1860s and 1870s, and slightly less than half thereafter. As geographical distribution widened, numbers increased, doubling each decade until the 1890s, when an even more dramatic jump occurred— from 58 in the 1880s to 167.

The editors were a varied lot. In age they ranged from thirteen-year-old Katherine Bagg, who published *The Bug-Hunter* in 1891, in Tombstone, Arizona, to Mary Hayes-Chynoweth, founder of the True Life Church in San Jose, California, who edited her church's magazine, *The True Life*, from 1890 until her death at eighty years of age in 1905. They came from all economic and social levels, but predominantly from middle-class backgrounds. In an era of limited educational opportunities, most had several years of schooling.

Usually they worked independently rather than with co-editors. Only 22 percent held joint positions. Of that percentage, about one-third shared the editorship with other women, half with women having the same last name. Two-thirds of the shared editorships were with men, and two-thirds of the men, judging primarily by last names, were the women's husbands. Some of them made light of their marital status. Caroline Romney, who founded *The Durango Record* in 1880, told readers, "The rumor . . . that the editor of this paper is about to be married is without foundation. In fact, we can't afford to support a husband yet."[8] Some of the women undoubtedly inherited their papers from husbands or fathers, but directories provide no way of determining how many. Often, they recruited family members to assist with writing and production of their publications.

Editorial careers usually lasted only a short time. *The Ladies' Mite*—published perhaps two or three times by The Ladies' Mite Association of Idaho City, Idaho, to raise money for the First Baptist Church of that city—was undoubtedly the only journalistic venture of its editors, identified in the paper only as Mrs. Butler and Mrs. Rees. At the other end of the longevity scale, Emmeline B. Wells had a thirty-seven-year career as editor of the *Woman's Exponent* in Salt Lake City, Utah. She took it over in 1877 when she was forty-nine and remained at the helm until she was eighty-six. However, 43 percent of the women identified acted as editors for less than two years. Another 26 percent edited publications for only two to three years, and 14 percent for four or five years. Only 16 percent worked as editors for more than five years, and only 2 percent for more than twenty years.[9]

Of course, many men also took up editing briefly and then abandoned it. Aspiring publishers could come by the modest amounts of capital required to start a periodical fairly easily, and journalism attracted entrepreneurs and idealists of both sexes who had little or no experience in the field. When readers or advertisers, or both, proved unresponsive, these editors moved on to other projects, in or out of journalism. A poem that Wyoming editors printed in 1870 memorialized the ephemeral publications:

> Leaf by leaf the roses fall,
> Dime by dime the purse runs dry;
> One by one, beyond recall,
> Mushroom papers droop and die.[10]

The types of publications edited by the women varied as much as did the women themselves. A few titles suggest their diversity: *Christian Workman, Insurance Sun, Revista Hispano-Americana, Political Age, Out of Doors for Women, Western Society, Indian Advance, Temperance Star, Music Life, Salt Lake Sanitarian, Pacific Boys and Girls*. Seven used lan-

TABLE 1.2

Types of Publications Edited by Women in the Nineteenth-Century West

State	Newspapers		Specialized Periodicals		
	Daily	Weekly or Semi-Weekly	Weekly	Monthly or Semi-Monthly	Quarterly
Alaska					
Arizona	1	2		1	
California	5	51	21	48	3
Colorado	2	32	5	11	
Hawaii		1			
Idaho		2	2		
Montana					
Nevada	2	2		5	
New Mexico		3			
Oregon	1	5	5	9	
Utah		9		6	
Washington		8	4	3	
Wyoming		5			
Total	11	120	37	83	3
Percentage of Total	4	47	15	33	1

Note: The total of 254 publications does not correspond exactly with the number of women working as editors, because some edited more than one type of publication. Each publication is given a separate entry in this table. In addition, periodicity could not be confirmed for ten publications (4 percent).

guages other than English, including Spanish, French, Italian, Hawaiian, and Norwegian and Danish.

Despite the exotic flavor of some of these titles, however, most of the women edited conventional small-town weeklies. As Table 1.2 shows, weekly or semi-weekly newspapers comprised nearly half of the publications edited by women. If daily newspapers are added, the proportion becomes just over half. The newspapers most often appeared in four tabloid-sized pages.

The specialized periodicals usually came out monthly or semi-monthly, with some weeklies and a few quarterlies. In size, they ranged from six-by-nine inches to tabloid, but the preferred measurements were about seven-by-ten inches. Their subjects defy classification in the case of hybrids like the *Medico-Literary Journal* and highly personal efforts like *The Queen Bee*, whose editor, Caroline Nichols Churchill, came to be known by the name of her paper. The specialized publications made up 18 percent of the total, and papers with unidentifiable subject matter comprised another 18 percent. Publications directed toward women totaled 23 percent, and another 6 percent addressed the topic of suffrage, also probably reaching an audience consisting primarily of women. Religious publications came next in number to those directed principally toward women, with 15 percent of the total. Temperance papers, with 10 percent, and literary and health periodicals, with 5 percent each, followed.

In all types of publications, the use of illustrations increased dramatically toward the turn of the century, although the small weekly newspapers adopted new technologies for reproduction of illustrations more slowly than did the monthly magazines of the cities. From an occasional woodcut used to embellish a title, an ad, or an article, the publications moved to use of engravings to illustrate the people and places they treated. Several magazines prided themselves on the number and quality of their engravings, and a few, as the century ended, even experimented with the new halftone photoengraving process.

In spite of such general trends, one searches in vain for the typical publication edited by a woman or the typical woman editor. An attempt to develop a definitive list of characteristics that differentiated women editors and their periodicals from men and the papers they edited also proves futile. At best, an examination of the women, their publications, and the situations in which they worked may reveal patterns that illuminate their experiences and their place in the nineteenth-century West.

Two broad contexts prove significant to this effort, those of the frontier woman and of frontier journalism. Writings concerning women's frontier experiences have proliferated in recent years, and journalism historians have begun to synthesize and generalize from the many histories of individual frontier editors and periodicals, but attempts to relate these two endeavors have been few. One may begin this effort by looking at the frontier woman.

Until recently few historians did. They told the story of the frontier in terms of its exploration and conquest by men. Women received mention in passing or not at all. If historians recognized women, they tended to depict them in stereotypes; the heroines of a work published in 1958 resemble those of one dating from 1876.[11] The frontier woman, in these versions, came West only to found a new home. She dreamed of a log cabin where she could guard the health and life of her household. She provided the cohesive force that held society together. A miracle of fortitude and patience, she soothed, strengthened, and cheered. A 1918 portrait is a classic of this genre:

> The chief figure of the American West, the figure of the ages, is not the long-haired, fringed-legging man riding a raw-boned pony, but the gaunt and sad-faced woman sitting on the front seat of the wagon, following her lord where he might lead, her face hidden in the same ragged sunbonnet which had crossed the Appalachians and the Missouri long before. That was America, my brethren! There was the seed of America's wealth. There was the great romance of all America—the woman in the sunbonnet; and not, after all, the hero with the rifle across his saddle horn.[12]

Granted, her civilizing mission sometimes took this heroine beyond the threshold of her log cabin, but as schoolmarm, rooming-house proprietor, or church fund-raiser she practiced a nurturing role.

Other stereotypes occasionally appeared—the woman of easy virtue or the strident crusader for suffrage or temperance, for example. Only with the publication of works by feminist historians in the late 1970s and early 1980s were the stereotypes attacked. Some writers aimed primarily to establish the basic fact of women's presence at all stages of frontier development, while others sought to debunk the myths that had grown up around the sunbonneted saint, or to demonstrate the overlapping of the stereotypical roles traditionally seen as mutually exclusive.

Interpretations differed. One book, providing historic photographs and commentary, emphasized the autonomy "never before dreamed of" that women found in the West.[13] A second came to the conclusion that "as equally active and capable participants in the family's struggle for survival, women earned the growing respect of their husbands, their children, and their communities."[14] An article suggested that frontier women spoke out on behalf of particular moral values and formed networks from which to construct movements and alliances, even though they held narrow views of themselves, their proper social roles, and their goals.[15]

Other authors wrote that men made the final decision to go west, that women depended upon men for status, and that they took up unfamiliar, demanding roles only reluctantly.[16] One concluded that women continued to value themselves and be valued for their traditional qualities and that the reality of the frontier, far from encouraging rejection of their civilizing mission, actually reaffirmed it.[17]

Between the extremes, one writer stated that women seized many opportunities for independence but continued to cling to their traditional roles.[18] Certainly, another concluded, western women did not restrict themselves to the traditional woman's place. While rarely attempting a complete break with past roles and even while giving lip service to ideas of the cult of true womanhood, they expanded their activities on the economic front and engaged in a number of unconventional careers. Sometimes from necessity, sometimes by choice, they entered into and succeeded at new professions.[19]

Such disparate viewpoints at least lead to the conclusion that no archetypal western woman existed. The frontier woman was not one, but a multitude. This realization represents one major contribution of recent scholarship. Another is the recognition that frontier women, along with men, thought and acted within a network of social, economic, and political influences, including the mass media, defined during the nineteenth century as books, magazines, and newspapers. Of these, the most pervasive and accessible was the weekly newspaper of general interest. As villages expanded into cities, specialized publications in newspaper or magazine format followed the general-interest weeklies.

Although the frontier press has received far less attention than the frontier woman, it also has had its historians, along with changes in perspective as recent scholarship has expanded the information available and suggested new interpretations. Journalism's stereotypical equivalent of the sunbonneted saints might be the migratory newspapermen, aiming "not at the known needs of an existing community but at the needs of some future community for which they desperately hoped." The newspaper, like the musket, "became a weapon and a tool, to conquer the forest and to build new communities." It functioned as a speculative enterprise, accompanying the earliest stages of settlement and concerning itself primarily with boosterism.[20]

Systematic studies are rare, but it appears that this view is at best simplistic. A journalism historian looking at the eight western territories of 1880 determined that the 47 percent of counties with newspapers had larger and more rapidly growing populations, higher assessed valuations and tax payments per capita, and more industrial activity than those without papers. Even towns with recently established newspapers had solid and growing population bases. Growth potential seemed to be the key. Some papers appeared in places with few residents and problematical prospects, but hopeful publishers usually tried to minimize their risks by seeking locations with stable, growing populations and evidence of financial prosperity.[21]

If one divides frontier development into two main stages, the first characterized by scattered populations living in primitive conditions and the second marked by community building with more developed economic and social life, the newspaper may have been more characteristic of the second stage than of the first. Specialized periodicals, the type produced by half of the women editors, usually came at an even later stage of community development and tended to be located in the larger population centers.

A 1981 study of the Rocky Mountain mining frontier, however, painted a different picture. The author examined papers founded between 1859 and 1881 and stated, "Realizing the golden journalistic opportunities inherent in mining communities, men of print rushed to newly discovered diggings with an eagerness and intensity almost equal to that of the goldseekers."[22] Still, the author gave no indication of just how soon after the mining communities sprang up the journalists arrived, what determined which boomtowns they chose, or even what percentage of the towns had newspapers.

Even the assumption that the town newspaper would boost settlement and economic growth must be questioned. A journalism historian found editors on both sides of the conflict between cowboys and homesteaders, with cowboys representing frontier freedom and homesteaders the expansion of settlement. In Tombstone, Arizona, for example, one paper supported the sheriff and the cowboys, while the other sided with Marshal Virgil Earp and the town's civic leaders.[23]

Another common idea, that it was relatively easy for an enterprising man or woman to break into the newspaper business, probably holds. The frontier publisher usually served also as editor and reporter and often as typesetter. With a minimum of capital, the entrepreneur could purchase a small printing press and type and begin soliciting for readers and advertisers in the chosen town. Success at starting a newspaper, of course, did not necessarily mean success at running it. More papers failed than succeeded.

A stereotype with less empirical foundation is that of the editor as lovable, or not so lovable, eccentric. Until recently, books about western editors concentrated on the flamboyant, particularly those who used their newspapers in the service of some personal or political cause. One author explained that she would describe eleven Arizona editors and continued, "To this land of beauty and death, men continue to stride in search of gold, fame, adventure, and escape. From these pioneers develop ranchers, miners, businessmen, and settlers. We are concerned here with a unique breed of men that develop in this frontier—fighting editors."[24] Another writer titled his book *Print in a Wild Land* and concluded that "the Western men of print were moved less by a desire to publish what would please others than by a yen to tell them what was what."[25] Not only does this stereotype overlook the less colorful, and probably more common, editor who intended first of all to turn a profit, but, by referring only to men, it ignores completely the women editors of the West.

They were among those western women who entered somewhat unconventional careers, although a tradition of women as editors dated back to colonial times, and a few women had edited publications throughout the first half of the nineteenth century in the East. Western women had at least some precedents for the decision to step into the world of publishing, even if that decision was uncommon.

Journalism in the West attracted women who wrote and set type for periodicals as well as those who served as editors and publishers. Some women publishers hired men or other women to edit their papers. Census tables on occupations do not list publishers or editors separately, but they do provide totals for journalists and printers, broken down by sex for the first time in 1890. The states and territories covered in this book had 85 women journalists (4 percent of the total) in 1890 and 196 (7 percent) in 1900. The more plentiful printers totaled 344 (5 percent) in 1890 and 959 (10 percent) in 1900.[26]

Perhaps the acceptance of women as journalists, and particularly as editors and publishers, had something to do with a subconscious perception that women and the press shared certain common functions. Women, after all, brought civilization to the frontier, at least in the eyes of those who accepted the traditional ideas of a woman's place. They initiated the recruiting of teachers and preachers and organized literary societies and amateur theatricals. Newspapers, for their part, brought the printed word. Either as evidence of the arrival of civilization or as its precursor, they demonstrated that a literate community had come into existence, and their editorials often agitated for the same improvements sought by the women

—libraries, opera houses, and law and order. Women may have seen the editorial role as compatible with their natural tendencies, and communities may have accepted them because that perception was shared. The presence of women in the editorial chair was unusual but not remarkable, and women contributed significantly to western journalism in the nineteenth century.

Little notice has been given that contribution. One positive result of the almost total neglect of western women editors is that no stereotypical image of them has developed. In seeking to paint their portrait one faces a blank canvas, rather than a picture to be painted over. The end product must be a group portrait. The pages that follow present the sketches on which it may be based.

CHAPTER 2

By Women,
For Women

The Contra Costa *commenced September 22d, 1854. It was printed at the* Evening Journal *office, San Francisco, and edited by Mrs. S. M. Clarke, an estimable lady and accomplished writer. The* Contra Costa *was intended to do service as a ladies' paper, as well as in the drudgery of a general news organ. It was edited with much ability, but only lasted about one year, the editor's ill-health, as well as the limited sphere of support compelling her to retire from the field she occupied so well.*[1]

—*Edward C. Kemble, journalist and historian*

As the first identifiable woman editor of the western United States, Sarah Moore Clarke contributed to a list of periodicals for women that reached back to Philadelphia and its *Lady's Magazine* of 1792. Not until the 1820s, however, did women's names begin to appear as publishers or editors, and many of the prominent eastern women's magazines continued to be controlled by men. By 1850, women across the land were starting small periodicals intended for readers of their own sex.

An enterprising woman could start such a journal with very little capital by writing substantial amounts of material for each issue herself, recruiting aspiring writers for little or no pay, and using a considerable number of items clipped from other periodicals—a standard publishing practice of the times.

Most editors chose a highly miscellaneous format. They might have combined household hints with news of an armed insurrection in India, serialized romantic fiction with editorial pleas for sensible clothing fashions, sentimental poetry with articles about notable accomplishments of women in a man's world, then added a few essays about history or natural history. They usually had a wide range of interests themselves and assumed that their readers would enjoy an eclectic mix of topics and treatments. They sought to educate, as well as to entertain.

The early periodicals for women were closely related to the magazines of general literature, with literature more broadly defined than it is today. Indeed, they competed strenuously for readers, and the competition forced "some of the merely masculine periodicals to print fashion plates and household hints."[2] The women's magazines also resembled a large group of publications with "home" or "household" in their titles, like the *Home Alliance* of Woodland, California, and the *Pacific Household Journal* of Los Angeles. Although these included men in their prospective audiences, they no doubt attracted mainly women. The suffrage papers also developed an audience composed mainly of women, even though their editors certainly sought to win male subscribers as well.

In addition, a large group of more specialized publications appealed principally to women. Magazines for mothers offered advice and encouragement for those engaged in rearing families. Fashion magazines brought women news and illustrations of the latest styles, sometimes including dress patterns. Society papers told them about the latest doings of the socially prominent and laid down rules of acceptable social behavior; some added articles about arts and amusements. *Out of Doors for Women* illustrates the extent of specialization. Published from 1893 to 1896 in San Diego by Olive L. Orcutt, it concentrated on the pursuit of floriculture, although it included some articles on travel and other outdoor activities.

The women's club movement contributed another large group of periodicals. As women organized to fight against slavery and then to fight for suffrage, they saw the political and social benefits of societies and clubs, and these proliferated during the latter half of the nineteenth century. A writer for *McCall's Magazine* observed in 1899 that "women's clubs are started nowadays for almost every conceivable object, from the meritorious wearing of a short skirt on rainy days to the study of the *Niebelungenlied*." Even small towns had their clubs, and cities had many of them. Club women gathered together to form the General Federation of

Women's Clubs in 1889, with a foundation of fifty clubs, and by 1892 that number had doubled.[3] The federation was national, but individual states also had organizations representing their club women. At all levels, the clubs sponsored publications ranging from informal newsletters to attractive magazines. For example, Mary L. Strong edited the *Colorado Club Woman* in Pueblo from 1898 to 1902.

All of the categories of publications mentioned above had representatives in the West. This chapter presents the editors of three different types of periodicals for women—a general publication, which also was the first women's paper in the West; a literary paper for women; and a society paper.

California's first English-language newspaper began in 1846. By 1854, the number of periodicals published there had increased to fifty-four. During that year, only six years after the state's first newspaper appeared, the West's first woman editor made her debut.

Sarah Moore was born in Maine, probably in 1821. When and where she met and married Henry Kirk White Clarke is unknown. By 1854 the Clarkes lived in Alameda County, and at some point she bore a son. In reference works at the Oakland Public Library, her husband is listed as rancher, journalist, and pioneer member of the California bar.[4]

Clarke started *The Contra Costa* as a four-page weekly in September 1854, in Oakland. The one surviving copy dates from November 10, 1854. The modern reader must rely on the judgment of Edward C. Kemble, a journalist and historian of the same period, for the conclusion that Clarke actually intended *The Contra Costa* to be a woman's paper, for the content of the only surviving number closely resembles that of many general weeklies of the time.

The serial romance which concluded on the first page would have held special interest for women. Titled "The Infant Heir," it featured the good and beautiful orphan Violet Brandon, who, as the story ended, discovered the secret of her parentage, inherited a fortune, and married an adored suitor. Clarke also included a column called "The Children's Corner"—with a fable in this number about a wise mother bird who teaches her little ones not to be afraid of the dark—and an apology for the loss by her printers of the final episode of a continued story, which the fable replaced. Editorially, Clarke commented favorably on a proposal by the principal of the College School in Oakland "to extend the advantages of that Institution of learning to girls, as well as boys."

Apart from those three items, Clarke used a variety of news notes from near and far, editorial comments, exchanges, jokes, poetry, and legal notices, as well as a healthy quota of advertisements. The paper was lively and attractive in appearance. One note consisted of an apology for the "many small articles in bad taste, and for which we are not responsible" that had "frequently found their way into our columns, and given us much annoyance," blaming the San Francisco printers upon whom she was forced to rely due to lack of a printing press on the Oakland side of the San Francisco Bay.

Clarke had *The Contra Costa* printed at the office of the daily *San Francisco Evening Journal,* which also no doubt handled any job printing she attracted through announcements in her paper. Perhaps in response to her dissatisfaction, her husband bought the *Evening Journal* and kept it going until March 1856, when it died. Kemble stated that Sarah Clarke edited the *Evening Journal* as well as *The Contra Costa.*[5] Surviving numbers of the *Journal* list her husband as publisher, but name no editor.

The Contra Costa survived about a year. As his 1858 work indicated, Kemble blamed its demise on limited support and on Clarke's poor health. He added, "Mrs. Clarke now resides in San Leandro and, we are pained to add, is slowly passing away under the ravages of her disease." In spite of heart disease and poor general health, she lived until 1880. Although bedridden after 1875, she contributed poems, stories, and articles to San Francisco periodicals.

In 1878 a series of events began which a *San Francisco Chronicle* reporter admitted "would be decried as a sentimentally overdrawn picture if dramatized."[6] Clarke's son, Frederick, killed his father in a shooting accident. The father lived long enough to make his will and absolve his son, who was "almost insane with grief," of guilt.[7] Clarke stayed with her son and his new wife for two months, then moved to the home of a cousin, later testifying that she thought Frederick would kill her if she stayed. Witnesses at subsequent legal proceedings blamed Frederick's conduct on his wife, whom one reporter described as much older and "of a grasping and avaricious temperament."[8] The reporter characterized Clarke as "a brilliant though bed-ridden and very feeble old lady of 58, whose literary work of late years has made her name not unfamiliar to the readers of local literary publications."[9]

By this time the large estate of H. K. W. Clarke had become the focus of a bitter struggle between mother and son. After her husband's death,

Clarke had given her son power of attorney. She intended to revoke it when she became well, according to her testimony in December 1879 at a court action seeking removal of her son as administrator of his father's estate. However, when she did revoke it, her son paid her a "horrifying" visit, railing at her and charging her with extravagance. The only extravagance she could remember, she told the judge and counsel who came to her sickbed to hear her testimony, was her request to have some photographs of her husband copied because she had none. Her son replied that he could not afford the expense. The argument made her very ill, and she essentially lost her memory for two months.

Without minimizing the trauma of the quarrel and the court case, one is tempted on the basis of Clarke's closing testimony to conclude that her literary and theatrical sense had survived the vicissitudes of illness and alienation. According to the court report, she said:

> I would rather die than testify against my own son; I have prayed for death, but I cannot die; I cannot go on; Oh, my God! I understand the wail of David when he cried, "Absalom! O, my son, Absalom!" [10]

Frederick denied that he had treated his mother cruelly. He testified that she had come under the influence of a spirit medium and had wanted to assign the property to parties outside the family after being influenced by the spirits to do so. He deemed it unsafe for the property to be under her control. The court's decision took a middle course, removing Frederick temporarily from the administratorship and ordering him to provide an accounting of it.

Ten days later, San Francisco police arrested a disguised Frederick at Truckee, Nevada, and charged him with embezzlement. He maintained his innocence, stating that he had intended to leave San Francisco for some time because of bad health and business conditions and that the opprobrium, to which he had recently been unjustly subjected, had hastened his departure. He had left behind an accounting of his administratorship, and it would show that the estate actually owed him money, he said. Still, he had expected his mother's attorneys to bring charges and, knowing he could never get a fair trial, had fled. In the meantime, his wife had disappeared and reporters speculated that he had intended to join her in the East.

Clarke died four months later, on April 16, 1880. An obituary noted that she "had written with considerable poetic talent." It added, "Her end was saddened, and perhaps hastened, by the unfilial conduct and unpleasant notoriety of her son."[11] It also stated that he was "now charged with murder," referring to the reopening of a case that had been abandoned ten years earlier. It concerned squatters who had been evicted from land owned by H. K. W. Clarke. When one of them returned for his possessions, Frederick shot and killed him. Legal maneuvers at the time delayed proceedings, witnesses left the area, and the case did not come to trial. The San Francisco papers carried no reports of legal actions involving Frederick during the months following his mother's death.

San Francisco developed early into a cultural center. A writer for *Putnam's Monthly* of New York observed in 1854 that, although "only five years old," it supported "two or three theatres, an opera, a monthly magazine, an Academy of Science, thirteen daily papers, and we don't know how many weeklies."[12] Four years after Sarah Moore Clarke started *The Contra Costa* across the bay in Oakland, other women founded periodicals in San Francisco. The first number of *The Athenaeum*, a weekly edited by Cora Anna Weekes and intended "For the Cultivation of the Memorable and the Beautiful," came out on March 20, 1858, but it lasted for only a month. *The Hesperian*, appearing as a semi-monthly on May 1 of the same year, led a longer and healthier life.

It joined two other literary periodicals being published in San Francisco. In fact, historian Hubert Howe Bancroft suggested that one of these might have lasted longer but for the rivalry of *The Hesperian*, a magazine of a higher order.[13] Its first number listed Mrs. A. M. Schultz as "Editress" and Mrs. F. H. Day as "Associate Editress," but Mrs. Schultz resigned within a month because of ill health, and Hermione Ball Day carried on as editor until she sold the magazine four years later.

Hermione Ball was born on July 18, 1826, in Buffalo, New York. Little is known about her early life. At the time of her marriage to Fidelio D. Parke in 1842, she was living with her older brother in Erie, Pennsylvania. Her daughter, Clara, was born in Buffalo about 1850, and they moved to California within the next year or two. Perhaps they traveled by way of Hawaii, for she later wrote of visiting the Sandwich Islands.[14] She became the proprietor of Brannan House in San Francisco and in 1855 married Franklin Henry Day, a bookkeeper from her hometown of Buffalo, who worked on the opposite corner of the intersection from the Brannan House.

In an autobiographical sketch written in 1903, Franklin listed his employers and his Masonic positions in full, but devoted only one sentence to his private life: "My domestic experience has been particularly unfortunate, having been deprived by death of two wives and two boys, and at the present time have only one relative on the Coast, a niece in the southern part of the State."[15] The second son was his and Day's. She announced his birth in *The Hesperian* in April 1861 and his death in August of the same year.

A passport application described her as five feet two and one-half inches tall, with a brunette complexion, black hair, hazel eyes, an oval face, and pointed nose and chin.[16] Another woman journalist called her "a bright, sweet, lovable little woman, with a cheery style of composition which has earned her that most unusual title for a woman of 'humorist.' "[17] The same writer called *The Hesperian* "a sincere and honest publication." That makes it sound too staid. As other writers pointed out, its contents ranged from Milton to muffin making.[18] It brought its readers fiction, poetry, articles on topics ranging from great women of history to the flora and fauna of California, travel sketches, engraved illustrations—sometimes in color— a juvenile department, and recipes. In 1859 it won the First Premium Award for book printing at the California State Fair.

The magazine's name referred to the mythological Hesperides, or western maidens, who were assigned to guard the trees in Juno's garden that bore golden apples. A sleepless dragon joined them after they yielded to temptation and took some of the apples for themselves. When she changed *The Hesperian* from a semi-monthly to a monthly in 1859, Day put an elaborate illustration of the myth on its cover and suggested her own interpretation of it: The Hesperides stretched forth their hands to pluck some of the "Golden Apples of Literature" from a branch "bearing golden apples of thought in the garden of Western Literature." In the background the dragon of ignorance lurked, trying to frighten them away from partaking of knowledge.[19]

In their first number, the editors challenged their readers both to combat ignorance by reading *The Hesperian* and to cultivate their talents by contributing to it. Writing "To the Women of California," they announced that their enterprise, "nothing less than the establishment of a literary paper upon a firm and respectable basis," called for "the talent and genius, latent and active, which the women of California possess." They continued:

> The present undertaking is in the hands of ladies, and will be conducted by our own citizens; those with whom we have toiled day by day for years past, those who have stood by California through her many vicissitudes,

and who are willing to give all their time and bring their energies to bear
in establishing a literary paper which will be a credit to the State. . . . Be
aroused, ladies, themes are clustering thick around us. . . . Come freely
forward then, and assist us with song and story as well as subscription.[20]

They went on to chastise the "few benighted individuals who think that
women are incapable of sustaining a literary paper by the productions of
their intellects" and suggested that great benefit would accrue to the social
circle if the ladies would occupy themselves with literature instead of the
latest fashions, the "distingué appearance of Mrs. So-and-So's turn out,"
or scandalous gossip.

A history of San Francisco journalism titled a sketch of *The Hesperian*
"Speaking Out, But Timidly." The author noted that the paper called on
woman to "enlarge her apprehensions" and "cultivate her range of thought"
that "each day she may add a new strain to the music of her march, and
shed a softened and mellowed light upon the broad landscape of human
life." But it also temporized:

> Her home is at once her Eden and her empire, and we would not tempt her
> to forsake that holy province for the untried fields of fame. To be womanly
> is woman's sweetest charm, and should be her highest aim.[21]

Whoever wrote that disclaimer, it fit into the philosophies that Day continued to espouse. She opposed woman suffrage, and most of the fiction
she published had spiritual overtones.[22] Still, "timid" seems the wrong
word to describe her. In the context of the day, her opinions represented,
if not the cutting edge of the quest for woman's emancipation, at least a
major step in that direction, and she expressed them clearly and forcefully.

She also showed no reluctance to promote herself, as well as her magazine. In it she published comments from the press to the effect that it was
the "very best literary publication in the State," and that she was "a most
capable editress."[23] She later claimed circulation from Maine to Minnesota
and announced that an entire printing of the first number of the expanded
monthly was gone within a week.[24]

The Hesperian evidently succeeded as a business enterprise, attracting
advertisers as well as readers. Day made it a policy not to issue a number
until the previous one had been paid for, and she was able to keep the
numbers coming out on schedule. She hired a business manager in 1860
but continued her travels to solicit subscriptions and advertising.

She wrote a great deal for the magazine throughout her tenure as editor, reporting her travels and producing historical articles. Basing her biographies of California pioneers principally on interviews, she intended to publish them as a book. She considered the essays on California's birds and plants—many of them written by Albert Kellogg, founder of the California Academy of Sciences—a major contribution.

In 1860 Day traveled to New York and arranged to include in each number of *The Hesperian* a full-size dress pattern by Madame Ellen Demorest, who had initiated the idea for her own magazine. She also opened a branch of Madam Demorest's Emporium of Fashion and further expanded her business activities by adding job printing to the services connected with her magazine.

Day sold *The Hesperian* in the spring of 1862. Elizabeth T. Schenck maintained it as a woman's magazine until mid-1863, when her associate, the Reverend J. D. Strong, and his wife took it over and directed it toward a more general audience, with the explanation that they disliked the idea of separating the sexes in literature as much as in schools, churches, families, or social life. They also changed its name to *The Pacific Monthly* to avoid having it called a ladies' magazine.[25] The change did not increase circulation or advertising, however, and they sold the magazine to Lisle Lester, who abandoned it in November 1864.

Day left San Francisco in the spring of 1862, attributing her departure to her daughter's poor health and choosing Europe "as the best place for the development of the work which we have in hand"—whatever that may have been. It remained uncompleted, for she died in Paris on July 3, 1865, at the age of thirty-eight.

The journalist who described her as sweet and lovable also wrote that someone said to her a few days before her death, "When you are dead I shall kiss this lily-white hand," leading her to sit up that night and write a poem titled "When I Am Dead." Its final stanza reads:

> Then welcome, Death! thrice welcome be!
> I am almost weary of waiting for thee;
> Life gives no recompense, toil no gain,
> I seek for love, and I find but pain;
> Lily white hands have grown pale in despair
> Of the warm red kisses which should be their share.
> Sad, aching hearts have grown weary of song,
> No answering echo their notes prolong;

> Then take me, oh Death, to thy grim embrace!
> Press quickly thy kiss on my eager face,
> For I have been promised, oh, bridegroom dread,
> Both love and fame, when I am dead![26]

Death disappointed on both counts, it seems, bringing neither love nor fame, although her husband, whom she left behind in San Francisco when she traveled to Europe, waited until 1872 to remarry. Occasional references in history books and scholarly journals constitute her only fame.

Another forgotten editor enjoyed considerable renown during her life, making a literary career and a reputation as a social arbiter. Agnes Leonard Hill worked in Colorado from about 1870 until some time after the turn of the century, contributing to various periodicals, assisting with the editing of two weekly newspapers, writing books and pamphlets, and editing her own publication.

Agnes Leonard was born in Louisville, Kentucky, probably during the mid or late 1840s. Her mother died when Agnes was quite young, so she attended boarding schools and, "having no home duties in her youth, Mrs. Hill developed literary tastes and habits," according to one biographical sketch.[27] She started writing verses when she was eight years old, and the Louisville *Journal* began to publish her poetry when she was thirteen, a year after giving her this notice:

> A young girl, twelve years old, sends us some verses written when she was only ten. Though hardly worthy to be published, they indicate the existence of a bud of genius which, properly developed, will expand into a glorious flower.[28]

Before she turned fifteen, the *Journal* editor wrote some verses to her, calling her "young minstrel girl" and wishing her a life blessed with joy and beauty. One verse went as follows:

> A soul of fire is thine, thou art a new star
>   Mounting in the sky,
> Whose beams in the meridian-hour will shine
>   Brightly on every eye.[29]

She was graduated in 1862 from the Henry Female College of New Castle, Kentucky, an institution of which her father was president, and she went to Chicago the following year. There she wrote editorials and other material for the *Tribune*, *Times*, *News*, and *Inter Ocean*. It also may have been there that she published her first three books—a volume of school-girl poetry, a novel titled *Vanquished*, and a children's story called *Heights and Depths*.

In 1868 she married Dr. S. E. Scanland, a fellow Kentuckian. He died about two years later—killed by her brother, if a story in the *Rocky Mountain News* of Denver is correct.[30] In May 1872, she remarried. This husband, Samuel Howe Hill, came from Bangor, Maine. By the late 1870s she had established residence in Colorado, where she had made successful lecture tours earlier. The *Rocky Mountain News* published in 1873 her first contribution to the Denver press—a memorial poem written in Golden, Colorado, for a couple whose child had died. A note in the same paper four years later referred to her as "late of this city" and reported that she was writing a continued story, to be called "One Man's Temptation," for the Chicago *Inter Ocean*.[31]

About 1880 Hill began assisting her brother, Percy A. Leonard, with the editing of *The Chaffee County Times* of Buena Vista, Colorado. Denver papers refer to her as "editor," "editress," and "associate editor" early in 1881. A history of Colorado, in a reference to the *Times*, described her as "well known in western journalism, contributing much to its fame and large circulation."[32] However, in April 1881, a Denver paper reported that she had dissolved her connection with the *Times*. Other sources state that she helped her brother with the Leadville *Dispatch*, which he edited from 1886 to 1892.[33] Her husband was listed as business manager or general manager of the *Dispatch* in Leadville city directories from 1889 to 1891.

At the same time, Hill continued her lecturing career. An announcement of a series of appearances at the University of Denver credited her with having spoken before the legislature of Missouri and before literary associations in the principal western cities. The Denver series began with a lecture on "Practical Advantages of Culture," went on to presentations about Charles Dickens, George Eliot, and Ralph Waldo Emerson, and closed with "Manners: Their Mission." A glowing report called Hill's style easy and pleasant, mentioned a large and delighted audience for the lectures, and concluded that "any community will be the wiser and the better after listening to them."[34]

The same report summarized the lecture on manners, although "no synopsis would do it justice." Hill said that "'manners are only the shadows of the soul'; they sum up the character of man; they are the balance-sheet showing the profit and loss that may result from his acquaintance." In 1887

The Queen Bee of Denver announced that Hill had assumed charge of the departments of rhetoric, composition, and literature at the Scott Saxton College of Elocution.[35] By the end of the decade, her concern with manners had led her to start a periodical that focused on that topic and to write pamphlets of advice.

The weekly publication, *Western Society*, began in December 1888, in Denver. It was one of many periodicals of the time that included reformation of Americans' bad manners as an aim. Journalism historian Frank Luther Mott wrote that "Ignorance of etiquette, 'tall talk,' faults of taste, crudities developed by a highly individualistic pioneer society, were firmly and sometimes severely condemned."[36] Proper speech received attention as a means of correct social intercourse. General, as well as specialized, magazines treated it.

No copies of *Western Society* appear to have survived, but a contemporary description in *The Journalist* gives an idea of what the magazine was like. It stated that *Western Society* was devoted to social aims, hints on behavior, and secrets of social success. This "tasteful and handsome weekly," which had received uniformly flattering press notices, contained a serial story in each issue, a department for young readers, brief fashion notes, art criticism, studies of standard authors, "and whatever is calculated to interest, instruct and stimulate to a higher standard of thought and life." The description gave special notice to "the sweet, graceful and tender poems written by Mrs. Hill" and suggested that her paper would be especially appropriate for home reading.[37] Another source indicated that *Western Society* became *Home and Society*,[38] which would seem to have been a more fitting title, given the contents listed above. However, the magazine lasted only about a year.

Perhaps Hill gave up *Western Society* in order to devote her time to *The Colorado Blue Book*, an ambitious effort that came out in 1892. It included not only "Names and Addresses of Prominent Residents on the most Fashionable Streets . . . with the full Membership of the Principal Clubs," but also an essay on "Good Form," "Hints on Behavior," and such useful information as a list of "Foreign Terms Used on Menus." It also contained many advertisements, including some for Hill's books and pamphlets: "Hints on How to Talk," "Principles of Behavior," and "Talks with Mothers."[39] In the preface to "Hints on How to Talk," the author wrote that her life and labor would not have been in vain if the book awakened any "to the necessity that exists for avoiding the atrocity of being a bore."[40]

Hill considered herself a social reformer because she encouraged cultivation of social graces, but she expressed scant tolerance for bores and provided an index to "The Elite of Denver." She stated in the *Blue Book*'s preface that readers should not consider it an effort "to establish old-world caste" or to define and label "the Elite," but simply an attempt to supply tradesmen with the addresses of profitable customers and social leaders with the names of those whom they might want to invite to large receptions.

The year after the *Blue Book* came out, she published a series of pamphlets on "Social Questions," intending "to interest, instruct and stimulate to a higher standard of thought and life." The titles ranged from "How to Give Gifts Acceptably" to "What Is Education?"[41]

Her final venture into journalism came in 1900, when she edited a Denver publication called *Society* for several months. Apparently it had no connection with her earlier periodical. Not even a description of its contents has been found. After its demise, Hill decided that she needed money, for in 1902 she published a book called *"Said Confidentially,"* described as a collection of things she secretly laughed about, written "for the amusement of the Precious Few." Her "frank and unblushing confession" was that she published it "for revenue only."[42]

An earlier novel, set in Colorado and called *The Specter of Grey Gulch*, seems never to have seen the light of publication. Another book, published but forgotten according to a Colorado historian, had the title *Divine Law of Divorce*.[43] Hill may have drawn from her own experience to write it. No listing for her husband appeared in the 1892 *Blue Book*, although she listed herself. She had children—three daughters and a son—and lived until 1917.

Thus, three western women added their voices to those of women across the country who sought to bring information, entertainment, and enlightenment to other women. Although remarkable in individual ways, they produced periodicals with aims and content similar to those of dozens of others published during the same period. As women practicing journalism, they seem not to have been considered unusual by their contemporaries. In writing his history of California periodicals up to 1858, Kemble did not so much as mention that Sarah Moore Clarke was the state's first woman editor.

While producing publications that had similar content in general terms—advice, essays, household helps, informational articles, fiction, and poetry

—Sarah Moore Clarke, Hermione Ball Day, and Agnes Leonard Hill led very different lives. That two of them seem to have had violent deaths in their families should be considered coincidental, not an indication that western women editors led violence-prone lives. That two of them were married more than once is less unusual. Their husbands faced the same limited life expectancies as did the general population, and widows often remarried. In addition, these relatively independent women may have found divorce a viable alternative to an unhappy marriage.

Few generalizations can be drawn even about a group as circumscribed as those who edited publications for women. Like the three subjects of this chapter, they often moved into and out of journalism, with editing careers occupying only relatively brief periods of their lives. They rarely expressed extreme views on the place of women in society, idealizing the home and woman's role as its preserver. They hoped, however, to contribute to the improvement of their readers' minds, as well as to the efficient operation of their households and, of course, to do so at a profit.

CHAPTER 3

Small-Town
Businesswomen

Those subscribers to The Recorder *who promised to replenish our wood pile in payment for the paper, are notified that this is a good time to remember their promises.*[1]

—The Idaho Recorder, *January 15, 1890*

 Weekly newspapers led the westward movement of the American press and set it apart from that of any other nation, spreading with the population and locating even in small and isolated hamlets. For those at the lower end of the circulation range—those which distributed as few as three hundred copies a week— editors gathered news, wrote it up, edited their own copy, sold subscriptions and advertising, set type, laid out the paper, and printed it. Like Ada Chase Merritt of Salmon City, Idaho, they might have bartered subscriptions for their winter supply of wood. Those at the other end of the range, whose papers sold as many as three thousand copies a week, could live comfortably and employ several assistants. Most often, however, the same person acted as both publisher and editor.

Circulations can be difficult to determine, given the understandable tendency toward exaggeration by the editors reporting them. However, a history and survey of United States periodical publishing commissioned in connection with the 1880 census made every effort to develop reliable figures and concluded that the most notable increase came among weekly newspapers, "an increase which was in such rapid progress at the time this census was taken that it was difficult, and indeed impossible, to trace all the new establishments that properly belonged in the enumeration of the census year."[2] This report showed that numbers of weeklies in the western states doubled each decade between 1860 and 1880 and that well over half of all periodicals published in the West during that period were weeklies.[3]

One explanation for the large numbers of small-town weeklies was the ease with which they could be established. It took little capital to start a paper. The prospective publisher needed only a rudimentary press, a few cases of type, an imposing stone, paper, and ink. Suppliers usually allowed credit to a new printshop.

To make full use of their equipment, most publishers ran a job-printing business in conjunction with their papers. Many had other businesses, as well. In fact, a real estate developer or a prospective state senator might see a newspaper as an ideal vehicle for making economic or political capital. Such entrepreneurs could either start a paper or contribute financial support to one that would advance their interests. They might become editors, or they might stay behind the scenes as silent partners. Although town promoters and political partisans sometimes were eager to subsidize newspapers, supplies and capital still could be difficult to obtain.

Many of those going into newspaper work on a subsidy—or on their own, for that matter—had little or no journalistic experience. A study of Washington state editors and proprietors found that, in the year 1889, 39 percent of them had no newspaper or related experience prior to their current positions.[4]

Although enterprising individuals started papers easily, they often abandoned them when hopes of fame and fortune proved vain. As the 1880 census report pointed out, the question of how many publications a town could support in many cases had to be tested by actual experience—at the expense of the experimenters. The overwhelming proportion of suspensions during the census year came among journals of recent establishment, often less than a year old.[5]

Many of the weeklies consisted of only four pages, becoming thicker toward the turn of the century. The standard subscription cost of two dollars a year had varied little since colonial times, when "the early rates established were low enough to prevent their proprietors from growing rich, and they have been kept low enough since to accomplish the same purpose."[6] Commonly, weekly papers circulated to fewer than one thousand subscribers.

The content of the weeklies, as well as their cost, varied little between 1850 and 1900. It consisted of local news, editorials, miscellaneous features, some national and international news, legal notices (in papers lucky enough to win a county printing contract), an occasional poem or work of fiction, and advertisements.

Local news gave the weeklies a raison d'être, and its quality and quantity often determined whether a paper would live or die; the more local names mentioned, the better. Most editors ran long columns of news notes chronicling the comings and goings, the triumphs and disappointments, the good years and lean years of the local populace.

Editorials usually had a local slant as well, and opinion regularly spilled over into the news columns, the editors making their positions on community issues and political questions abundantly clear. Most of them listed their papers as being affiliated with one or another of the political parties. Even those who styled themselves "Independent," and their numbers increased toward the end of the century, spoke out at election times. Virtually all of them, as champions of social and material advancement, "boosted" their communities with great enthusiasm.

The original material in each number might range from one-fourth to three-fourths of the paper's contents. Special postage rates made exchanging of papers with other publishers attractive, and editors culled both news and features from other publications and printed them as "exchanges," usually with credit to the source. Another tactic, the use of "patent pages," came into prominence after the Civil War when cooperative printing companies began to make available sheets already printed on either the inside or the outside pages, so that the local publisher could simply print the blank pages and have a complete paper ready to distribute. As the companies attracted advertisers eager to reach the huge market offered, they could supply the patent pages, containing a variety of short feature articles, almost as inexpensively as the publishers could buy blank paper. By 1880, twenty-one companies sold patent pages to more than three thousand periodicals, most of them weeklies and most of them in the West.[7]

In 1875 one of the companies began offering stereotype plates, which could be used with more flexibility in conjunction with locally set type and then returned to the manufacturer. After an initial payment for metal, this "boilerplate" cost only twenty-five cents a column.[8] Publishers also saved money in some instances by printing essentially the same paper for neighboring towns. They changed only the name and a few columns of local news.

While the press survey report of the 1880 census called all editors "men," among them were a significant number of women, and nearly half of the western women editors edited weekly newspapers. The census grouped weekly magazines with weekly newspapers and reported that together they accounted for 70 percent of all publications. The proportion of weekly newspapers and magazines among the western periodicals edited by women was about two-thirds. The report's generalizations about weekly publishing apply to papers run both by men and by women and raise questions about the stereotype of the flamboyant editor rushing in with the first prospectors or settlers to set up shop in a tent or lean-to.

Mining led to the settlement of Salmon City, Idaho, and mining brought the Henry Clay Merritt family there in 1883, so that Henry could become superintendent of the Kentuck Mine, downriver from the town. A year later he fell from a supply boat and drowned, leaving his wife, Ada, with two children to support.

Two years after the accident, in 1886, J. E. Booth founded *The Idaho Recorder*, with the subtitle "Official Journal of Lemhi County," to encourage settlement and investment in the area. Profits may not have met his expectations, for in July 1888 he sold the paper to the partnership of Ada Merritt and O. W. Mintzer, staying on as their printer. That marked the beginning of Ada Chase Merritt's newspaper career. She bought out Mintzer in October and ran the paper on her own until 1906.

Ada Chase was born on February 24, 1852, in Louisiana. The stockraising business brought her family to Nevada, where she married Henry Merritt in 1871 and where their two children were born. The Chase family moved to Salmon with the Merritts in 1883. Henry's parents had settled in nearby Shoup a year earlier.

The first number of *The Recorder* under Merritt and O. W. Mintzer contained their greeting:

With no little trepidation we take the pen (and scissors) in hand and salute you. . . . To successfully conduct and edit a live local paper in an intelligent community like ours, will be readily recognized—by any but a vain egotist —as a task almost Herculean. Conscious of the magnitude of the work before us, with its difficulties, its demands and embarrassments, we boldly "strike out," encouraged by the fact that others have gone this way before us and that our entire community wish us success.[9]

The editors went on to promise that readers could depend on a "good clean paper, free from small gossip and wholesale slander," one that would awaken interest both at home and abroad "to the boundless mineral, stock raising, agricultural and other material resources of our county." Departments would feature regular correspondence from each section of the county, and the paper's appearance would be improved. Readers could rely on its political independence because one editor was a Republican and the other a Democrat, "without a vote, being a lady."

Additional content included a schedule of mail deliveries, a directory of county and state officials, lists of county financial disbursements and license approvals, county and state news notes, mining notes, general news culled from other publications, an editorial, a column titled "Local Intelligence," and a generous portion of advertisements. This first number set the pattern for the entire period of Merritt's editorship. She continued to concentrate on local activities, paying particular attention to the comings and goings of the county's residents and commenting on county and state politics. The "Local Intelligence" column undoubtedly contributed greatly to the paper's success by featuring a series of short, sprightly notes. Here readers could learn that haying was in full swing, that the circus would be in Dillon on Friday, or that Henry Monroe had come in from Pine Creek to meet his friend from Missouri, who arrived on Saturday's stage.

Another quality that made *The Recorder* appealing was Merritt's sense of humor. One of the many welcomes from other editors that she published concluded, "Sister Merritt now has but to change her politics and we shall embrace her principles as well as enterprise," signed "Keystone." Merritt replied, "Thanks Mr. Keystone for your very kind and favorable notice. You may embrace our enterprise and our politics (and no doubt you will do so when you learn that Sister Merritt represents the Democratic side of this journal) but not our avoirdupois."[10]

Having a Democrat and a Republican as editors supported claims of impartiality, but it also may have led to an uneasy atmosphere around the office, especially after O. W. Mintzer began an active—and successful—campaign for a position in the state assembly. Perhaps he had seen Merritt as more malleable and the paper as more of a promoter of his political career than either turned out to be. With the October 4 number, he severed his connection with the paper. The next week Merritt explained that "various reasons may be assigned for this action, the chief one being the presence of other matters which would require so much of his attention as to prevent him from giving the time required to keep *The Recorder* up to the standard of its initial numbers." [11]

Beginning in 1889, Merritt stepped more boldly into the political arena. Judging by their inauspicious showing in the 1888 elections, Lemhi County Democrats formed a minority, but Merritt did not hesitate to call the majority to task. She criticized the county's representatives for their failure to get money for the region and mentioned her erstwhile partner by name, accusing him of partisanship and adding, "It is a notorious fact that the Democratic vote of this county elected, or at least went a long way to elect our representative to this position, an honor which he has so poorly repaid." [12] Endorsements of candidates included a note of support for her brother, Hal H. Chase, who ran for county assessor in 1890 and won, one of two county Democrats elected.

In 1889 she advised voters to approve the proposed state constitution but noted that, as a woman, she would be unable to follow her own advice. That comment might be taken as an indication that she supported woman suffrage, but in 1895 she wrote that she opposed it:

> We are not in sympathy with the movement, we are just old fashioned enough to think that women now have more rights than they use intelligently. What more right does a true woman want than the right to be loved and protected as the wife of an honorable man and the right to mold the characters of her sons and daughters. [13]

Merritt's feud with her former partner heated up at the end of 1890 with the publication in *The Salt Lake Tribune* of a letter from "Perihelion," later identified in *The Recorder* as O. W. Mintzer. It not only attacked the Salmon paper but went on to make disparaging personal remarks about its editor. The paper did not represent the community, the letter claimed, and therefore would have to be replaced. Something had "soured" *The Recorder*—not politics, because the recent Democratic victory had "set every nerve and fibre of its great editorial bosom quivering with delight," and not matrimony, "for we know of one who has been passionately camping on its trail for years, longing to fill the aching void of the disconsolate widow's heart, and still waits its beck and call." [14] Merritt published a scathing reply a month later, pointing out that the character of the correspondent— a "wolf in sheep's clothing"—was so well known the length and breadth of the county that comment was unnecessary, and the writing of the letter under an assumed name was "quite in keeping with his former notorious record." [15]

In 1894 the Republicans started their own paper, *The Lemhi Republic*, which immediately called for a boycott of *The Recorder*. Merritt frequently answered its charges against her and launched a few of her own. By this time she supported the Populists.

She played a leading role in 1902 in a grand scandal with both political and personal ramifications. By this time *The Recorder* had moved to semi-weekly publication, and its competition was *The Lemhi Herald*. Merritt had a new assistant, George W. Walsen, and he went with her late in 1901 to purchase a new press and other equipment in Omaha and Chicago. She then made him business manager of her publishing company.

In May 1902, she reported a malicious attack by *The Herald* and then published a reprint from *The Pocatello Advance* to explain the situation. The *Advance* story stated that she and her assistant had been quietly married in Omaha in December, but had kept the marriage secret. On March 26 Walsen had left for Boise, saying he was going on to the East to promote the Salmon City route to Thunder Mountain, a new mining district.

Soon after he left, the *Advance* story continued, Merritt discovered that $6,000 of the money with which she had been entrusted as county treasurer also had disappeared. Only she and her son, the deputy treasurer, had known the combination to the county safe, but she had it written on a piece of paper "concealed on her person," and Walsen apparently had stolen both the paper and the money. Merritt spent several hundred dollars tracking Walsen down and, without indicating that she suspected him of stealing the money, tried to persuade him to meet her in Denver. This attempt failed, but he finally agreed to see her at her daughter's home in Salt Lake City, and there she had him arrested. The *Advance* had discovered that Walsen had served three terms in the Colorado penitentiary and a fourth term in Utah for forgery. It added an expression of support:

> Mrs. Merritt has the sympathy of her many friends in Idaho, and she deserves great credit for the determined effort she made to apprehend Walsen.

Not many women could have exhibited the nerve and cool judgment shown by her during the time she was compelled to play the devoted wife in getting him to meet her.[16]

The Lemhi Herald, on the other hand, showed no compassion. It called for an investigation and auditing of the books of county officials and suggested that Merritt had written the letters she claimed to have received from supporters. It quoted Walsen as saying the accusation represented a conspiracy against him, because he didn't want to live with his wife, and added it was not reasonable to suppose that Merritt had nothing to do with the theft. It reported indictments returned by the grand jury, against Walsen for grand larceny, and against Merritt for embezzling county funds. It accused her of being "proud, empyrical, disdainful, having at times abused some of our best citizens in the most unmerciful manner." It suggested that more money was missing than officials had announced and that the affair was being whitewashed. It noted that the sheriff had taken possession of *The Recorder*'s printing plant.[17]

In November, the district court met and released Walsen because of insufficient evidence. It brought Merritt in to plead not only on the embezzlement charge but also on an accusation of furnishing a prisoner in jail with ways and means of escape. She pleaded not guilty to both counts. Her lawyers obtained a postponement of her trial, and the court received a petition signed by a long list of county citizens asking that the cases be dismissed if the deficit were made good.[18]

In December, at the same time *The Recorder* went back to weekly publication, a judge granted Merritt "absolute divorce," adjudged her all property, and found that Walsen stole the $6,000 missing from the county treasury.[19] The following May, the court dismissed the embezzlement indictment, its opinion stating that the money had been restored, it was difficult to find an unbiased jury, and important witnesses had left the state permanently. In the case regarding delivery into prison of things useful to an escape attempt, Merritt changed her plea to guilty and implored the mercy of the court, which fined her $50. As *The Herald* concluded, "Thus ended the most sensational chapter of this county's history."[20]

In spite of both personal and editorial vicissitudes, Merritt seems to have maintained *The Recorder* at a reasonably prosperous level during the entire period of her editorship. She reported in June 1889, as the paper began its seventh volume, that she had "no kick coming,"[21] although she claimed in December to have insufficient funds for a trip to the state press association meeting at Caldwell. The subject of the meeting came up when she replied to an exchange from *The Cassia County Times*, which announced that she would be at the convention. It continued, "This announcement will allow bachelor editors the privilege of sleeking up for the occasion. We will attend if we have to borrow the minister's clothes and wade through snow knee deep." Merritt replied, "We are very sorry indeed to disappoint Brother Times, but circumstances over which we had no control, viz. lack of collateral, prevented our appearance in Bunion precinct. Brethren, can't you pass the hat?" [22]

Merritt traveled frequently to solicit advertising and subscribers for the paper, sometimes taking her son or her daughter with her on trips throughout northern Idaho and into Montana. She also ran promotional campaigns in *The Recorder*, like bargain offers for combined subscriptions to her paper and other publications or contests requiring coupons clipped from the paper. She reminded readers of appealing features coming up: "The charming serial story entitled 'Delinquent Tax List' will appear in our next issue and continue for six weeks. Subscribe now and get this entertaining tale." [23] Some readers exchanged services for subscriptions, like those who promised to replenish her woodpile during winter months.

Along with the paper, Merritt ran a job-printing shop and the Salmon City News Depot, a store in the express office which sold stationery, periodicals, novels, and writing materials. The county printing contract undoubtedly proved a significant source of income. Awarding of the contract to *The Lemhi Herald* in 1904 may have influenced her decision to sell her paper. Or, at the age of fifty-four, she may have decided she needed a rest. H. E. Frost took over as editor and proprietor in June 1906.

Merritt had edited the paper with skill, enthusiasm, and a sure instinct for the interests of her community for eighteen years. She also had taken an active role in church and community affairs. She participated in concerts by the Methodist Episcopal church choir and sang at Independence Day celebrations, served as vice president of the Salmon City Chautauqua Literary and Scientific Circle and as secretary of the Woman's Relief Corps of the Grand Army of the Republic, belonged to the Washington Reading Club, was elected associate conductress of the Order of the Eastern Star and representative to its Grand Lodge, and won the post of county treasurer in the election of November 1900. As a delegate to the state silver convention in 1893, she was perhaps "the first lady receiving the honor of being elected a delegate to a public convention in Idaho." [24] Members of the Idaho State Press Association chose her as vice president in 1905.

After selling *The Recorder*, Merritt moved to Caldwell, Idaho, where she spent two years, and then to Salt Lake City. There, in 1912, she married Joseph Crain, who died seven years later. Between 1920 and 1928 she traveled extensively, at least part of the time as companion to a wealthy heiress, eventually moving to California, where her daughter lived. She died in Santa Monica at the age of eighty-one in November 1933. An obituary in the Salmon *Recorder-Herald* called her "one of the city's most influential citizens," "a woman of unusually brilliant intellect," and "a pleasing personality" who had lived "a remarkably active life full of colorful incidents."[25]

Such public recognition came only rarely to another woman editor, Maude Hulbert Horn, although she edited *The Georgetown Gazette* in California's mining country for thirty-three years. Historians ignored her, giving credit for the paper's operation to her father or her husband, until 1980, when a graduate student wrote a thesis about her life and career.[26] She represents an unknown number of women, including her own mother, who edited periodicals without official acknowledgment.

Maude Aleah Hulbert was born April 10, 1875, in Yuba City, California, where her father had founded a weekly paper. Both of her parents worked on that paper and on others that her father owned in Colusa and Auburn. Then her family moved to Georgetown, where her father could combine publishing with prospecting for gold. There he founded *The Georgetown Gazette* as a mining journal in 1880, but his Bright Hope Mine claimed more of his attention. In 1885 he was spending half his time there, and in 1886 he announced that he had "turned the Gazette over to our better half who will . . . ask only one day of our time each week to make up and do press work."[27]

By this time his ten-year-old daughter had been taught to set type. Soon she began doing other chores around the office—actually the front part of the Hulbert home—and gathering local news. Her father noted in 1889, "The extra amount of reading matter in the Gazette is due from the efforts of Miss Maude Hulbert who is beginning to take quite an interest towards making the Gazette a better paper. Miss Maude is already talking of obtaining a half interest in the paper."[28]

In the meantime, the future editor attended local public schools, but Georgetown had no high school, so at sixteen she planned to move to nearby Placerville. If her father offered her the editorship in order to keep her home and working for him, his stratagem succeeded, although he first listed her as manager on the paper's masthead two years later, in 1893.

In 1894 he wrote, "Miss Hulbert has a will distinctly her own, and we can assure you that she will conduct the policy of the paper to suit herself."[29] From diaries and items in *The Gazette*, her biographer concluded that she was running the paper virtually alone by 1895, receiving help only on press day.

She continued her education as well, studying French, astronomy, and literature in her spare time. She also learned telegraphy and shorthand to prepare for a career as a court reporter for the state legislature and, in fact, had passed the state exam in 1896 when her mother died and she became responsible for care of a younger brother and sister. Another younger brother had left home.

Although she removed her name from the masthead of *The Gazette* after her mother's death, she appeared to be running it again within a year. Her father wanted to leave for Oregon, if she could find another printer. She hired thirty-two-year-old John C. "Jack" Horn, her future husband. Her name appeared in the paper as publisher beginning in May 1897.

She kept the paper politically independent and continued its strong focus on local news—the comings and goings of residents, their social and religious activities, school projects and pupils' grades, church and lodge directories, railroad timetables, and lists of government officials. She occasionally used the patent pages mass produced for weekly newspapers. Her editorials focused on community improvement, with some comment on national or international affairs. She favored woman suffrage, and when Georgetown voters supported an unsuccessful state suffrage amendment in 1896 by a margin of four to one, she boasted, "I think our precinct not only the banner one in the county, but also in the state on the woman question, and I am proud of it."[30]

Jack Horn left for a job in Los Angeles late in 1897. Maude had agreed to marry him, but they disagreed on where to live. Her father, back from Oregon, resumed the title of publisher, with his daughter as business manager and local reporter. But he produced the paper only briefly, although his name remained on the masthead until 1900. In a letter to Jack, Maude wrote, "I should prefer that papa's name be at the head of the paper—it pleases him, though he does not admit it." In April 1898, her father sold out to her for $5 in gold coin, and Jack Horn decided to come back.[31]

Maude Hulbert and Jack Horn were married on July 31, 1898. Several papers referred to her journalistic career in notices of the wedding. A story in the *Sacramento Bee* stated, "The bride, who has for several years had charge of the management of *The Georgetown Gazette*, is one of the brightest newspaper women in California. She has displayed considerable ability as a writer and shrewdness in business affairs."[32] This represented rare public recognition for Maude Horn, although she remained owner, editor, reporter, manager, and typesetter. Her husband received the credit and was listed as publisher from 1900 until his death in 1921. It must be added that she acquiesced in this arrangement.

Maude bore three children in rapid succession, the first in June 1899. It was a press day, so "Dr. was cautioned to keep the event quiet until the papers were printed—so the first that was known of it in Georgetown . . . was through *The Gazette*, at about 3:30 that afternoon."[33] The children were trained not only to help with the housework but also to assist with the paper. According to her daughter, she would have the children write down at mealtimes what each had seen and done that day, whom they had talked to, and what was new in town. Names had to be spelled correctly and information verified. Good manners prohibited taking notes at funerals, so the children memorized names of out-of-town relatives and pallbearers.[34]

The Horns supplemented income from the newspaper by taking other jobs. Jack sold insurance and real estate and ran a photography business. Maude was a stringer for the *Sacramento Bee* and other papers. Both were notary publics. The family worked together to prepare and ship fancy packs of home-grown cherries.

Maude participated actively in community affairs, as well as boosting Georgetown in her paper. She liked to serve as secretary in the groups she joined, on the theory that this post gave her access to news. She went as an honorary delegate to the League of Nations meeting in San Francisco, participated in the first county superior court jury that seated women, and was the first woman justice of the peace in El Dorado County.

Jack died in a hotel fire in 1921, and Maude once again listed herself as publisher and took full responsibility for the paper. She also continued her husband's insurance business and kept her jobs as notary public, job printer, and newspaper stringer, maintaining the paper primarily to support her son in college. She suspended it in 1922, leased it to someone else in 1923, and then returned to run it when the new publisher suffered a back injury. In 1924 she sold it and used the $1,500 she realized from the sale to take a long vacation in Hawaii.

The Mountain Democrat of nearby Placerville published a feature article about her in 1922, beginning, "Job printer, editor of a country newspaper, notary public, insurance agent, housewife, farmer and community hostess —these are some of the occupations of Mrs. M. A. Horn of George-town." [35] The article went on to quote her to the effect that her real vocation was homemaking. However, the *Sacramento Bee*'s obituary notice, written by her daughter and approved by Maude before her death, emphasized her newspaper work. Perhaps, upon reflection, she concluded that she left a journalistic legacy equally as significant as the legacy of a successful family.

Her journalistic instincts remained strong to the end. She complained that the papers in Placerville ignored the smaller communities nearby, and she attempted to remedy the situation by posting typewritten funeral notices in the window of Georgetown's post office. When her daughter revived *The Gazette* in 1933, Maude Horn contributed a column called "Happenings of the Past." She died in June 1935, in a Sacramento hospital. Even her daughter was unaware that she had actually owned *The Gazette* during the years she listed her husband as publisher.

Ada Chase Merritt worked alone; Maude Hulbert Horn worked with her father and her husband, as well as independently; the Huntington sisters of Saratoga, Wyoming, exemplified yet another working arrangement. Three of them cooperated to produce the *Platte Valley Lyre* from 1890 to 1902.

Gertrude Mary and Laura Charlotte Huntington, with financial support from their father, bought the paper from W. B. Hugus, a Saratoga business-man who had purchased it a short time earlier from its founder, George R. Caldwell. Caldwell started the *Lyre* in 1888, after having owned a paper in Lander, where he earned the title of "Lurid Liar of Lander" with his tall tales of life in the wilds of Wyoming. His pride in the title may have influenced his choice of "lyre" as the name of his new venture. It was one of many western newspapers with unusual names. The 1880 census report stated that the tendency toward "unique and fantastic" newspaper titles had become excessive, particularly in recently settled sections, where it had been carried "to extremes bordering on the absurd." [36]

Gertrude and Laura Huntington had returned from studies at Kansas State Agricultural College in Manhattan just before they bought the *Lyre*. In 1889 their father had moved the family to Saratoga from Rawlins, where he had settled three years earlier, upon completion of an Episcopal church in Saratoga. A native of Vermont and a graduate of Cambridge University in England, according to one source he had written for and edited newspapers for several years before his marriage in 1865 and his subsequent decision to enter the ministry.[37]

Gertrude Huntington was born on October 6, 1866, in Indiana, the oldest of nine children. She was twenty-four when she and her sister Laura bought the paper. Laura Huntington was twenty-two, having been born on September 2, 1868. Their younger sister, Carolyn Virginia Huntington, born on July 28, 1879, assisted Gertrude as business manager after Laura married in 1898. The six sisters and three brothers of the Huntington family grew up in what one writer later called a "wholesome and wonderful atmosphere," referring to "chores, school work, and of course family games in the evenings." The sisters "had beaus, they danced, and were involved in all of the community projects."[38]

Gertrude Huntington took chief responsibility for the paper as editor and publisher; Laura served as business manager. They ran a lively four-page paper, setting all the type themselves. It featured the standard miscellaneous exchanges from other papers, legal notices, advertisements, and a page of local news. It boosted the Platte Valley continuously, taking advancement and upbuilding of the area as a prime goal. In 1896 a series of illustrated articles described the valley's mineral and agricultural resources in detail. Judging both from the quantity of ads and from a brief reminiscence written late in life by Laura Huntington, the paper succeeded financially.[39]

The *Lyre* had a rival in the *Saratoga Sun* but apparently the rivalry was friendly. The *Sun*'s "Observer" called Saratoga the "Drunkard Settlement," and the *Lyre* created a "Mrs. Annie Bush" to defend the community's honest, industrious citizens. When the *Lyre* appeared in a new typeface, the *Sun* reported that "the paper was changed in appearance as a tramp fresh washed," and the *Lyre* responded by questioning the boast of the *Sun*'s editor that he was a descendant of a British lord.[40] A Saratoga historian wrote that the editors of the two papers "were of very different outlooks and backgrounds" and that "many subscribers took both papers just to see what the editors chose to argue over each week."[41]

Laura Huntington told of the flood of comic valentines that came to the sisters each Valentine's Day, picturing everything from pretty girls to old maids looking for a man. They decorated the walls of the newspaper office for several weeks each year.[42]

Like most of the West's weeklies, the *Lyre* announced its political preference and made its leanings plain in both editorials and articles. As Laura

Huntington wrote, "We were the first women to edit a newspaper in Wyoming, and from that date the *Lyre* was straight Republican in politics, never on the fence for a moment."[43] Shortly after the Huntingtons bought the paper, they ran the following note:

> The Cheyenne *Sun* says: "Gertrude has joined the g.o.p." That the *Platte Valley Lyre* has done so, is true, but "Gertrude" has not "joined the g.o.p." for the reason that she has been a member of that party from her cradle.[44]

Laura Huntington married Alfred Heath, a forty-two-year-old attorney from England, in August 1898 and turned her share of the *Lyre* over to her sister Gertrude. Heath had settled in Saratoga in 1883 and may have been in poor health at the time of the marriage, because an obituary in 1903 stated that he had been "almost helpless and dependent on his devoted wife" of late and added, "It was unquestionably her devotion and tenderness that was the means of prolonging his life for the past three or four years."[45] Laura Huntington Heath returned to Rawlins with the rest of her family, her father having retired. She took an active part in community affairs, as deputy clerk of court, deputy assessor, deputy treasurer, and then for fourteen years as treasurer of Carbon County.[46] She died in 1962.

After serving as the Carbon County superintendent of schools for six years and as a delegate to Republican conventions, Gertrude Huntington sold the *Lyre* in 1902. A later owner merged the *Lyre* into the *Sun*.

In December 1903 Carolyn Huntington married A. L. Clendenan, a rancher from Dillon, Colorado, where she had put skills learned at the *Lyre* to use by working as a compositor for the *Dillon Doublejack*. She contracted typhoid fever only a few days after the wedding and died in March 1904.

A year later, Gertrude Huntington became the second wife of Homer Merrell, a Rawlins judge in whose office she had worked. He earlier had been a justice of the Wyoming Supreme Court. Her father performed the ceremony, his last act as a clergyman before his death in May. Merrell lived until 1916, and his wife continued his insurance and notary business after his death with the assistance of her sister Laura, who maintained it until her own death. Gertrude taught in the Episcopal church Sunday school and sang in the church choir, chaired the Ladies' Auxiliary of the Carbon County Memorial Hospital, started the local chapter of the American Red Cross in 1918, and headed it until her death in February 1925.[47] An obituary called her "an inspiring personality" and praised her as "a Rawlins booster in all regards."[48]

And so small-town women editors came and went, some staying with journalism through most of their lives, more trying it only briefly, some becoming embroiled in local scandals, and others never swerving from the path of rectitude. They both represented and championed their localities, and most became forces in their communities. This occurred partly through the power of their papers, whose "potency as an educating and informing medium is conceded by the preachers, teachers, politicians, and philanthropists who seek their agency as affording a wider method of inter-communication than any other agency of civilization,"[49] to quote the 1880 census report, and partly through their interest in and dedication to the communities where they lived, worked, and served.

CHAPTER 4

Causes Great and Small

The rank hot-bed of civilization seems to send forth poisonous plants even more profusely than useful ones. Millerism, Mesmerism, Mormonism, Bloomerism, and Spiritualism, all have flourished amazingly among us.[1]
—De Bow's Review, *1854*

 Not even the writer quoted above from *De Bow's Review* would have characterized all the causes that spawned magazines as "poisonous plants," but certainly the unconventional occupied a prominent place among them. Of course, the ideas of one generation's radicals might become the conventional wisdom of the next, but many reformers remained on society's fringes, their movements waxing and waning more or less rapidly.

Even the earliest American magazines devoted considerable space to the reforms of the day. Slavery came in for its share of attention well before 1800. Temperance also interested readers over a long period of time. Early magazines spoke out against dueling and swearing. A magazine crusade against the unattractive and unhealthy clothing which fashion decreed for women continued for more than a century.

During the first part of the nineteenth century, more and more reformers started their own magazines. Often denied access or treated with contempt and ridicule by the conventional press, they sought an alternative means of propagating their ideas. Publications proliferated until every "ism" had its printed voice. An 1858 article reported, for example, that "a score or more of periodicals devoted exclusively, or nearly so, to the defence and propagation" of spiritualism circulated at that time.[2] The American Peace Society had its *Advocate of Peace*; prison reformers sponsored the *Prisoner's Friend*; *Tip of de timz* called for spelling reform.

The West proved a fertile field for radical and reform publications. It probably spawned no more of them per capita than the East, but virtually every national reform movement of the latter nineteenth century had western, as well as eastern, periodical voices. The West saw the development of its own peculiar causes, as well. Perhaps, as some historians have suggested, the youth and rawness of its communities made it more tolerant than the East of those who expounded unconventional ideas and promoted social experiments.

Western women supported causes and joined and led movements. They organized and carried out campaigns for woman suffrage, and they took the lead in temperance crusades as well, but they also involved themselves in battles for education and labor reform, in communitarian experiments, and in religious societies like those devoted to spiritualism.

In the interests of all of these causes, and many others, they edited periodicals. A few titles, in addition to those treated at length in this and other chapters, suggest the variety of their enthusiasms: *The World's Advance-Thought*, edited by Lucy A. Mallory in Portland from 1886 to 1918; *Indian Advance*, managed by May Longenbaugh in Carson City, Nevada, in 1899; *Ridgway Populist*, edited by Ellen G. Cassidy in Ridgway, Colorado, from 1894 to 1905; *Christian Workman*, edited by Nannie M. Arnold in Whittier, California, in 1892 and 1893.

Many publications promoted more than one cause. The suffragists usually supported temperance; the educational reformers wanted better job opportunities for women and less extravagant clothing styles; the spiritualists campaigned for the election of liberals to political office. This chapter examines the careers and publications of three editors, the first of whom started a periodical to battle polygamy as it was practiced by members of the Mormon church. The second represents at least thirteen women who edited temperance papers, and the third founded and operated the publication of the Puget Sound Co-operative Colony.

Jennie Anderson was born in Ireland on December 6, 1849, and came to the United States with her family, who settled in New York. In 1866 she went to Europe, staying for five years to study at convents in Berlin and Florence. Shortly after her return, in 1871, she married Bernard Arnold Martin Froiseth in Brooklyn. The couple moved to Salt Lake City's Fort Douglas, where Bernard, a surveyor and mapmaker, had been assigned two years earlier by the U.S. government. He later left government service to establish a real estate and map-publishing business.

During the next several years, Utah became the focus of national outrage as Mormons openly followed what they believed to be a divine revelation received by church founder Joseph Smith, directing men to take more than one wife at a time. Mormons and others called this polygamy, although that term actually describes multiple mates of either sex, the correct term for the Mormon practice being polygyny. By the early 1870s Congress had passed anti-polygamy legislation, and distaste for polygamy, along with fear that political and economic activities of the Mormons would make them all-powerful in the areas they dominated, had led to opposing political parties for church members and nonmembers in Utah. As the decade progressed, Congress gave the federal judiciary increasing power to enforce the anti-polygamy acts, and the Supreme Court upheld their legality.

Mormon women joined Mormon men in defending polygamy. The *Woman's Exponent*, founded for Mormon women in 1872, devoted space to the benefits of polygamy as attacks intensified. Writers upheld its morality, described their own favorable experiences as plural wives, and chided critics for hypocrisy. An 1879 article quoted and praised an unidentified author who wrote that "the difference between the Mormons and the christian statesmen is that the Mormons marry their mistresses, the congressmen don't."[3]

Jennie Anderson Froiseth soon became embroiled in the effort to bring Mormons to their senses or, failing that, to have polygamy completely outlawed. She helped organize The Ladies' Anti-Polygamy Society of Utah and served as its vice president. After it went national in August 1880, as the Woman's National Anti-Polygamy Society, she made lecture tours around the country to strengthen sentiment against the practice and to set up new branches of the society. Apparently, the state society later evolved into the Utah Association for the Advancement of Women, for a 1930 obituary article about Froiseth referred to it by that name.[4]

In April 1880, the Utah society began publication of the *Anti-Polygamy Standard*, with Jennie Anderson Froiseth as editor. Although the paper provided only the names of society officers, with no editor listed, she later claimed responsibility in a compilation of anti-polygamy writings drawn largely from its pages and published in 1886.[5] A monthly of eight pages with a subscription price of one dollar a year, the *Standard* carried a biblical verse from I Corinthians 7:2 as its motto, "Let every Man have his own Wife, and Let every Woman have her own Husband."

Froiseth noted in her "Salutatory" that the object of the paper would be the same as that of the society, "to plan and execute such measures as shall in the judgment of its members tend to suppress polygamy in Utah and other Territories of the United States." An editorial, also in the first number, assured readers that society members felt only "kindness and good will" toward Mormon women, but hated the system under which they suffered. The editor stated that the articles in the paper would be written, or at least have facts furnished by, "women who have had personal experience in the system and consequently may be relied upon as true in every particular."[6]

True to this promise, Froiseth included many exposés of polygamy, with titles like "How Wives Are Coerced into Giving Consent for their Husbands to Enter Polygamy" or "A Letter From an Old Mormon Lady." A poem in Scots dialect was called "The Wail of a Mormon Wife." Several articles focused on Ann Eliza Young, the last and youngest wife of church president Brigham Young, who sued him for divorce on grounds of neglect, cruel treatment, and desertion, thus presenting the federal courts with the interesting dilemma of whether a divorce could be granted to a woman not officially married.[7] The case attracted great notoriety, and Ann Eliza Young went on the lecture circuit with sensational accounts of her experiences as a plural wife. As its general agent, she also took subscriptions for the *Standard*.

Many anti-polygamists disapproved of allowing Mormon polygamists to vote, reasoning that they would cast their ballots as directed by the church. Mormon women had voted since 1870, and Froiseth found herself in the position of supporting woman suffrage for all states and territories except Utah. She seemed to find no contradiction in this stand.

The *Standard* also contained material unrelated to polygamy, such as miscellaneous news notes telling readers that a young ladies' reading club had been organized in Washington, and household hints, like one advising that to make a proper soup one must use the proper herbs. A series on "Woman as a Benefactress" consisted of sketches of noble women who had labored for the cause of humanity. For its first two years, the paper featured a mining page, and it always included news of Utah's non-Mormon churches.

The final number, for February and March 1883, mentioned plans for an enlarged and improved fourth volume, but admitted that the *Standard* had been "struggling against fearful odds, right in the midst of the enemy's camp."[8] Froiseth offered no explanation of the paper's demise, but she may have surmised that her cause was on its way to victory even without her organization and its paper, for in 1882 Congress had passed the Edmunds Act, which specified fines and prison sentences for those convicted of polygamy or unlawful cohabitation and removed their right to vote or hold public office, as well. The 1887 Edmunds-Tucker Law abolished woman suffrage in Utah, required male voters to sign an oath of obedience to anti-polygamy laws, provided that wives must testify against their husbands in polygamy cases, and dissolved the church as a legal corporation.

Perhaps Froiseth simply decided to spend more of her time on another project—the construction of a refuge for Mormon women and children who abandoned polygamy. The U.S. Congress gave the Industrial Christian Home Association of Utah $40,000 to rent a temporary building and appropriated additional money for construction of the Industrial Christian Home in Salt Lake City in 1888 and 1889. According to one report, Mormon women held indignation meetings instead of flocking to the home, and only three took advantage of the refuge, which later became a residential hotel.[9]

Froiseth continued both her literary and philanthropic interests after the demise of the *Standard*. She aided in the founding of a group from which the Salt Lake Ladies' Literary Club evolved, and participated as an active member in the Poetry Society. She also established a local reputation as a dramatic reader.

Her obituary reported her association with the Orphan's Home and Day Nursery, but gave primary emphasis to her role in the founding of a home for the aged. She conceived the idea and interested a donor in bequeathing money for it. A bronze plaque placed at the home five years after her death commemorated "her devotion and energy."[10] She died at the age of eighty in February 1930, at the home of one of her five children.

Mary Frank Browne also engaged in a variety of philanthropic activities, but the temperance movement took first place among her interests. Along with abolition, it had become a major object of concern for reformers early in the nineteenth century. During the 1820s and 1830s temperance societies multiplied, and the movement's first prominent publication appeared in 1826. By the mid-1850s thirteen of the thirty-one states had passed temperance or prohibition laws, and more than 20 periodicals preached the virtues of abstinence. Organization of the Prohibition party in 1884 gave impetus to the crusade, and a periodical directory for 1886 listed 134 temperance publications.[11]

Other organizations that played major roles in the movement and sponsored publications were the International Order of Good Templars, a fraternal organization founded in 1851 to promote temperance, peace, and brotherhood, and the Woman's Christian Temperance Union (WCTU), which grew out of the Women's Temperance Crusade of 1873. The temperance campaign sent women church members into saloons to sing hymns, pray, and ask saloonkeepers to stop selling liquor. The National Woman's Christian Temperance Union got under way in 1874, and that same year Californians organized their first local chapter at Grass Valley. Through her work with that chapter, Mary Frank Browne became an editor.

She was born in Warsaw, New York, on September 9, 1835. After completing her education, she taught there in a school sponsored by the Presbyterian church. In 1858 she married Philo D. Browne, a banker from Montreal, Canada, and established her home there. She assisted in the organization of the Young Women's Christian Association of Montreal and served as its president; helped form the Ladies' Canadian Foreign Missionary Society and was one of its officers; aided in the establishment and management of an infants' home; and worked as a founder and officer of the Canadian Board of Missions.

The Brownes and their three children moved to San Francisco in 1876. She organized and presided over a YWCA there, moving to Oakland and setting up another YWCA the following year. She developed ambitious plans for an Oakland YWCA building, which would include a home for young women, a day nursery for working mothers, a kindergarten, and a room for gospel services. She also served for quite some time, beginning in 1877, as president of the Woman's Occidental Board of Foreign Missions. For several years she presided over The Ebell, an Oakland art and literary society, and the first free kindergarten in Oakland grew out of her young ladies' Bible class. Although probably not involved with religious reform to any great extent, she expressed sympathy with the Hyacinthe movement founded by a dissident and defrocked French priest to liberalize organized religion.[12]

Mary Frank Browne became involved with the WCTU almost as soon as it started. The local chapter developed into a state organization in 1879, and delegates elected her president during an 1880 convention held at the First Congregational Church in Oakland. A resolution that all meetings be presided over by the president inspired considerable discussion, "some holding that it was unfeminine for a woman to preside at a public meeting," but it eventually passed. The new president refused to pledge herself to preside or even to sit on the platform, although it was only a step above the floor. The church pastor presided at the evening meeting "to spare the president's feelings."[13] The recorder of this incident went on to state that "Mrs. Browne's views changed, however, and she afterwards became a most successful presiding officer and a fine platform speaker, distinguished for her fluency and readiness of speech."

She remained WCTU president for five years, with only a brief respite when she served as vice president before moving up to replace a president who had resigned. In the course of her duties, she decided that the state association needed a publication and started *The Bulletin* early in 1885. With a committee to manage its finances, she produced it monthly, changing its name to *The Pharos* to avoid confusion in the mails with a major daily newspaper. The new name recalled a lighthouse built about 300 B.C. in Egypt, one of the seven wonders of the ancient world. *The Pacific Ensign*, an eight-page weekly with more reliable funding, replaced *The Pharos* at the beginning of 1891, and other women continued the work that Mary Browne had started.

No copies of *The Bulletin* survive, and only one of *The Pharos*—the number for November 1889. It contained twelve pages of essays, news reports, editorials, fillers, book reviews, and advertisements. As the official WCTU paper, it listed names of officers, covered local and state meetings, and encouraged subscriptions and support. It claimed to be the largest WCTU state paper in the United States, with a circulation of four thousand and a paying subscription list of twenty-six hundred.

The paper used much material from other publications, principally in the form of short articles on subjects related to temperance. One, written by reformer Washington Gladden for *The Forum*, suggested that "The Only Way to Become a Capitalist" was to save and use more wisely the money spent on beer, tobacco, and baseball. Another, based on a *Chronicle* story, decried the backbreaking labor demanded of French country women to produce wine. A filler stated, "The liquor traffic begins by hanging a sign over the door, and ends by hanging a man on a gibbet." [14]

Browne wrote introductory paragraphs for some of the reprinted articles, compiled the news reports, and prepared editorials. She no doubt had a hand in sponsoring the *Pharos* teas, which, she wrote, had become symposiums on important questions like "how shall the law that liquor shall not be sold near the University of Berkeley be enforced?" [15] In a lengthy travelogue she described a trip to Chicago, where she visited the national WCTU office, digressing from comments about the scenery to include support for the cause:

> The mountains are round us on every side but there are none so high but the engineer found some way around or through or over them. So let it be with us this coming year. There are thousands of women in our State unenlisted in this work, feeling that they have but little influence individually. This may or may not be true but unitedly what a power may our California women become. [16]

Browne's writings also included a temperance book, *Overcome*, which, according to a biographical sketch, portrayed "the evils of fashionable wine-drinking and intemperance." [17] It may have collected articles and editorials that were originally prepared for *The Pharos*.

Sometime near the turn of the century, Browne moved from Oakland to Sonoma County. She lived in the town of Camp Meeker for four years before she died there of heart failure on June 2, 1910, at the age of seventy-four.

Laura Etta Crane Hall Peters lived during the same years as Mary Frank Browne, but their interests and accomplishments differed considerably. Laura Hall started out as a campaigner for temperance and woman suffrage, but moved on to labor reform, the more radical causes of communitarianism and spiritualism, and, finally, populism. In the service of the Puget Sound Co-operative Colony, she became an editor.

The colony followed a venerable tradition. One writer considers the Puritans to have been America's first utopians, explaining that they saw the New World as a promised land where they could establish an ideal society. [18] After them came many other dreamers and seekers, convinced that they could perfect society and determined to put their ideas into practice. Robert Owen established socialist communities during the 1820s, notably New Harmony on the banks of Indiana's Wabash River. Brook Farm in Massachusetts attracted followers of transcendentalism from 1841 to 1847. John Humphrey Noyes gathered groups in Connecticut and Vermont and then established his best-known colony at Oneida, New York, in 1848. The West had its own utopian communities, and the Puget Sound area of Washington attracted more than its share, five of them between 1885 and 1915. Like their predecessors in the East, they drew idealists who intended to build a new social order, and who published newspapers.[19]

Utopian periodicals varied widely in content, style, and quality. They usually served three main purposes—to spread the ideas and plans of their sponsors; to attract converts or, in the case of the communitarian groups, colonists; and to maintain communication among the committed. Laura Hall made sure that *The Model Commonwealth* met all of those goals.

Born in Fountain County, Indiana, in 1840, Laura Etta Crane moved with her family to Iowa and there married Isaac M. (Ike) Hall. Her parents migrated to Seattle, Washington, in 1864, and the Halls went with them, stopping in San Francisco for the birth of their first child. In Seattle, Ike Hall established himself as a lawyer and earned a reputation for his wit and good legal mind.[20] He also took up journalism and, during 1866 and 1867, ran a succession of short-lived newspapers, including Seattle's first daily, before taking political office as county auditor. In 1871 he briefly ran another newspaper. Although many frontier periodicals were family affairs, there is no evidence that his wife assisted him. She probably kept busy running their home and taking care of their two children, although a granddaughter remarked many years later that Laura preferred writing and painting to cleaning and cooking.[21] She also had to cope with her husband's drinking, which became increasingly troublesome, in spite of his association with the International Order of Good Templars. In 1874 she filed for divorce, but a reconciliation resulted in the birth of a third child, and the couple postponed their divorce until 1883.

Laura Hall, too, had been active in the Order of Good Templars, holding office and traveling around the state to organize new lodges, but suffrage efforts soon came to occupy more of her time than temperance. In 1871 her name appeared among those who sponsored a suffrage convention in Olympia, and delegates appointed her to the convention's constitution committee. After Washington State gave women the vote in 1883, she served on the first mixed jury in King County, and when the Washington Supreme Court overturned the suffrage law four years later, she spoke out:

I have been in a number of meetings, and have heard the votes ring out loud and clear for woman suffrage. I was paralyzed when I saw the *Post-Intelligencer* extra announcing that the rights had been taken from us, and I have hardly got over my paralytic shock yet. . . . I believe we should go into the war and fight against the war on women. If we show we are earnest, the men will help us.[22]

The war lasted twenty-three years. Hall battled as vice president of a group of local societies in 1888, president of the Port Angeles suffrage club in 1896, and vice president in 1898 of the state association, which had been formed three years earlier. Appointed to take charge of the suffrage bill presented to the 1897 legislature, she steered it through both houses and then discovered that a worthless bill had been substituted for the genuine one. On the last day of the session, she arranged to have the correct bill signed by the speaker of the house and the president of the senate and then asked the senate president to make her a special messenger to take the bill to the governor for his signature. She described her mission in these words:

As I happened to hold the peculiar position of having voted (at the State convention) for both those gentlemen, and as I had taken pains to remind them of that fact, and as both the Governor and Lieutenant Governor were suffragists, I found no difficulty in having my request granted. I said that the bill had been delayed, deformed, pigeon-holed and stolen, and I would not feel safe until it was made law by the Governor's signature.[23]

The measure still had to go before the state's voters, however, and they failed to approve it. Not until after Hall's death did suffrage finally come to Washington.

At about the same time that she began working actively for suffrage, she also joined the Knights of Labor, attracted perhaps by that organization's advocacy of cooperative institutions and government ownership of utilities, as well as by its support for equality of the sexes. Her father and her son became members before her, the son and two of her nephews having started a daily newspaper in 1885 which they ran as a semi-official organ of the Knights for about a year.

Another relative who joined the Knights, Peter Peyto Good, had the idea for a communitarian organization in which all would be equal, no person could employ another, and each would work for the good of all. A Seattle lawyer, George Venable Smith, possessed the organizational skills to carry out Good's vision, and in 1886 he put together the Puget Sound Co-operative Colony with himself as president of the board and Laura Hall as corresponding secretary and education officer, responsible for publicity. Almost immediately she started a newspaper, *The Model Commonwealth*.

Its first number appeared in Seattle on May 21, 1886, three months after the colony was organized. The board selected Port Angeles as the site for the community, and in May 1887 Hall and the paper moved there. She and her eleven-year-old daughter settled in rooms over the printing offices, and the eight-page paper went from biweekly to weekly publication.[24]

For her paper's motto, Hall used "Let the many combine in co-operation as the few have done in corporations." The first number stated that *The Model Commonwealth*, as the official paper of the colony, would be devoted to its interests. It gave considerable space to recruiting efforts; colonists would find employment, abundant supplies, good wages for an eight-hour day, physicians and lawyers paid by the colony, a home, and free libraries and schools. There would be no rent, taxes, mortgages, debts, saloons, or churches. In its boosterism the paper differed but little from weekly newspapers throughout the West.

Hall reprinted materials from other periodicals, also in keeping with newspaper practice of the day, but her exchanges usually came from publications of the Knights of Labor and other like-minded papers. She kept readers informed of developments at the colony with reports giving names of new colonists and share purchasers and rules developed for colony governance. Many articles appeared without bylines, but Hall signed a column she wrote for children. She also may have been responsible for frequent comments about the happy lot of the colony's women, who would receive equal pay for equal work, the right to vote, and, with meals prepared in a cooperative kitchen by colonists, a solution to the servant problem. The kitchen would rid home life of drudgery and provide varied menus. When not taking a turn at cooking, women could devote themselves to loftier pursuits.

While still in Seattle, Hall sent out one number of the *Commonwealth* with a flower petal enclosed. She had hosted the first colony social, a pot-luck dinner with music and dancing, and a guest had brought a bouquet of flowers. From it she took the petals, explaining,

> It will give us great pleasure to contribute a small portion to each of our subscribers, who, when they find a petal of a flower in their paper, can begin

to understand how lovely they can make *their homes* when they have become established in the colony, where the hours of labor will be few enough to allow them some time for the cultivation of the beautiful, and where their homes will be *their's* in the broadest sense.[25]

With the move to Port Angeles, Hall began to include much local news in the paper. She reported the colony's July 4 celebration, at which she sang the national anthem; its ethical culture meetings; results of school elections; the progress of building construction; and, with great enthusiasm, music and theater performances, in which she frequently appeared. Colonists could find out from the paper when wild blackberries were ripe and where the new settlers came from. Or they might be taken to task for their tendency to find fault and criticize each other within their homes and families.

In July 1887 *The Model Commonwealth* boasted a circulation of two thousand, but both the paper and the colony had problems by this time. Colonists expressed discontent with the president and his board, and only a favorable response from proxy voters kept them in power after a September election. In a special election early in 1888 their opponents took control. Hall either resigned or was removed from her editorship, although she kept the post of education officer. The paper soon took a more radical stance.

In her "Valedictory," Hall explained that the paper required more time and attention than she could give it and that she had been awaiting the arrival of an assistant. However, she continued, "It is now thought better that I retire altogether from the paper in order that I may have more time to attend to my correspondence and other duties." She promised that the paper would improve with an experienced journalist as editor but admitted that editing it had been "a pleasant duty." Leaving it would be "like bidding farewell to a beloved friend."[26] The colony limped along for only a few more months, with *The Model Commonwealth* evolving under new ownership and other names into a standard rural weekly.

While still editor, Hall had accepted assistance from a new colonist, Charles J. Peters. Thirteen years her junior, he moved to Port Angeles from Texas but soon became disillusioned with the colony, and purchased farmland. They were married in 1888, made a trip to Europe, and then settled down to farm. Laura Hall Peters chaired the local women's committee charged with arousing support for Washington's exhibit in the Chicago

Columbian Exposition of 1893, while Charles served as county exposition commissioner. She enjoyed gardening and won a blue ribbon for her strawberry preserves at the 1895 county fair.

By this time she had become a leader in the state suffrage movement and also had taken up the cause of populism. In 1896 when the Populists, Democrats, and Silver Republicans held a fusion convention, she attended as one of the Clallam County representatives—the only woman delegate. Undoubtedly she supported the suffrage cause at the convention, but her only recorded speech concerned railroad passes for legislators.[27]

Laura Hall Peters turned away from organized Christianity and probably agreed with the decision not to have churches in the Port Angeles colony. Whether her acceptance of spiritualism was a cause or a result of her change of heart regarding Christianity, she apparently espoused wholeheartedly the belief that the spirit lives on after physical death and can communicate with living persons. A Seattle spiritualist minister read the service over her grave after her death in 1902, and her obituary reported that shortly before she died she had urged friends to be glad, for, she asked, "Am I not about to step off into a higher and better life?" The obituary writer characterized her as "radical, aggressive and progressive, strong and positive in her conviction and plain mannered to an unusual degree." She wanted only a simple burial. A friend built her coffin, and a neighbor's wagon was her hearse.[28]

The enthusiasms of Laura Hall Peters ranged across a broad spectrum of the causes that attracted the allegiance, or at least the interest, of nineteenth-century Americans. Mary Frank Browne concentrated on temperance but took up the banner of other reforms as well, most of them of the sort that society found appropriate outlets for the exercise of women's civilizing influence. Jennie Anderson Froiseth worked in a more restricted sphere. While she engaged in philanthropic efforts throughout her adult life, her one major crusade was to rid the country of what she and other respectable citizens considered a morally and socially degrading practice —Mormon polygamy.

All three were convinced both of the value of their ideas and of the power of the press. Like most editors with a cause, they saw their papers not as a means to make a living but as a way of promulgating their beliefs. They attracted neither large circulations nor substantial amounts of advertising, and they found no wealthy donors to subsidize them. Only the WCTU supported its publication consistently, but not until after Mary Frank Browne's editorship ended. The editors worked without salaries and suffered, to varying degrees, the ridicule or contempt of their contemporaries.

To their readers, most of whom shared similar convictions, they offered information and encouragement. To the unconverted, they suggested the possibility of a better life. To the modern audience, they left a record of a different world and of woman's place in it.

CHAPTER 5

The Suffragists

Before returning to Oregon I resolved to purchase an outfit and begin the publication of a newspaper myself, as I felt that the time had come for vigorous work in my own State, and we had no journal in which the demands of women for added rights were treated with respectful consideration.[1]

—Abigail Scott Duniway

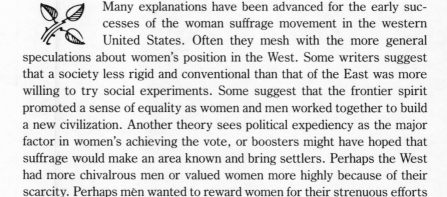 Many explanations have been advanced for the early successes of the woman suffrage movement in the western United States. Often they mesh with the more general speculations about women's position in the West. Some writers suggest that a society less rigid and conventional than that of the East was more willing to try social experiments. Some suggest that the frontier spirit promoted a sense of equality as women and men worked together to build a new civilization. Another theory sees political expediency as the major factor in women's achieving the vote, or boosters might have hoped that suffrage would make an area known and bring settlers. Perhaps the West had more chivalrous men or valued women more highly because of their scarcity. Perhaps men wanted to reward women for their strenuous efforts during the pioneer period.

While historians have examined and debated these assumptions and looked at the progress of woman suffrage both in individual states and in the West as a whole, little attention has been paid to the publications that the suffragists founded or to the women who founded them. Much more has been written about the suffrage periodicals of the East, and most discussions of suffrage ideas are based on eastern sources.

The West had at least twelve suffrage papers, all edited by women. Copies of eight of them survive. No doubt others existed, as directory listings of such titles as *Equal Rights Champion* suggest. The twelve papers identified were published from 1869—when Wyoming gave women the vote—to 1914. Thus, this chapter includes a few editors active after the turn of the century in order to provide coverage of the group as a whole. By the end of 1914, all of the western states and territories except New Mexico and Hawaii had adopted suffrage.

Suffragists founded papers because the conventional press denied them access. They hoped to give the movement a voice, to expand its influence, and to win converts. This chapter focuses on two editors: Emily Pitts-Stevens and Abigail Scott Duniway. Like others who founded papers to support causes, they worked actively in organizations and lectured widely to advance their ideas.

The presence of alternative voices in the press of the United States is a venerable tradition, and women's rights periodicals are readily identifiable as part of that tradition. Certainly, the suffrage papers shared the traits one historian identified as characteristic of the dissident press: they were underdogs, at least until well into the twentieth century; they held views that diverged from the mainstream; they wanted to effect social change; and they were excluded from the traditional media marketplace, but their ideas gradually filtered into it.[2]

A few periodicals devoted to women's rights appeared in the East before the Civil War. *The Lily*, for example, was published from 1849 until 1859 in Seneca Falls, New York. After the Civil War, in 1868, Susan B. Anthony and Elizabeth Cady Stanton founded the most notorious of the woman suffrage papers, *The Revolution*, in New York City. Its rival, the more conservative *The Woman's Journal* of Boston, began under the leadership of Lucy Stone in 1870.

At about the same time, western suffragists got their own publications under way. In 1869 Emily A. Pitts, a twenty-five-year-old schoolteacher who had moved to San Francisco from New York in 1865, bought a half interest in the *California Weekly Mercury* and transformed it into the West's first suffrage paper, taking full control and renaming it *The Pioneer* later that year. Her "Salutatory" established the tone for *The Pioneer* and for the suffrage periodicals that followed:

> We defend the rights of women fearlessly and to the best of our ability. We shall insist upon woman's independence—her elevation, socially and politically, to the platform now solely occupied by man. We shall claim for her each privilege now given to every male citizen of the United States. In short, we shall claim for her the right of suffrage—believing that by this she will gain the position for which God intended her—equality with man.[3]

Emily Pitts had come to San Francisco to help establish and then teach in the Miel Institute, a female seminary. She wrote in *The Pioneer* that she built up the public evening school for girls but resigned her position when her health failed. She spent some time tutoring "in one of the most prominent families in this city" before resuming work with the evening school. This lasted until

> the value and importance of woman's industrial enlargements and political enfranchisement so filled our entire mind, heart and soul, that we were constrained to abandon all other interests and to consecrate ourselves to the promotion of that great movement that held within its sacred embrace, the destinies of half the human race.[4]

Not long after she changed the name of her paper, the editor changed her own name as well. At the beginning of 1870 she started listing herself as Emily Pitts-Stevens, having married August K. Stevens. The *San Francisco Chronicle* implied that this was not her first marriage in an 1872 note that read, "The population of Lima numbers 38,704 more males than females in a total of 160,059. What a chance for Sister Emily Pitts Stevens and other muchly marrying women."[5]

At the same time she worked to establish her paper as a voice for suffrage, she led attempts to organize women in San Francisco, the rest of California, and Nevada into associations that would agitate for woman suffrage. She served as vice president of the San Francisco organization and conducted the first meeting of the California Woman's State Suffrage Association in January 1870, until a temporary president was elected. As a member of its board of control, she jumped into the disputes among its members that apparently began almost immediately. The *San Francisco Chronicle* faithfully reported proceedings of the meetings in a manner calculated to make the suffragists look ridiculous, stating that "two rings" had formed.[6] Pitts-Stevens gave few details in *The Pioneer*, but lamented that "the men and women friendly to our movement cannot see through the cunning and craft of those who would make the woman-suffrage cause a stepping stone for their individual advancement" and that the convention and state society "have been captured by a ring, and the whole movement subordinated to other people's quarrels!"[7]

In June she wrote that the opposition ring had urged county associations to withdraw from the state group because they had insufficient voice in its decisions, and in October she charged that those who had failed to gain control of the movement or *The Pioneer* now sought to destroy the influence of both by attacks on her character.[8]

The editor did not reveal the exact nature of her rumored impropriety. The *Chronicle*, however, named her in 1872 as a member of the Radical Club, an institution "composed exclusively of Socialists, Spiritualists, Free Lovers, Woman Suffragists and all who by reason of their sentiments are ostracised from the society which they so much condemn."[9] From then on Pitts-Stevens refuted the free-love charge at frequent intervals. Apparently it did not arise at the 1872 state association meetings, when she was president, but at the Pacific Slope Woman's Suffrage Convention held that year she reminded the delegates that they had met not to discuss "free-love or anything of the kind; but to talk of the ballot, and the best way to get it."[10] That same year, dissatisfied with views on women's rights held by the candidates of the major political parties, Pitts-Stevens organized the Woman Suffrage party of the Pacific Coast and was elected its president. As November approached, she published many articles supporting presidential candidate George Francis Train, the eccentric reformer who had provided financial support for *The Revolution* in New York.

At the state association meetings in 1873 the free-love accusation came up again. Along with other issues, it caused a complete split among those attending. The officers adjourned the convention two days early, before new officers could be elected, and the editor and her supporters—a majority of those present, according to the *Chronicle*—reconvened and held meetings as a continuation of the official sessions, electing their own officers. Pitts-Stevens made a speech "with tears in her eyes," disclaiming any belief in free-love heresies and denouncing the *Chronicle* reporter who put her in that camp.[11]

She avoided direct treatment of the subject in *The Pioneer* until after the *Chronicle* published a statement from the deposed officers of the state association, in which they referred to the editor as "an instrument . . . under the guidance of artful conspirators, to capture this State Suffrage Association, in order to subject it to the Woodhull phase of woman suffrage and to vaccinate the holy cause in this State and on this coast with the virus of that modern social pest denominated 'Free Love.' "[12] In response, Pitts-Stevens printed a notice "To the Public," signed by ten prominent women in the suffrage movement, denouncing the "vile and scurrilous attack upon Mrs. Pitts Stevens" and pronouncing "many of the charges, particularly that relating to Free Love, UNFOUNDED AND UNTRUE." Once again, the editor attributed the association's problems to persons who wanted to use the organization for personal aggrandizement, under the leadership of "a *certain* Masculine Member, whose ambition is to rule all creation."[13]

The California disputes reflected disagreements among leaders of the national suffrage movement. Pitts-Stevens reported regularly and at length on national meetings and claimed initially that she would stand aloof from dissension in the national groups, but it soon became obvious that she supported the liberal views of Susan B. Anthony and Elizabeth Cady Stanton, rather than the conservative position of Lucy Stone and her Boston followers. The question of how to respond to Victoria Woodhull, who espoused her free-love views in *Woodhull & Claflin's Weekly*, the paper she edited in New York with the assistance of her sister, Tennessee Claflin, bedeviled the national leaders, as well as the Californians.

The *Chronicle* predicted that the arguments would be "the end of the suffrage movement in this state for the present,"[14] and certainly a lull occurred that lasted for several years. Pitts-Stevens abandoned *The Pioneer*, giving ill health as her reason.[15] Perhaps the slurs on her morals coupled with the power struggle in the state association had taken a physical toll. Perhaps she simply tired of the editorial grind, or she may have lacked financial means to keep the paper going.

With no concrete evidence available, it is impossible to determine whether the free-love rumors had any basis in fact. One is tempted to conclude that Pitts-Stevens made herself a target for speculation by supporting Train and the liberal wing of the national suffrage leadership but that the press and her opponents in the state organization jumped to unwarranted conclusions. Although an ardent campaigner for woman suffrage, she also upheld the sanctity of the home in terms that could have come straight from the lexicon of the ideal of true womanhood. She agreed that "there is nothing so beautiful as home life" [16] and published comments by other writers from time to time praising her own achievements as a homemaker.

Abigail Scott Duniway, Oregon editor of *The Pioneer* for a few months in 1871 and later publisher of her own women's rights paper in Portland, wrote one of these. Duniway had spent a day with Pitts-Stevens in August and reported that she found the lodging to which she had been invited "dainty" and "cozy," peopled by "the twin sisters, Love and Harmony," and the husband "a genial, happy, whole-souled gentleman, with love-light in his eyes, and a pardonable pride of his gifted wife in his heart." [17]

The Pioneer survived Pitts-Stevens's departure by only a few months. Details of her activities after 1873 are scant. She founded the Woman's Pacific Coast Publishing Company that year, and the *San Francisco Directory* for 1873 listed her as its president, but it may have been connected with the paper. *Directory* entries between 1874 and 1877 refer to her simply as "writer" or "journalist." With her husband as president and herself as an officer, she instituted the Seamen's League in 1874,[18] but its exact purpose is unknown. Perhaps it was a forerunner of the Sailors' Union set up a decade later by the Woman's Christian Temperance Union to sponsor socials and gospel temperance meetings and to supply temperance literature for the library at the Seamen's Bethel, a gathering place for sailors.

The *Directory* for 1880 listed Pitts-Stevens as a "temperance lecturer." She joined the prohibition party in 1882 and led a movement in 1888 to persuade the WCTU to endorse that party. Active in the California Lodge of the Sons of Temperance as a lecturer, she served as grand vice-templar for the Independent Order of Good Templars. *The Queen Bee* of Denver credited her with "an eloquent discourse" on temperance there in 1883.[19] She wrote for WCTU publications and labored as state superintendent of foreign work for that organization in 1887. In 1897 a directory listed her as a national organizer for the WCTU. According to one writer, she also ran a successful business during these years, presumably in job printing, and required all stockholders to join the WCTU.[20] Still traveling the temperance lecture circuit in 1892, she attracted a favorable notice from Annie Martin of the *Carson Daily Morning News* in Nevada, who credited the lecturer's oratorical powers with gaining her "the name of 'Our Demosthenes' among that noble band of women leagued together for 'God and home and native land.'" [21] In 1894 she was a member of the Equal Rights

League and the board of the state suffrage society, and the following year she participated in the state woman's congress, which passed a unanimous resolution favoring suffrage.[22] Although she did not revive *The Pioneer*, she apparently remained a staunch supporter of the suffrage cause.

Abigail Scott Duniway fought for suffrage in Oregon even longer and more tirelessly. She began her weekly paper, *The New Northwest*, in Portland in 1871 and kept it going for sixteen years, later editing two other suffrage papers and living long enough to see suffrage finally adopted and to receive recognition as its premier champion in the Northwest.

Born in 1834 in Illinois, Abigail moved west with her family in 1852. Her mother and a younger brother died during the journey, but her father pushed on, and she obtained a teaching position in a small town near Salem after the family arrived in Oregon, although she had less than a sixth-grade education. After only one season of teaching, she married Benjamin Duniway, another recent emigrant from Illinois. Nine years later, with four children, the Duniways lost their farm, which Ben had offered as security for a loan, and a short time later a back injury left him unable to farm.

Abigail Scott Duniway first tried running boarding schools as a means of supporting the family, then opened a millinery shop in Albany. This provided funds sufficient to move the family to Portland, where Ben Duniway got a job at the customs house through the influence of his wife's brother, Harvey Scott, editor of *The Oregonian* in Portland and lifelong opponent of woman suffrage. Abigail Scott Duniway was thirty-six and had six children —five sons and one daughter—when she started *The New Northwest*.

She had not started out as a suffragist. However, she came to see her mother as a victim of the backbreaking labor to which pioneer women were subjected, and the first years of her own marriage strengthened her conviction that women were little better than serfs under the laws and customs of the time. In her millinery shop she met customers from whom she heard stories of husbands who abandoned their wives, leaving them with debts about which the wives had known nothing. Others appropriated money that the wives had earned selling butter and eggs. When her husband suggested during a family conversation that women could remedy such situations if they had the vote, Abigail Duniway saw the light. Of course! If women could vote, they could not only ensure their own independence, they could clean up politics and perhaps even usher in an era of world peace. A periodical seemed the ideal vehicle for sharing her insights with others.

Duniway had tried her hand at writing even before she became Oregon editor for *The Pioneer*. She had kept a diary of the Scotts' journey to Oregon and had published a novel based on the journey in 1859. Called *Captain Gray's Company, or Crossing the Plains and Living in Oregon*, it collected bad reviews and lost money.

Like Emily Pitts-Stevens, Duniway published a paper that used articles, editorials, fiction, poetry, and fillers to promote suffrage, but both papers treated other subjects as well. They published general news, practical advice of many kinds, articles of wide interest, and advertising. They also reminded readers frequently that the papers needed financial as well as moral support. At the end of 1886, Duniway wrote that she had produced more than four hundred original columns of printed matter for *The New Northwest* and other papers during that year and had canvassed every town she had visited for subscriptions and renewals, adding,

> we do feel abused, and insist that we have a right to say so, when suffragists, many of whom, as in Washington Territory, have received their liberties mainly through these efforts, and many others, as in Oregon, who owe their property rights and whatever of fame they have gained to the influence of this journal, withhold from it their support. We confess that we do feel abused and outraged when they let their subscriptions expire unless personally solicited to renew them, and they often even then . . . make some other vain and vapid excuse to "let go." [23]

To help with publication of the paper, Duniway recruited her family. Her older sons set type under the direction of a printer. The younger ones ran errands and filled paste pots. When her sons came down with measles in 1872, she discontinued publication for three months. Her younger sister, Catharine Coburn, served as associate editor from 1874 until 1879, when two of the sons became co-publishers of the paper. A third son joined them in 1882. (Catharine went on to edit the Portland *Evening Telegram* from 1883 to 1888, then worked as associate editor at the *Oregonian* until her death in 1913.)

Duniway consistently upheld the values of the traditional family. One of the advantages of a woman's activities outside the home was that they made her a more interesting wife and mother. Giving women the vote would not make them masculine, she promised, agreeing that there was "nothing more detestable to be seen or endured upon the earth than a feminine man, unless it be a masculine woman." [24] No taint of free love arose to tarnish the reputation of Duniway or her paper. Her disputes with other suffragists lay in different directions.

The first concerned the question of uniting the suffrage and temperance causes. While not opposed to temperance, Duniway insisted that each battle had to be fought separately. She feared that linking suffrage to temperance would lead the liquor interests to oppose suffrage, and she believed the suffragists could not afford to alienate any significant power bloc. She opposed prohibition, the goal of most temperance workers, for philosophical reasons as well, seeing suffrage as a form of freedom and prohibition as a form of force:

> Every attempt of men to prohibit economic rights for women has ever since increased my feeling of opposition to any sort of Prohibition which would destroy the moral responsibility or individual right to self-control in any man or woman.[25]

In the later Oregon suffrage campaigns, Duniway had differences of opinion with the national suffrage leadership over the organization and operation of the state drives for suffrage. She served as vice president of the National Woman Suffrage Association in 1884, but resented attempts to impose eastern ideas upon campaigns in the Northwest, and the national leaders criticized her for failing to create an extensive and highly visible organization.[26] She withdrew from the unsuccessful 1906 campaign after the national association sent its organizers to take charge. But she again led the Oregon Equal Suffrage Association, which she had founded in 1873, for the 1908 and 1910 campaigns.

Duniway had sold *The New Northwest* in 1887, reminding readers that she had warned them she would sever her ties with the paper unless they remitted subscription payments more promptly. She also mentioned increasing calls in the lecture field that demanded her time, energy, and money. Perhaps the death of her only daughter and the illness of her husband also had something to do with her decision to join two sons who had taken up ranching in Idaho.

However, she still spent most of her winters in Portland, and in 1891 she returned to journalism with a short-lived publication called *The Coming Century*—Oregon's second suffrage paper. She became editor of Frances Gottshall's weekly, *The Pacific Empire*, in the fall of 1895 and made it a near duplicate of *The New Northwest* until she retired from journalism in 1897.

In spite of the cool reception of her first novel, Duniway continued to write fiction, as well as poetry, both for her papers and for publication in book form. *Musings*, a collection of poems, came out in 1875, and a year later she published *David and Anna Matson*, a book-length poem. She revised the ill-fated *Captain Gray's Company* for republication in 1905, and completed her autobiography, *Path-Breaking*, in 1914.

In addition to such literary efforts, she found time for activity in the Portland Woman's Club and served as president of the Oregon State Federation of Woman's Clubs. In 1873 she announced her candidacy for mayor of Portland. But the battle for suffrage continued to occupy the major portion of her time. She wrote that she had spoken an average of four times a week during her editorship,[27] and she traveled frequently to Washington and Idaho to guide suffrage campaigns there both during and after her years as editor.

In 1912, Oregon voters finally approved suffrage. Duniway, ill and in a wheelchair, wrote the suffrage proclamation and signed it jointly with the governor. Suffrage had come to Idaho in 1896 and to Washington in 1910, with her help. She died in 1915.

From what is known of their lives, one can conclude that the main similarity between Abigail Scott Duniway and Emily Pitts-Stevens was their common devotion to the cause of suffrage. Both had sufficient education to be literate and eloquent, both taught school for a time, both had husbands, and there the similarities in their personal lives ended. Both traveled, lectured, and led state suffrage associations, but, like other editors, they were independent individuals, and a composite portrait would obscure important differences. They borrowed from each other only to broaden the range of their arguments for suffrage.

The mottoes of the papers suggested their orientation. *The Pioneer* used "Devoted to the Promotion of Human Rights" and, under that, "Liberty, Justice, Fraternity." Pitts-Stevens explained that she used "fraternity" only because "the paucity of our language . . . has no word to express the brotherhood and sisterhood of the race."[28] The motto of *The New Northwest* was "Free Speech, Free Press, Free People." For *The Pacific Empire* Duniway chose "A Journal of Freedom."

A Colorado paper founded by Caroline Churchill claimed on its masthead to be "The only paper in the State advocating Woman's Political Equality and Individuality." Caroline Nichols Churchill used the title of *Queen Bee* both for her paper and for herself. She had founded a monthly in 1879 and called it *The Colorado Antelope*, but three years later she made it a weekly and changed its name. It remained *Queen Bee* until it ceased publication in 1895. Churchill urged women to go to the polls in force, whether they were allowed to vote or not, and she carried "individuality" beyond the masthead of the paper to its content, expressing her definite opinions in colorful prose. Chapter 7 describes her career.

The researcher finds less information on most of the other editors of suffrage periodicals. Sometimes all that remains is a name on a masthead. *The Alki*, published twice a month in Puyallup, Washington, in 1895, came next chronologically after the *Queen Bee*. Its editor was Ida LeFevre. The number for April 15, 1895, demonstrated the existence of a woman suffrage network functioning among the western publications and often reaching out to include the eastern ones as well. On its first page appeared a poem by Abigail Scott Duniway and a report of a reception given for her. The poem, a tribute to Lucy Stone titled "Make the World Better," concluded:

> Let us up and to duty! Let us do our work well;
> And wherever the story of freedom we tell,
> We will make the world better, as Lucy Stone said,
> Who made the world better, then smiled and was dead.

The editors of these publications not only read and clipped one another's papers, they met and conferred as they traveled to lecture at public meetings and to recruit supporters. The eastern suffragists also made many trips through the West, and the westerners quoted them liberally.

Next in line after *The Alki* came a monthly paper in Nevada. In Reno during 1897 and 1898 Frances A. Williamson and her daughter, Mary L. Williamson, published *The Nevada Citizen*, subtitled "A Journal Devoted to the Best Interests of Our Commonwealth," with the motto, "As in union there is strength, so in action there is progress." Frances Williamson spearheaded organization of the Nevada State Equal Suffrage Association in 1895, served as its first president, and used her paper—published at her own expense—as its official organ.

Another official paper of a suffrage association may have been the first of the new century, but not even its name has survived. *The History of Woman Suffrage*, published by the National American Woman Suffrage Association, reports that Lida P. Robinson, president of the Arizona suffrage organization from 1902 to 1905, promoted suffrage "through a little paper which she published and distributed herself throughout the Territory. This well-edited paper kept alive the favorable sentiment and through it the leading men and women suffragists in Arizona were in touch with each other." When Robinson left Arizona in 1905, both the paper and the association languished.[29]

By that time Oregon suffragists had embarked on another campaign to persuade male voters to admit women to their ranks. The movement's newspaper voice was Clara Bewick Colby's *The Woman's Tribune*. She started the paper in Nebraska in 1883, moved it to Washington, D.C., at the time of the International Council on Women in 1888, kept it there until 1904, and then changed her base of operations to Portland. At about the same time, the officers of the National American Woman Suffrage Association, displeased at the low-key campaigns organized by Abigail Scott Duniway, decided to take an active part in the Oregon effort. A fortnightly, the *Tribune* was not the sort of local or regional paper that its western predecessors had been. Although Colby included news of suffrage events in Portland and Oregon, she emphasized the national organization and state developments in the East and Midwest. Oregon voters defeated the amendment in 1906, but she kept the *Tribune* going until 1909.

The next push for suffrage came in California after several years of inactivity on the part of suffragists there. Katharine Reed Balentine, daughter of a congressman from Maine, founded *The Yellow Ribbon*, another official organ of a state organization, in 1906. She intended it to be the organ of the state and auxiliary societies in California, and in Washington and Oregon too, if they cared to cooperate. Washington did, and the monthly's motto was "Official Organ of the Washington and California Equal Suffrage Associations."

In July 1907, the paper changed its name, its editor, and, briefly, its frequency of publication. Laura Bride Powers, the new editor, called it *Western Woman*, "Weekly Advocate of Political Equality and Allied Interests," and adopted a much lighter, breezier writing style. She also expanded its content with a lineup that included "Equal Suffrage News," "Civics—Local Politics," "Clubs and Club Women," "Art and the Artists," "Worthwhile Books," "Foyer and Footlights," "Good Roads—Motoring," and "Happenings." The paper lasted until 1908.

Votes for Women, a Washington State paper, was issued for a year before and a year after Washington voters approved suffrage for women in 1910. Mrs. M. T. B. Hanna, its editor, changed the name of her monthly to *The*

New Citizen after the election.[30] No copies have been found. An assistant at *The New Citizen*, Adella M. Parker, published her own monthly, *The Western Woman Voter*, from 1911 to 1913. Designed "to be a journal of information for the women voters of the West," it discussed questions of government and of the legal rights of women both in and out of the home.[31] Colorado also had a paper for its newly enfranchised women, according to references in Caroline Nichols Churchill's *Queen Bee*. In 1894 she commended the Denver Woman's Club for publishing *The Woman Voter*.

The Nevada suffragists entered another period of activity in 1911, reviving their state suffrage organization. They obtained approval of a suffrage amendment by two consecutive legislatures, as required, and the amendment went to voters in 1914. During the campaign, they published a *Weekly Bulletin of the Nevada Equal Franchise Society*. A one-page collection of brief news articles, it may have been intended more for the press than for society members. It listed no editor.

Publications of state organizations were the norm, but at least one county had a paper of its own. A copy of the Ely, Nevada, *White Pine Suffragist*, edited by Mrs. W. E. Collins and dated October 31, 1914, survives, although it is unclear whether the *Suffragist* functioned as a continuing publication or as a short-term, pre-election effort to arouse enthusiasm for the state's suffrage amendment. It may have been a project similar to that of a group of Montana newspaperwomen who cooperated to issue a daily suffrage paper during the Montana State Fair in 1912.[32]

From the beginning of the western campaigns for woman suffrage, editors of many different orientations joined the crusade. The early ones in particular were highly individualistic. Even though they printed news of national suffrage leaders and organizations, they concentrated on the local scene and clearly stamped their personalities on their papers. Rarely did they have independent incomes, so their papers battled for survival as well as for suffrage. Subscribers, mostly middle-class women like themselves, had no funds to make donations beyond the price of a subscription, and editors had trouble collecting even subscription bills. They also found subscribers hard to come by, which resulted in low circulation revenues that usually were insufficient to support the papers. Most accepted advertisements, but small readerships and their unpopular point of view made the papers unappealing to advertisers.

An examination of the papers confirms the thesis that the editors had no common or official ideology. They developed arguments in response to the arguments of their opponents, as did their eastern sisters,[33] but they always had as a basic assumption the premise that justice would be served by the extension of the vote—a natural right—to women. This contention, frequently and passionately asserted, underlay all of their arguments.

One way of looking at their ideas is to divide them into categories suggested by a historian who used California as a model. He developed a framework referring to "social feminists," who argued that enfranchised women would humanize society, protect the home and family through social legislation, and purify politics; "personal feminists," who focused on women's quest for dignity and independence; and "natural rights feminists," who emphasized equality and condemned taxation without representation.[34]

The editors of the western suffrage papers fit into these categories, but in actuality they showed little interest in developing logical frameworks or philosophical underpinnings for their beliefs. Their aim was to gather and present all possible justifications for suffrage. They bolstered their views and answered their opponents with every idea at their disposal. Inconsistency might result, as when one article stressed natural right arguments and another in the same periodical lamented the fact that inferior men of other races had the vote when superior white women did not, but that never seemed to trouble the editors. Emphases changed somewhat over time. However, variations of the themes elaborated and stressed in the twentieth-century papers had been around since the first western suffrage editors took up journalism.

For example, an early article by Emily Pitts-Stevens combined all three themes:

> We believe that those who still refuse to recognise the civil rights of women strike at the foundation of equitable government, . . . for women are taxed but not represented; authorized to hold property, but not to control it; permitted to form political opinions, but not allowed to use them. We believe that the feminine element is necessary to complete the harmony of life in government as in other departments. If our government is a protector and educator, then does it need the peculiar characteristics of woman. . . . Not the interests of woman alone, but the interests of all humanity are involved in this great question of Suffrage.[35]

In fact, hardly an article or editorial mentioned only one idea.

Still, the natural right argument remained the firm foundation for all the

others. A rhyme that ridiculed the specter of the abandoned home offered
a variation of it:

The Same One

When woman goes to cast her vote—
Some miles away, it may be—
"Who then," is asked, "will stay at home
To rock and tend the baby?

Since the matter seems to turn
On this, as on its axis,
Just get the one who rocked it when
She went to pay her taxes.[36]

Particularly in the early days of the suffrage movement, the editors represented a dissident view. Only when capitulation of the last holdout states
neared could they claim to speak for a majority of their fellow westerners.
As dissidents, they faced ridicule and harassment of themselves and of
their papers. Perhaps their greatest problem, however, was obtaining the
means to keep publishing, and the papers generally led short lives.

Although they might hope to support themselves with their publications,
the editors usually saw journalism not as a professional goal but as a means
to the end of winning the vote for women. Despite their difficulties, they
persevered. Along with their supporters, they maintained their faith in the
power of the press, and major campaigns brought new publications as well
as increasingly extensive publicity of other types.

While it is impossible to demonstrate conclusively the total impact of
the papers, one can examine the kinds of roles they played and assess
possible areas of influence. Their main goal was to win support for suffrage from the uncommitted or opposed. Because readers were much
more likely to come from the ranks of sympathizers, it seems unlikely that
the editors achieved notable success in converting their opponents. Even
the educational function of providing exposure to ideas and issues that the
popular press overlooked or distorted probably did not function among the
unconverted.

Still, the fact that the movement could support publications at all must
have lent it some substantiality in the eyes of the general public, and over
time the public caught up with the suffragists as their ideas penetrated
mainstream thinking. Suffrage campaigns succeeded when they became
mass movements among middle-class women. By adding the force of the

printed word to the speeches and conversations of the suffragists and by providing ammunition for their proselytizing efforts, the editors promoted growth of middle-class support.

They also articulated and refined the ideas that became the bulwarks of the suffrage cause. The most basic of these, that simple justice required extension of the natural right of suffrage to women, remained a mainstay in all of their publications. The editors added to the natural right arguments, according to their own preferences and the temper of the times, appeals that emphasized the need for dignity and independence or the benefits that enfranchised women would bring to society.

Perhaps most important in terms both of ideas and action, the papers enabled suffragists to solidify a base from which to extend their efforts. A paper lent prestige to the cause in the eyes of subscribers and the general public. It boosted morale and offered information and support. It urged action and suggested exactly what that action might be. It provided a means of communication among suffragists at local, state, and national levels and helped keep the organizational networks functioning. It gave the establishment press something to react to, and even a negative reaction at least kept the issues alive.

The editors led the way in the campaigns for suffrage wherever their papers were published. They helped develop ideas and organizations. They provided a forum for a cause which had time—and justice—on its side. Perhaps they thought of themselves in Abigail Scott Duniway's terms, as "presumptuous dreamers" struggling to bring progress to a recalcitrant society:

To Readers

Presumptuous dreamer, vain, am I
To dare attempt Parnassus' hights,
My Pegasus untrained and shy,
My muse unnerved to lofty flights;
But there be hearts that choose to sing,
Albeit their lays are lowly ones,
That only to their authors bring
Compassion from Fame's favored sons.
I've penned my sad and simple song,
And to my Muse lend heart and ear,
Because I deprecate a wrong.[37]

CHAPTER 6

For the Sake of Religion

I wish you would look about you a little more and try to jot down something
every time that you think might be of public interest. . . . for your own good, I
want you to make an effort to do some other good thing than to raise boys for
missionaries in Zion. I know that is a great thing to do, but you have ability
to add to it.[1]

—Lula Greene Richards

Religion played an important part in the earliest American periodicals and continued to attract interest throughout
the nineteenth century. Even though its latter years saw
a decline in the power and influence of organized religion, religious controversies still made newspaper headlines and occupied many magazine
pages. New religious movements flourished, and they too received attention in the press. A writer estimated in 1840 that "of all the reading of the
people three-fourths is purely religious . . . of all the issues of the press
three-fourths are theological, ethical and devotional."[2]

The period before 1800 saw the publication of at least 5 American magazines devoted exclusively to religion, and this number grew rapidly. By
1828 the total had expanded to 101, by 1850 to 191, and by the early
1890s to more than 1,000.[3] Some of them took a nondenominational or
interdenominational stance, but the majority performed in the service of a
particular religion. The traditional denominations led the field in publishing

activity, having from 25 to 50 periodicals each, but the smaller groups also relied on newspapers and magazines to spread the word.

At first, the religious monthlies published mostly learned commentary on theology and philosophy, while the weeklies included much general news, competing with nonreligious weekly periodicals for readers. However, as daily newspapers became increasingly available, the weeklies also concentrated on religion and moral living, although they usually maintained a livelier style than the more academic monthlies. After the mid-1800s, the types of publications multiplied. A list might include: general magazines with a church background; scholarly reviews in biblical and religious studies; interdenominational periodicals; denominational journals of many kinds—official, liberal, regional, local, theological, women's, children's; organs of religious action groups, like the Salvation Army; and journals of missionary societies. Perhaps the peripheral movements, like spiritualism and theosophy, deserve a category of their own.

The spiritualist movement began in 1848 in Hydesville, New York, where sisters Margaret and Katharine Fox heard rappings that they identified as communications from the spirits of the dead. Spiritualism attracted many women in the vanguard of the women's rights movement, including editors, and women edited a large proportion of the spiritualist periodicals in the West. Perhaps women who sought independence in the political and economic spheres also looked for it in religion, and their activities in suffrage organizations and spiritualist societies may have worked together to reinforce the sense of self-sovereignty that allowed them to express their convictions in public settings.[4]

The West had representatives of most types of religious publications, with at least twenty women editors. *The Pacific Churchman*, edited between 1899 and 1904 by Mrs. E. R. Oliver, served the "Protestant Episcopalians," according to its masthead. *The Pacific Methodist Collegian*, edited in 1892 by Mercie A. Tucke, had a more restricted but still denominational audience. The title of *Sabbath School Worker*, edited by a succession of women from 1891 to 1900, explained its purpose, but the modern reader might not guess that the *Carrier Dove*, edited by Mrs. J. Schlesinger from 1883 to 1895, focused on spiritualism.

One might expect that the typical religious editor would work for an established denomination and produce a conventional paper for its members. In the West, however, fewer than half of the women religious editors fit this pattern, and little information about them is available. Perhaps women found unconventional religious movements more accepting of their efforts and more willing to award them positions of responsibility.

This chapter will follow the lives and careers of two women who lived and worked outside the mainstream religions. The first, Louisa Lula Greene Richards, belonged to the Mormon church and edited a publication for its women. While Mormonism could not be counted among the mainstream religions of the nineteenth century, it was highly organized and politically conservative, in spite of its espousal of an unconventional marital arrangement. Louisa Greene Richards remained absolutely faithful to the church throughout her long life. Mary Folsom Hayes-Chynoweth had a long life and definite religious convictions as well, but her career developed outside the bounds of organized religion until, just two years before her death, she founded her own church.

Louisa Greene was born on April 8, 1849, in Iowa, the eighth of thirteen children. Both of her grandmothers were sisters of Mormon church president Brigham Young, who led the exodus of church members from Nauvoo, Illinois, to Salt Lake City, Utah. The Greene family moved to Utah in 1852, settling in Smithfield in 1864. Even before that time Louisa had begun to compose poetry. A "poetical dialogue" between "Princess Aurora" and the "Mountain Queen" that she composed at fourteen and recorded years later has been preserved, with an apology for its crudeness. "Childish and absurd as it really seemed," she wrote, "it always met with great applause wherever we could be induced to give it in public assemblies."[5]

Her first venture into journalism came when she edited the "Smithfield Sunday School Gazette," one of many handwritten papers produced and distributed by church organizations in the West. Given each Sunday to those who would "come to Sabbath School, keep order and pay attention,"[6] the four-page paper lasted for six numbers, from October 24 to November 28, 1869. It included advice, short notes of miscellaneous information, poetry, tributes, congratulations to classes that had performed creditably, and a few contributions from readers. In the final number, the editor explained that, after having attended school in Salt Lake City the two previous years, she now wanted to pursue her studies at the University of Deseret. By fall 1871, she had obtained a teaching position, but then she received a letter calling her home because of family illness. Lacking the money she needed to get there, she sat up all night writing poetry and took it the next day to the office of *The Salt Lake Daily Herald*, asking the editor, Edward L. Sloan, to buy it for the $7.50 she needed.[7] He did, and "Tired Out" became her first published work. It made a melancholy addition to the poetry corner of the *Herald*'s front page, asking if the author might return home to die.

A few days later, back in Smithfield, Greene received a letter from Edward Sloan asking if she would be interested in editing a paper for Mormon women. She later wrote that he had contemplated giving her work on the *Herald* but, since other staff members protested, conceived the idea of the women's paper. She pleaded inexperience, but the editor persisted, so she wrote Eliza R. Snow, the most influential woman in the church, to find out what Snow thought and to ask her to get Brigham Young's reaction. If President Young approved, Greene would like him to "appoint the duties of that calling" as a mission for her. Snow replied that both she and the president "heartily sanctioned the undertaking" and that President Young would gladly appoint Louisa Greene the mission and bless her in it. He agreed to this after inquiring about her capabilities and being assured that what she lacked in education she could learn and that she was "stanch."[8]

During the first months of 1872, planning for the new publication went forward. Snow and Greene corresponded about printers, financial matters, subscription prices, and content. The paper would be published twice a month. Greene moved to Salt Lake and set the publication date for early April to coincide with a general conference of the church, but delays in shipments of type postponed the first number until June 1—happily the birthday of Brigham Young.

The first numbers of the *Woman's Exponent* were printed in the *Herald* plant, and Edward Sloan probably assisted with preparation of a prospectus which appeared as an advertisement in the *Herald* and went to all local presidents of the church's organization for women, the Relief Society. The twenty-three-year-old Greene set herself a considerable task, for the paper would discuss, according to the prospectus,

> every subject interesting and valuable to women. It will contain a brief and graphic summary of current news, local and general; household hints, educational matters, articles on health and dress, correspondence, editorials on leading topics of interest suitable to its columns, and miscellaneous reading.

It also would present reports of the Relief Societies, while endeavoring "to defend the right, inculcate sound principles and disseminate useful knowledge."[9]

The first number came close to meeting the promise of the prospectus. In its eight pages, it contained a column of "News and Views," the first installment of a history of the Relief Society, a report of Relief Society activities, household hints, poetry, news notes under the heading "Splinters," exchanges, editorials, articles on woman's place and on suffrage, fillers both witty and whimsical, advertisements, and brief essays advocating hard work and a cheerful attitude and warning of the danger of relying on first impressions.

The editor listed herself as "L. L. Greene," changing this to "Louise L. Greene" after six weeks, with the explanation that

> there appears to be a misunderstanding on the part of numbers of our readers, in regard to the Editor of the *Exponent*. "Mr. L. L. Green, Dear Editor," and "Editor *Woman's Exponent*, Dear Sir," are honorable appellations, but we are not entitled to either "Mr." or "Sir," being simply a woman, which our name as it now appears over the editorial department will indicate.[10]

Greene probably wrote a substantial portion of the *Exponent*'s content herself. She camouflaged this fact to some extent by use of the pen names "Geranium," "Mary Grace," and "Mignona," following standard practice in the women's and literary magazines of the time by adopting pseudonyms for some of her work. Her subjects ranged from health advice, like getting sufficient sleep and bathing daily, to defenses of polygamy. A proponent of woman suffrage, she frequently stressed the importance of educational opportunities for women, as in this statement from an 1873 article:

> If there be some women in whom the love of learning extinguishes all other love, then the heaven-appointed sphere of that woman is not the nursery. It may be the library, the laboratory, the observatory. . . . Does such a woman prove that perfect liberty of education unspheres woman? On the contrary, it has enabled that woman to perceive exactly what God meant her to do.[11]

Her comments on short items she chose for the regular *Exponent* columns also revealed her ideas and opinions. She suggested, in connection with a report that half the servant girls in Philadelphia were said to be drunkards, that giving them "a chance to become honest wives and keepers of their own houses, instead of having to keep irregular hours waiting on fashionable mistresses" might solve the problem. She criticized the flamboyant Tennessee Claflin, co-proprietor (with her sister, Victoria Woodhull) of *Woodhull & Claflin's Weekly* in New York, calling her "a sad spectacle of a talented woman setting modesty, purity of feeling, and womanly grace at defiance, that she may secure the applause of the reckless and the indorsement of those who set proper restrictions at defiance." She approved of Harriet Beecher's remark that "there is nothing which so distinctly marks the difference between weak and strong minds as whether they control circumstances or circumstances control them."[12]

A year after Greene began her editorship, she changed her own circumstances by marrying Levi Willard Richards, a bookkeeper and local church leader. She bore two daughters during the next four years, but both died in infancy. In 1875 another woman, Emmeline B. Wells, began sharing editorial responsibility for the *Exponent*, and in August 1877, Louisa Greene Richards resigned. Emmeline kept the paper going as sole editor until 1914.

Before she resigned, Richards wrote Brigham Young to request a release from her mission as editor:

> Four years ago, you sealed upon me a higher and holier mission—to be a wife and to become a mother!
>
> My object in addressing you now, is to acquaint you with the fact, that I find I have not sufficient strength to perform both missions at the same time, with satisfaction or credit to myself. . . .
>
> In years to come, I hope to be prepared to enter again upon such labors, with renewed energies and increased capabilities.[13]

This is not to say that Richards intended to retire completely from the public sphere. She still endorsed the advice given her sister in the letter quoted at the beginning of this chapter, but she intended, "during the years of my life which may be properly devoted to the rearing of a family," to "give my special attention to that most important branch of 'Home Industry.'" She concluded her farewell to *Exponent* readers with this statement, "But every reflecting mother, and every true philanthropist, can see the happy medium between being selfishly home bound, and foolishly public spirited."[14]

Richards continued to contribute frequently to the *Exponent* and sometimes assisted Emmeline Wells with editorial responsibilities. She also wrote for other Mormon publications and composed poetry and song lyrics for special occasions. Her next major journalistic responsibility was a department begun in 1883 in *The Juvenile Instructor*, a Mormon church magazine designed for Sunday school workers and members. Starting as a

"Chapter for the Little Ones," with a single story or essay, it soon evolved into "Our Little Folks" and included, in addition, contributions and letters from readers, poetry, charades and puzzles, and a series of articles on Mormon leaders. It included many features in a humorous vein, such as when Richards described a "cheeky little fellow" who came to a Mormon conference uninvited, revealing at the close of her description that he was a bat who lived, she surmised, on top of the organ in the Mormon Tabernacle.[15]

In 1905 the *Instructor* offered fifty dollars for the best poem honoring Joseph Smith, Mormon church founder, on the hundredth anniversary of his birth. Richards won first prize and a prominent Mormon composer set her verses to music. The magazine continued to publish her poetry, but in 1907 the editors discontinued "Our Little Folks" when they modernized the publication. Disappointed and hurt, Richards wrote church president Joseph F. Smith, who also served as official editor of the *Instructor*, requesting that some explanation be given to the children all over the world who sent letters and contributions, and suggesting that she would be gratified by some indication that her work had been satisfactory.[16] He sent a gracious handwritten reply, blaming the changes on the need to place the magazine on a firmer financial footing.[17]

Three years earlier, Richards had published a collection of her poetry and prose called *Branches That Run Over the Wall*, a title taken from the opening epic poem based on the Book of Mormon. Paintings by her artist son, Lee Greene Richards, illustrated each of the three sections of the book. A prefatory poem, "At the Door," expressed the trepidation with which all writers launch their works:

> Upon the threshold, ere I touch the bell,
> I pause, and listen—and my heart beats quick.
> Who are within? How shall I be received?
>
> * * *
>
> I ring courageously, then calmly wait.[18]

By this time many changes had occurred in Richards's personal life. Four sons had been born between 1878 and 1885 and had grown to adulthood. A third daughter, born in 1888, had died. A second wife had been added to her husband's household, an arrangement which apparently worked well for all concerned. Levi Richards married Persis Louisa Young, Louisa's

THE HESPERIAN

EDITED
BY
Mrs F. H. Day
SAN FRANCISCO, CAL.

VOL.   IV.

1860

Cover of an 1860 issue of *The Hesperian*, a San Francisco monthly magazine intended primarily for a female audience. Hermione Ball Parke Day edited it during most of its five-year life. (*Courtesy California State Library*)

Front page of *The Contra Costa* for November 10, 1854. Sarah Moore Clarke, the West's first woman editor, produced the weekly paper in Oakland, California, during 1854 and 1855. Historian Edward C. Kemble wrote that it was intended both as a "ladies' paper" and a "general news organ." (*Courtesy State Library of Pennsylvania*)

"*Said Confidentially*"

By AGNES LEONARD

"If people do not like you, do not ask what you have
done—but what you have said."

———

Some things cost too much; and some people's
"liking" is one of them.

"When in doubt, tell the truth."—*Mark Twain.*

Denver, Colorado
The Smith-Brooks Printing Company
1902

Title page of "*Said Confidentially*," by Agnes Leonard Hill, who wrote in its preface that she published it "for revenue only." With her monthly magazine, *Western Society*, and pamphlets on manners and morals, Hill aspired to be Denver's social arbiter. (*Courtesy Colorado Historical Society*)

Portrait of Maude Hulbert Horn at age twenty-two. Horn published and edited *The Georgetown Gazette* in Georgetown, California, over a thirty-three-year period, although she generally gave credit first to her father, then to her husband. This portrait was taken about a year prior to her marriage to John C. "Jack" Horn. (*Courtesy Maude Hulbert Horn collection, California State Library*)

Georgetown home of the Hulbert and Horn families in 1900. A front room served as the office of *The Georgetown Gazette* during the editorship of Maude Hulbert Horn. Pictured on the front porch are (from left) Horace W. Hulbert, Maude's father and founder of the *Gazette*; John C. "Jack" Horn; Maude; the Horns' daughter Amy; and Celia Hulbert, Maude's younger sister. (*Courtesy Maude Hulbert Horn collection, California State Library*)

Portrait of Agnes Leonard Hill from frontispiece of her book *"Said Confidentially."*
Hill worked with her brother on two Colorado weekly newspapers before she
founded *Western Society* in Denver in 1888. (*Courtesy Colorado Historical Society*)

Front page of the *Platte Valley Lyre* of Saratoga, Wyoming, for July 10, 1890. Gertrude Mary Huntington served as editor and publisher from 1890 to 1902. Her sister Laura Charlotte was business manager until her marriage in 1898 to Alfred Heath, who advertised as a justice of the peace and notary public on this front page.

Emily Pitts-Stevens (right), founder and editor of *The Pioneer* in San Francisco, California. Shortly after buying it in 1869, she made *The Pioneer* the West's first suffrage paper. It survived only until 1873, but Pitts-Stevens continued to campaign for suffrage, as well as temperance. (*Courtesy Humboldt State University Library*)

Gertrude Huntington
Merrell (right) and
Laura Huntington Heath
(below) as pictured in
a 1927 work, *Women of
Wyoming*. By the time of
publication Gertrude, as
well as both women's hus-
bands, had died. Laura
carried on the insur-
ance and notary business
founded by Gertrude's
husband in Rawlins,
Wyoming. (*Courtesy
University of Wyoming
Library*)

Abigail Scott Duniway (seated) signing Oregon's equal suffrage proclamation on November 30, 1912, with Governor Oswald West and Dr. Viola M. Coe. The doctor had been Duniway's longtime ally in efforts to win suffrage for Oregon's women. (*Courtesy Oregon Historical Society, Oreg. 4590*)

Edited by
LOUISA L. GREENE RICHARDS.

Address: Mrs. L. L. Greene Richards, 160 C. Street, Salt Lake City, Utah.

THE HURRY OF THE TIMES, AND NEED OF RELAXATION.

 "HOW is it Maudie, that you are so careless about things at home?" asked little Maudie's father. "You throw your things down anywhere, it seems to me, and off you go without showing the least consideration for others who may have to 'pick up' after you, and who may be just as hurried or busy as yourself."

"I am real sorry, papa, for all my faults," answered Maudie, "and I hope to correct them. But just now I can't stop another second, or I shall be late and lose five points, and you and mama, as well as I should be sorry for that. Goodby, papa, my dear, patient papa!" And with a hasty hug and kiss, which her father received with an affectionate smile, the child was off to school.

At the gate, while she opened it and passed out, she looked back and called to her father who was watching her, "Papa, please read the things I have marked for you in the book you gave me for Christmas, it will do you good."

When Maudie's father thought he could take a few moments for reading that day, he remembered his little daughter's request, and took up the book she had mentioned. And, for a wonder, Maudie's mother sat down with some light work in her hands, and listened while her husband read aloud from the book. Following are some of the things he found and read:

"Every one has heard the old story of the silent man, who, riding over a bridge, asked his servant if he liked eggs, to which the servant answered, 'Yes.' Nothing more was said about it till the next year, when, riding over the same bridge, he turned to his servant and said, 'How?' 'Poached, Sir,' was the immediate answer."

"Of President Abraham Lincoln it is said that in the most serious of situations, sometimes of grave national importance, with lines of pain deep written on his countenance, he would often interrupt the proceedings of his Cabinet to tell a laughter-provoking story. Once when asked by an impatient statesman why he did it, he suddenly ceased laughing, and in a voice well nigh pathetic said, 'To relieve the strain. There are times when my heart would break if I should not lift the burden for a moment, and there is nothing else that does it so well as a diverting story.'"

"Maudie was right," said the mother, "you do need some relaxation from all the strain and worry of business and work that you carry. I hope you will take the hint given in the anecdote told of President Lincoln, and often refresh yourself

"Our Little Folks," a column written by Louisa Lula Greene Richards from 1883 to 1907 for *The Juvenile Instructor,* published for Mormon church Sunday school workers and members. Richards also wrote poetry and worked in church organizations after her term as editor of the *Woman's Exponent.* (*Courtesy Church Archives, The Church of Jesus Christ of Latter-day Saints*)

Louisa Lula Greene Richards, founding editor of the *Woman's Exponent*, published from 1872 to 1914 in Salt Lake City, Utah, as a periodical for women of the Mormon church. As editor until 1877, Richards sought "to defend the right, inculcate sound principles and disseminate useful knowledge." (*Courtesy Church Archives, The Church of Jesus Christ of Latter-day Saints*)

Mary Hayes-Chynoweth, in a portrait published several times in *The True Life* from 1903 until 1906, the year it ceased publication. Hayes-Chynoweth died in 1905, after devoting her life to healing troubled minds and bodies. (*Courtesy The Bancroft Library*)

THE TRUE LIFE

AS LIVED AND TAUGHT BY

MARY HAYES CHYNOWETH.

| VOLUME I. | EDEN VALE, CAL., FEBRUARY 1, 1891. | NUMBER 5. |

PUBLISHED SEMI-MONTHLY.

For many years past Mrs. Chynoweth—formerly Mrs. Mary Hayes—has been in the habit of frequently addressing upon spiritual subjects, not only public audiences, but also little gatherings composed of members of her family and such of her friends as daily gathered about her. By the aid of the art of stenography some of these addresses have been imperfectly preserved. And the principles of many more that have otherwise been lost have settled deeply into the hearts and lives of those who heard them. In many other ways, Mrs Chynoweth by reason of the purity, unselfishness and nobility of her life, and the knowledge and power which such qualities will always develop, has been able to bring help, elevation and happiness to many. Suffering bodies have been healed ; troubled minds and heavy hearts have been relieved ; poverty has been dissipated ; discord and inharmony have been banished from home and heart ; dissipations, with their attendant evils, have been overcome ; and where was suffering and unhappiness, in their place have grown peace and joy. The many lives that have thus been changed by her help and ministrations make us feel sure that could they be extended to many, even by imperfect and indirect methods, the good that might be done would be very greatly multiplied. And this is the only excuse for this publication. Neither Mrs. Chynoweth nor the other promoters of the enterprise desire any recognition or pecuniary profit for themselves. Nor have they any creed or ism which they wish promulgated or upheld. The only object they have in view in the matter is the good of their kind. They fondly hope that the principles and the inspiration of God which have touched their lives and built them up from the hard and unbeautiful elements of the world into some degree of harmony and happiness may reach some, at least, of those who may read " THE TRUE LIFE," and make them also feel that life is worth living.

Aside from Mrs. Chynoweth, those who will be the principal contributors lay no claim to originality. They will merely strive to reproduce the principles they have learned from her, and relate what they have seen and the experiences they have had while under her guidance. This number comprises chiefly papers and addresses read or delivered at the meetings either here or in the East. And doubtless many if not all the future numbers will be made up in the same way.

No charge will be made against any one to whom this or future numbers may be sent. But as its publication is attended with no inconsiderable expense, any one receiving it who does not care to read it will confer a favor upon the publishers by notifying them of that fact. The publishers will also esteem it a favor if those who receive the paper will send them the names and addresses of others, to whom it is not accessible, who in their opinion might be benefitted by it. All such will be added to the list, and the paper sent to them thereafter. The publishers will also be glad to send it to any one *who desires to read it*, and who will send his name and address with the request that it be sent to him.

The paper will be issued on the first and fifteenth of each month. All communications should be addressed,

"THE TRUE LIFE,"

HILLSDALE,

Santa Clara Co., Cal.

Front page of *The True Life* for February 1, 1891. The same first page introduced all early issues of this publication founded in 1890 by Mary Folsom Hayes-Chynoweth to ensure permanence for her religious teachings, which culminated in the organization of the True Life Church in 1902 in Eden Vale, California. (*Courtesy The Bancroft Library*)

Caroline Nicholas Churchill at forty and at seventy-six. Churchill used these photographs for *Active Footsteps*, her autobiography. She had founded *The Colorado Antelope* in 1879, renamed it the *Queen Bee* in 1882, and continued it as a weekly voice for "women's political equality and individuality" until 1895. (*Courtesy Special Collections Department, University of Utah Libraries*)

ACTIVE FOOTSTEPS

BY

CAROLINE NICHOLS CHURCHILL

Author of

"Little Sheaves," "Over the Purple Hills,"
"Class Legislation," Etc.

AND

Editor and Proprietor of

"The Antelope," a Monthly Published Three Years,
and "The Queen Bee," Established 1879, Devoted to the Interests of Humanity,
Woman's Political Equality
and Individuality.

COLORADO SPRINGS
MRS. C. N. CHURCHILL, PUBLISHER
1909

Title page of *Active Footsteps*, the autobiography of Caroline Nichols Churchill, in which she detailed the vicissitudes of conducting "a traveling business," which consisted of publishing books about her journeys and then traveling to sell the books, and of founding a publication in Denver, Colorado. (*Courtesy Special Collections Department, University of Utah Libraries*)

Rowena Granice Steele—actress, elocutionist, singer, poet, novelist, and editor. This portrait appeared in the *History of Merced County, California*, published in 1881 when she was fifty-four and serving as associate editor of the *San Joaquin Valley Argus*. Her husband's illness left her in complete charge of the paper both before and after this time. (*Courtesy California State Library*)

PRINTING OFFICE.

OFFICE OF SAN JOUQUIN VALLEY ARGUS,
ROBERT J. STEELE, PROP.
MERCED, CAL.

The Merced, California, office of the *San Joaquin Valley Argus*, another illustration published in the *History of Merced County, California*. Rowena Granice Steele married Robert Johnson Steele in 1861 and worked with him on several other weeklies before they founded the *Argus* in 1869. (*Courtesy California State Library*)

DIRIGO.

Equal Rights Party.

FOR PRESIDENT OF THE UNITED STATES
BELVA A. LOCKWOOD.
FOR VICE–PRESIDENT,
MARIETTA L. STOW.

Campaign advertisements for the National Equal
Rights Party and its 1884 nominees for president
and vice president of the United States, Belva A.
Lockwood and Marietta Stow. The ads appeared
in Stow's monthly *Woman's Herald of Industry
and Social Science Cooperator*, founded in 1881
in San Francisco and renamed *National Equal
Rights* during the 1884 campaign. (*Courtesy The
Bancroft Library*)

"A being breathing thoughtful breath,
A traveller between life and death.
The reason firm, the temperate will,
Endurance, foresight, strength and skill;
A perfect woman nobly planned
To warn, to comfort and command."

OUR EQUAL RIGHTS
NOMINEES,

LOCKWOOD AND STOW.

BELVA A. LOCKWOOD.

CALIFORNIA
Woman's Social Science Association.

INSTIGATED, ORGANIZED AND FOUNDED BY MRS. J. W. STOW, AUGUST 7, 1880.

HEADQUARTERS, 304 Stockton St., San Francisco.
PRESIDENT—Mrs. J. W. Stow, 304 Stockton St., S. F.
HON. SECRETARY—S. Gertie Smyth, Oakland, Cal.
MEMBERSHIP.—Life, $25. Annual, $1.

S. S. S.

ORDER AND TRADE MARK.

BADGE OF THE S. S. S. ORDER.—Double scarlet satin ribbon, fringed at the ends and top. S. S. S. is embroidered in gold on the longest end, and the official initial or a flower on the short end. It is worn on the left breast with a star spangle or a badge pin. Those of the Reception Committee are made with a blue ribbon between the scarlet, showing an inch below and half an inch above. Ribbon one and a fourth inch wide.
Officers badges, $1, members 50 cts., post-paid.

Order, trademark, and description of the badge of the Social Science Sisterhood, founded along with the Woman's Social Science Association by Marietta Stow. Her sister, S. Gertrude Smyth, served as honorary secretary and also assisted Stow with the *Woman's Herald of Industry and Social Science Cooperator*, organ of the association. (*Courtesy The Bancroft Library*)

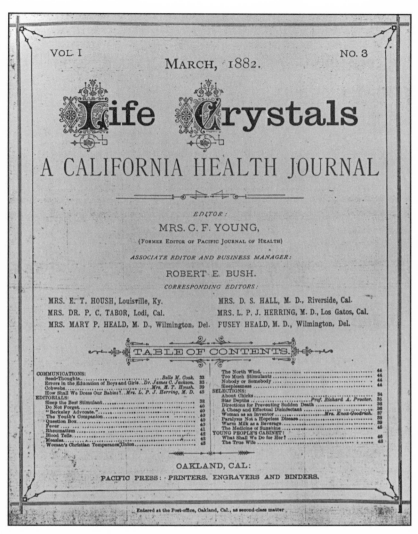

VOL. I   MARCH, 1882.   NO. 3

Life Crystals

A CALIFORNIA HEALTH JOURNAL

EDITOR:

MRS. C. F. YOUNG,

(FORMER EDITOR OF PACIFIC JOURNAL OF HEALTH)

ASSOCIATE EDITOR AND BUSINESS MANAGER:

ROBERT E. BUSH.

CORRESPONDING EDITORS:

MRS. E. T. HOUSH, Louisville, Ky.   MRS. D. S. HALL, M. D., Riverside, Cal.

MRS. DR. P. C. TABOR, Lodi, Cal.   MRS. L. P. J. HERRING, M. D., Los Gatos, Cal.

MRS. MARY P. HEALD, M. D., Wilmington, Del.   FUSEY HEALD, M. D., Wilmington, Del.

TABLE OF CONTENTS.

OAKLAND, CAL:

PACIFIC PRESS: PRINTERS, ENGRAVERS AND BINDERS.

Entered at the Post-office, Oakland, Cal., as second-class matter.

Cover of *Life Crystals*, a monthly health journal published in Oakland, California, from 1882 to 1885 by Carrie Fisher Young, with her son, Robert E. Bush, as associate editor and business manager. *Life Crystals* was Young's second venture into journalism. (*Courtesy The Huntington Library*)

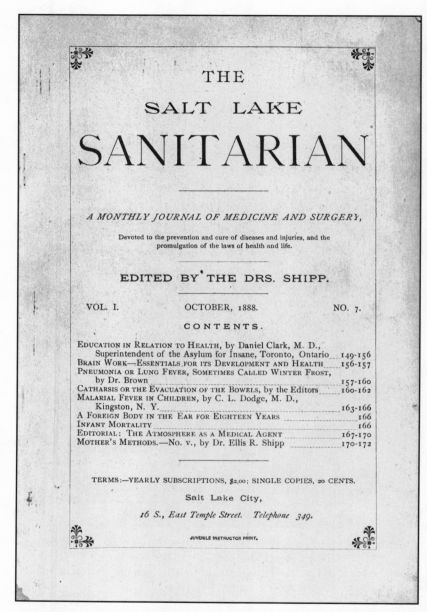

THE

SALT LAKE

SANITARIAN

A MONTHLY JOURNAL OF MEDICINE AND SURGERY,

Devoted to the prevention and cure of diseases and injuries, and the
promulgation of the laws of health and life.

EDITED BY THE DRS. SHIPP.

VOL. I.   OCTOBER, 1888.   NO. 7.

CONTENTS.

TERMS:—YEARLY SUBSCRIPTIONS, $2,00; SINGLE COPIES, 20 CENTS.

Salt Lake City,

16 S., East Temple Street. Telephone 349.

JUVENILE INSTRUCTOR PRINT.

Cover of *The Salt Lake Sanitarian*, published in Salt Lake City, Utah, from 1888 to 1890 primarily for members of the Mormon church. Its editors used many reprints from other medical periodicals and urged readers to refer to their dictionaries for help with medical terminology.

Carrie Fisher Young, editor of two California health journals between 1870 and 1885. She started the first, *Woman's Pacific Coast Journal* (later *Pacific Journal of Health*), in San Francisco after traveling by wagon from Idaho with her husband and two children. This portrait appeared in a 1913 book titled *A History of the Woman's Christian Temperance Union*, an organization Young actively supported. (*Courtesy Humboldt State University Library*)

Ellis Reynolds Shipp (above), Margaret Curtis Shipp (top right), and Milford
Bard Shipp (right)—physicians who founded *The Salt Lake Sanitarian*. Ellis and
Margaret were "plural wives" of Milford Bard, who suspended publication of *The
Salt Lake Sanitarian* early in 1889 while he served a ten-week prison sentence
for "unlawful cohabitation," then continued it as sole editor. (*Courtesy Utah State
Historical Society*)

VOL. III, No. 3.   SECOND SERIES.

THE
Overland Monthly

DEVOTED TO

THE DEVELOPMENT OF THE COUNTRY.

MARCH, 1884.

CONTENTS:

SAN FRANCISCO:

SAMUEL CARSON, PUBLISHER,

120 SUTTER STREET.

NEW YORK:
The American News Co., 39 and 41 Chambers St.

LONDON:
Trübner & Co., 57 and 59 Ludgate Hill.

Cover of *The Overland Monthly* for March 1884, when it was edited by Milicent Washburn Shinn. Writer Bret Harte had edited the original *Overland*, founded in San Francisco in 1868. Shinn managed the revived version from 1883 to 1894 as a showcase for western literature. (*Courtesy Humboldt State University Library*)

Milicent Washburn Shinn (center), editor of *The Overland Monthly*, and her associates Charles S. Greene and Mrs. M. F. Upton. Shinn assumed the editorship at twenty-five and became the target of humorist Ambrose Bierce, who called the magazine the "Shinnplaster." (*Courtesy Humboldt State University Library*)

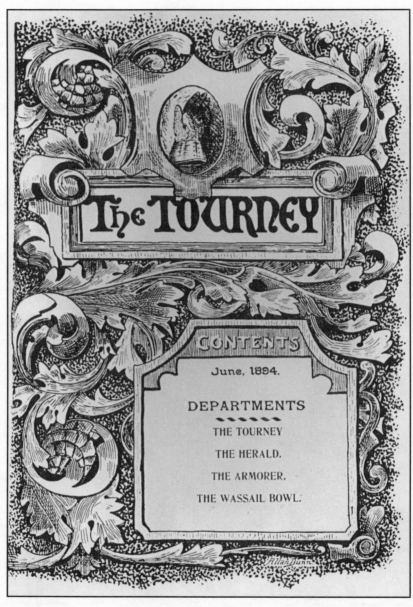

Cover of *The Tourney*, published during 1894 in Fort Collins, Colorado, where its twenty-seven-year-old editor, Grace Espy Patton, taught courses at the State Agricultural College (now Colorado State University). Patton moved her monthly magazine to Denver in 1895 and renamed it *The Colorado Woman*. (*Courtesy Special Collections, Colorado State University Library*)

Grace Espy Patton Cowles, Colorado educator and editor. By the time this photograph was published in the 1898 *Portrait and Biographical Record of Denver and Vicinity,* she had interrupted her journalistic career to campaign for and win the post of state superintendent of public instruction in 1896. (*Courtesy Colorado Historical Society*)

Front page of *Ke Aloha Aina (The Patriot)*, a Honolulu weekly published and edited by Emma Aima Nawahi and her nephew, Edward Like, after her husband's death in 1896. The paper was written principally in Hawaiian. (*Courtesy Hawaiian Historical Society*)

Newsboys in front of the printing office of *Ke Aloha Aina* in Honolulu. The paper under Emma Nawahi expressed commitment to Hawaiian institutions and culture and supported home rule after annexation by the United States in 1898. (*Courtesy Hawaii State Archives*)

Emma Aima Nawahi, editor and publisher of *Ke Aloha Aina* between 1896 and 1910. Nawahi's father was a pioneer Chinese sugar miller, her mother a Hawaiian chiefess. She married a Hawaiian lawyer and legislator, Joseph Nawahi, who founded the paper in 1895. (*Courtesy Hawaiian Historical Society*)

THE BUG HUNTER

Published in the Interest of Tombstone Agassiz Associations

VOL. 1.   TOMBSTONE, ARIZ., JUNE, 1891   NO. 2

ARIZONA BUG-HUNTER

(PUBLISHED MONTHLY)

CARRIE BAGG,   EDITOR.

PRICE PER ANNUM .... $.50

Hints to "Bug Hunters"

Although the BUGHUNTER is devoted to all branches of natural history, that of entomology or the study of insects, seems more suitable to the title of this sheet so hints to boys and girls who would fancy collecting the members of the insect world are given first Hints in collecting other specimens will soon be given.

It is not at all peculiar that the great majority of the juvenile members of the A. A. should have chosen entomology as their study, girls especially being much interested in this for who does not love the beautiful hued butterflys, moths and beetles that seem so tempting. Let us then hasten to answer the three questions so perplexing to those who start with no help in this line: how catch? how kill? how keep?

One great essential in the catching of butterflys, etc. is a net. A very good one can be made of silk veiling and a bamboo rod but one just as good, I find, is made of mosquito bar. Get a piece 2½X3 feet and have it sewed into a bag which is 2½X1½ feet. Then get a bit of common bailing wire 4 feet long and bend it in the form of a circle w ose circumference is 3 feet, th extra 6 inch wires on both ends b ing twisted around each other to form a handle. A bamboo pole is of course very good but something that can be had for the getting, the pole of the yucca or Spanish Bayonet that blossoms out in large white flowers in the spring here, is just as good.

Now sew this net bag all around to the circle of wire and attach the wire ends to your pole and you have a net that is light and whose cost has been about 10 cents Sev-

Page 1 of *The Bug Hunter*, published briefly as a monthly magazine "in the interest of the Tombstone Agassiz Association" in Tombstone, Arizona, by thirteen-year-old Katherine Bagg, daughter of a Tombstone newspaper editor. (*Courtesy Arizona Historical Society*) niece, on the eleventh anniversary of his first wedding. Persis's only child died, and she spent her time helping with family and household tasks while Louisa pursued more public interests. His two wives continued to share the same house after Levi died in 1914.

Richards held many church positions and continued to write for church publications almost until her death in 1944, when she was ninety-five. A description of her written by another prominent Mormon woman could apply equally to many of the West's women editors:

> Lula Greene possessed courage, initiative and considerable fire of poesy and self-expression, modified greatly by a placid, obedient spirit which often hid the steely strength of her will and determination to press forward always in the path of duty.[19]

Certainly most of that description could apply to Mary Folsom Hayes-Chynoweth.[20] One might want to downplay "placid" and "obedient," although Mary no doubt considered herself perfectly obedient to the spiritual voices that guided her. Perhaps they came as an inheritance from her father, a minister of the Free Will Baptist faith who had the power of mesmerism, according to one source.[21] He left Vermont to preach the gospel on the frontier in Erie County, New York. There, Mary Folsom was born on October 2, 1825.

She demonstrated possession of spiritual qualities at the age of five, after her younger sister had an accident that left her seriously burned. Nothing could be found to ease her pain until, at about 1:30 A.M., Mary took the younger child into her arms and lulled her to sleep. Her reputation spread, and townspeople soon began to seek her help.[22]

When she was ten, a distraught neighbor came to tell her that he feared for his wife's life, and Mary rushed back to his house with him. They found the woman with jaws set, apparently dead. After rubbing the body, the girl asked for angelica, with which she made tea, forcing a small amount of it into the woman's throat. The patient regained consciousness and, before long, normal health. The chronicler of the event considered the cure remarkable, since Mary knew nothing of medicine nor of the effects of angelica, the idea of using it having come as an inspiration. When a physician arrived, he praised her timely action and credited her with saving the woman's life.[23]

Limited means and a remote location prevented Mary from attending school—her entire formal education totaling less than a year—but she studied on her own and announced at the age of twelve that she wanted to support herself by going out to work. Her father convinced her that she was too young. A few weeks later, however, a neighbor who suffered from rheumatism called on her for aid, and her remedies proved so successful that the woman persuaded her to stay on. From then on, Mary Folsom made her own way in the world. At eighteen she took over a teaching position that her brother had held, and continued teaching for the next seven years, moving with her parents to Waterloo, Wisconsin, when she was twenty-three.[24]

The spiritualist movement was attracting attention by this time. Fearing that friends or family would be deceived by it, Folsom prayed that she might know the truth as to the immortality of the soul. No immediate answer came, but she felt encouraged and continued to pray until, on a Sunday morning two years later while washing dishes, she fell to the floor, feeling pushed down by a great weight, and began to pray in an unknown language. She and her father considered this experience the answer to her prayers. Her power to heal increased and brought many sufferers to her door. She used herbal medicines or massage, or simply moved her hands over an injured limb. Sometimes she took upon herself the suffering of those who sought her aid, seeming to relieve their pain by undergoing it for them. She also began to preach in churches and schoolhouses, at first refusing any remuneration but eventually accepting voluntary gifts and contributing them to the maintenance of the family farm.[25] At twenty-eight she married Anson Everis Hayes, continuing her spiritual ministrations while taking charge of their home at Waterloo, Wisconsin, and rearing three children.

One of her followers reported that Hayes-Chynoweth said she had a great desire for wealth even as a child, not for herself, but so that she could alleviate some of the suffering and poverty she saw around her.[26] Certainly her revelations sometimes took a practical turn. At the beginning of the Civil War she felt that the conflict would be long and bloody and that prices would rise, so she purchased supplies to last the family for two or three years, saving a considerable sum of money. She also suggested that wheat crops be stored instead of sold immediately, and the wheat brought $2.85 a bushel rather than $0.75.[27]

Mary Folsom Hayes made the family fortune, however, by directing her lawyer sons to look for iron ore deposits in nearby areas that proved to be rich with ore. They developed the Ashland and Germania mines during the late 1890s, establishing a school and a reading room for the miners and holding Sunday services as well. When lifting of tariffs in 1893 made the mines unprofitable, Mary used her personal fortune of $450,000 to keep them operating so that the workers would continue to have employment. The next federal administration restored the tariffs. Her mines had iron ready for immediate delivery, and the family soon became wealthier than before.

About 1872 she made her first visit to California, moving with her sons to Santa Clara County after the death of her husband. They purchased land south of San Jose and called it Eden Vale (sometimes spelled Edenvale), building a house and a chapel and again setting up a school for her workers. She married her second husband, forty-three-year-old attorney Thomas B. Chynoweth, on July 9, 1889, when she was sixty-five. He had come to Eden Vale four years earlier after illness compelled him give up his practice in Madison, Wisconsin, and she had cured his partial blindness. He died a year and a half after the wedding, and his wife officiated at the funeral, preaching a sermon on life after death.[28]

The magazine *The True Life* may have been her idea, or her sons may have instigated it. Both became journalists, purchasing the daily San Jose *Herald* and the weekly *Mercury*. *The True Life* first appeared in December 1890 as a semi-monthly with the subtitle, "As Lived and Taught by Mary Hayes Chynoweth." Later it changed to monthly publication, being advertised as "a monthly periodical devoted to liberal religion." At first Hayes-Chynoweth distributed it free of charge, but soon instituted a subscription price. Individual numbers ran from twenty-four to thirty-two pages, with miscellaneous advertisements on the inside front cover and both sides of the back cover.

All numbers for the first year carried the same first page, explaining who Mary Folsom was and what she intended the magazine to do. It stated that she had been able "by reason of the purity, unselfishness and nobility of her life," to heal suffering bodies, relieve troubled minds and heavy hearts, dissipate poverty, banish discord and inharmony, and bring peace and joy where suffering and unhappiness had prevailed. Neither Folsom nor other promoters of the publication desired recognition or pecuniary profit. They wished to promulgate no creed or ism, but only to extend the happiness they felt to others.

If one subdivided the categories of religious periodicals listed earlier, a significant type of denominational publication would be the compilation of sermons. *The True Life* consisted in large part of Hayes-Chynoweth's sermons and writings. In addition, it featured sermons and essays by her followers, many of whom were related to her, judging by the large numbers of Hayeses and Chynoweths among their authors. Some typical titles include "Nothing Impossible with God," "What We Believe," "Forsake Not the Right," "True Happiness," and "Man's Relation to God." A regular "Questions and Answers" column might contain a question like, "There are great numbers of different churches, yet all professing to be founded on the Bible. Has God established all of them, and if so, why so many and so different?" The answer would be, in part, ". . . the churches are all created by God; one a little in advance of another so that all shall have an opportunity to have a belief, and a home where they can hear God talked about." [29] Another questioner asked, "Do you think it wrong to mingle with the people of the world? If one keeps away from them, how can he benefit them?" Mary answered, "You should not mingle with these low people for their society, but you should mingle with them to do them good." [30] "A Talk to Patients," another continuing feature, had content such as a warning against unwholesome foods and drinks and a reminder that "man should not live to eat; he should eat that which is best, and just enough of it to sustain life." [31] Early numbers sometimes had recipes for medicines, ointments, and healthful foods. Students from the Germania and Eden Vale schools contributed short essays, and testimonials by those whom Mary Folsom had healed appeared throughout the magazine's life, as did brief aphorisms by her. A sample of the latter follows:

> If we are fortified with God's truth and life in our hearts, we can triumph over evil with good, bringing out that which is false to the world so plainly that no man can stand against our principles. [32]

Publication gave Hayes-Chynoweth's teachings permanence and, in December 1902, she further institutionalized her ideas by forming a church, which met in the chapel on the family estate and named her pastor for life. The Eden Vale chapel burned in 1903, resulting in a move to the San Jose Unitarian Church, where 165 members officially incorporated as the True Life church in a ceremony on November 22. The statement of principles for the church started out, "We hold that religion consists in pure and holy living and unselfish doing, and not in professions," and went on to affirm belief in God, prayer, and human perfectibility. Members pledged to try to overcome the physical elements in their natures and to induce others to do likewise. [33]

Three years later, on July 27, 1905, Mary Hayes-Chynoweth died at the age of seventy-nine after an illness of three months. A funeral sermon by the president of the University of the Pacific praised her as "preeminently a religious woman," "intensely careful about the soul being open to God and responsive to His Spirit," aiming for the true life.[34] "She never sought truth for truth's sake, but for humanity's sake," he added, reporting that her last words were, "I have never harmed anyone."

Her sons, one of them a state congressman by that time, continued the church, alternating the task of preaching sermons, and kept *The True Life* going for another year, until they had exhausted all of the theretofore unpublished writings of their mother. In the final number, for December 1906, they suggested the possibility that the magazine might someday be revived, apparently in response to many letters, some of which they published, that expressed regret at its demise.

The funeral sermon for Mary Hayes-Chynoweth also characterized her as an apostle, one selected from among the disciples to gather strength and transmit it to others. The speaker, in the florid language of the time, talked of trees that absorb energy "from the sun and soil and dew and rain, and transmit it into the ripening flower, until with distended capsule it bursts and sends its seeds everywhere." That makes an apt metaphor for the work of the women who edited religious periodicals.

Of course, they absorbed their energy from sources other than the sun and probably more from their own inner resources than from those around them. But they certainly felt the need to go beyond the private expression of their religious convictions and marshalled the strength to speak out for their beliefs. They scattered seeds, and their publications enabled them to scatter those seeds more widely.

CHAPTER 7

The Queen Bee and Other Characters

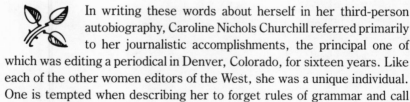

Mrs. Churchill has performed a wonderful work under most difficult circumstances. It is not at all likely that another woman on the continent could under the same conditions accomplish as much.[1]
—Caroline Nichols Churchill about herself

In writing these words about herself in her third-person autobiography, Caroline Nichols Churchill referred primarily to her journalistic accomplishments, the principal one of which was editing a periodical in Denver, Colorado, for sixteen years. Like each of the other women editors of the West, she was a unique individual. One is tempted when describing her to forget rules of grammar and call her "more unique."

While avoiding the stereotype of the editor as colorful eccentric, it seems important to recognize the accuracy of that description for a few of the women editors, as well as for their male counterparts, and to add their sagas to those of their more conventional sisters. This chapter looks at three of them: Caroline Churchill, who assumed the title of her paper, *Queen Bee*; Rowena Granice Steele, who juggled careers as actress, novelist, and journalist; and Marietta L. Beers Stow, who used her paper to promote her candidacy for vice president of the United States. Their unusual efforts contribute to a rounded portrait of the western woman journalist.

While enjoying accounts of their colorful lives, however, one must also consider the possibility that some of the editors appeared eccentric because they saw discrimination and injustice ignored or condoned by the majority and had the courage to act on their vision in unconventional ways. Others found themselves in unusual circumstances and simply refused to let the circumstances control them. They took the initiative and became pathbreakers for the women who followed. If they had few imitators, they at least confirmed the possibility that women could move in uncommon directions.

Caroline Maria Nichols[2] was born December 23, 1833, to American parents living in the Canadian town of Whitby, forty miles from Toronto. In her autobiography, *Active Footsteps*, she wrote of gathering beechnuts and maple sugar, traveling by sleigh in frigid winter weather, and watching her mother perform tooth extractions for country neighbors. Her parents sent her to the United States to live with her grandmother when she was thirteen. She attended school for a few months and then began teaching. She taught school in the summers, did family sewing in the winters, and studied every spare moment.

In the early 1850s Caroline Nichols married a man named Churchill, apparently chosen for her by her parents. She included no details about him in her autobiography, not even his first name, stating only that he died after eleven or twelve years of marriage. By that time she had borne a daughter and moved to Minnesota, where she established a millinery and dressmaking business and spent, from 1857 to 1862, "the longest five years" of her life,[3] facing pioneer hardships that included an Indian war. No reference to a second husband and two more children, mentioned in an obituary for her,[4] appears in her published writings.

During her Minnesota years, Churchill found a role model in Jane Grey Swisshelm, a crusading feminist and former Washington correspondent who had been editing a paper in St. Cloud since 1857. When Swisshelm died in 1884, Churchill wrote, "Our first ideas of the wrongs which women suffer from the absolute power of a ruling class, were put in shape by reading the *St. Cloud Democrat*, edited by Mrs. Swisshelm."[5] By 1869 Churchill had developed her own ideas, and in that year she found herself free to carry out her plans for advancing the thought she saw "ripening and materializing all over the civilized world."[6] Although in poor health, she left her daughter in the care of a married sister and set out for California to begin what she always referred to as "a traveling business."

This consisted of traveling, writing about her experiences, publishing her works, traveling to sell them, and gathering material for new sketches in the process. After starting her newspaper several years later, she used her travel writing as staple content and then sought customers for both her books and her paper as she canvassed Colorado and neighboring states. In California she contributed sketches to San Francisco and eastern newspapers and wrote two books, *Little Sheaves Gathered while Gleaning after Reapers* in 1875 and *Over the Purple Hills* in 1877. She later wrote that Emily Pitts-Stevens offered her the position of editor and manager of *The Pioneer* in San Francisco, but Churchill had decided that the coast climate did not agree with her.

Her books contained a miscellany of essays and a few poems inspired by her travels. They might describe scenery or economic activities or use some experience as the excuse for a lecture on manners or morals. She returned often to the topic of women's rights, her encounters with the unenlightened having sharpened her sense of injustice. In "The Traveler's Bell," for example, she offered a set of rules for regulating hotels and boardinghouses which specified that they should not charge women more than men, take liberties with women traveling alone, inform an inquiring man of a woman's whereabouts without asking her, or expect anyone to pay for rooms infested with mosquitoes or bedbugs.[7] She later took credit for arranging defeat in the California and Colorado legislatures of bills detrimental to single professional women, as well as for passage of a Texas bill to prevent street sales of *The Police Gazette*.[8]

In 1876 Churchill went east. She found a publisher for *Over the Purple Hills* in Chicago, then traveled through Texas, Missouri, Kansas, and Indian Territory until 1879, when she visited Denver. The climate impressed her and, at the age of forty-six, she decided to settle there and start the paper she had been contemplating for several years. She assessed the social and business climates, as well as the weather, writing that she chose a newly settled region because "all reforms take root in new countries sooner than in older communities, and in inaccessible places there is not the same means at hand for getting rid of money. There is more money in the community and less competition."[9]

The first number of her monthly, *The Colorado Antelope*, appeared in October 1879. She explained the title the following month:

In the first place we wanted a name never before given to any paper under the sun; we wanted something that had the least feminine suggestion; something graceful and beautiful, and above all something that was alive and had some "git up" to it.[10]

Also, she concluded, "the *Antelope* is a little deer, and is so difficult to overtake."

As for her purpose in founding the paper, she believed that "every State in the Union should have a live feminine paper published at the Capital" and that "as the acquisition of women to the educational department has raised the standard of education and general cultivation, so acquisition of women to the journalistic department will advance the standard of journalism. It is not good for man to be alone in journalism any more than in any other enterprise."[11] The motto that appeared under the *Antelope*'s title was "A paper devoted to the interests of humanity, woman's political equality and individuality."

In a list of the advantages the *Antelope* had over all other papers, Churchill included:

Its editor is the oldest and handsomest in the United States.

It has the only lady editor who wears a seven by nine boot and dares tell her own age.

It has the only lady editor who dares so far defy underlying principles of political subjection as to write and publish a joke perpetrated upon herself.

It is the most original paper published in the United States, . . . it is the wittiest, spiciest, most radical little sheet published in the United States.[12]

Along with considerable editorial comment, the four-page *Antelope* contained travel sketches, news notes from near and far, essays, columns, fiction, correspondence, recipes, household hints, and advertising. In a column titled "Laconic Sermons," Churchill gave advice to readers on topics ranging from the necessity of women's involvement in community affairs to the importance of tempering hard work with recreation.

She credited her travel sketches with "doing more to advertise the state than is done by any local paper in the country; or for that matter any dozen local papers."[13] They sometimes combined fiction with fact. "The Way the Future Historian will write up Leadville," continued for more than a year and featured Romeo and Juliet. Romeo, having lost his way, wandered into Leadville, where he discovered such oddities as "men wearing night shifts and men wearing day shifts who worked for the most part in holes in the ground."[14] In another episode she reported that, with every other building in town a successful saloon, Romeo had encouraged his father, the merchant of Venice, to move there and set up shop.[15] Churchill told readers in a note that she intended to write a humorous history of every community in Colorado, a goal she did not reach. She also projected a volume of Colorado travel sketches to be titled *Over the Evergreen Hills*. That, too, apparently remained uncompleted.

Churchill used humor in supporting women's rights and other causes, as well as in her travel sketches. In reply to someone who asked the politics of her paper, she replied:

> We are a Democratic-Republican, a Greenback-Know-Nothing, Pro-China-Woman Suffragist. We are also Anti-Polygamist. . . . They say that people "talk about us," we should feel dreadful if they did not; let them talk, we have lived in the world long enough to realize that the pathway of life is literally lined with snarling *curs,* and we should remember that the same Creator made the cur as made the thorough-bred, and if they can stand being a cur and behave like one, we can stand being snarled at, because we are a thorough-bred.[16]

In a more serious vein, she described her view of woman's sphere, "to seek every good place and good thing in life and to shun the evil and the bad." A man's sphere was no more and no less, "and all acknowledge these facts except the bigot and the individual, whether man or woman, not capable of comprehending the situation."[17] Even her opinions about proper spheres for the sexes she laced with humor, however, as when she admitted that "there is no one who thinks more of a man than the *'Queen Bee'* does, but we want him to keep his proper sphere, and we propose to decide what that sphere is."[18] As the author of a thesis about woman suffrage in Colorado wrote, the 1880s might have been dull on the Colorado suffrage scene had it not been for Caroline Nichols Churchill.[19]

Although she considered her paper to be the voice of the Colorado suffrage movement, participated in state suffrage conventions, and wrote a woman's column for *The Denver Republican* in 1881, she never became part of the suffrage establishment. Neither did she win popularity with the WCTU, although she supported its aims, "because popularity was not what she was looking for," she later wrote. Her methods were her own and "she made no effort to curry favor."[20]

By selling out each number of the paper before printing the next, Caroline managed to make a profit and increase the number of pages. She set up an office in her home and hired a printer, the first of many to whom she entrusted production of the paper during her absences. Some proved to be unreliable or dishonest or both, and a portion of her autobiography devoted to the vicissitudes of running the paper from a distance described some who caused her grief. Over the years she employed several women, both as printers and as editorial assistants. From 1892 to 1894 the *Queen Bee* listed Miss Hattie Nichols as publisher, with Caroline as editor and proprietor. Hattie must have been a relative, but the editor never explained the relationship.

By mid-1882, the *Antelope* had eighteen pages, almost four of them full of ads, but Churchill found that the book format made it expensive to publish and mail and decided to transform it into a four-page weekly. Eastern readers had objected to the name of the *Antelope*, so she decided to call the new weekly *Queen Bee*. Perhaps she had already adopted the same title for herself. At any rate, "Queen Bee" became her popular name soon after she started the paper, if not before.

The new paper continued the numbering of the *Antelope* and carried the same sort of content. From news notes to serial novels, it bore the stamp of the editor's personality. She continued the regular feature titled "What Our Editor Encounters" and tried columns such as one for "Young Folks," one to promote "Fonetik" spelling, and one on "Woman Suffrage" by the president of the Nebraska Woman Suffrage Association. She also offered recipes and household hints. "Locals" boosted businesses that advertised in the paper. Illustrations brightened its appearance.

Favorable notices from individuals and other papers came in and Churchill used them liberally. Sometimes they referred more to the editor than to her paper, like this one from the Las Vegas, New Mexico, *Daily Optic*: "With all her crankisms and vagaries, Sister Churchill is a brainy woman, and the tongue of scandal has never assailed her, although she has been snubbed and insulted by men thousands of times all over the West."[21]

Churchill carried on barbed exchanges with other editors, but she balanced these with humor. Fellow editor Dave Day, of the Ouray *Solid Muldoon*, became her favorite adversary. Upon the occasion of a "neck-tie party," he "could have described the toilets to perfection, and the fancy steps of the dancers would have been a poem to his soul."[22] When a mule kicked him in the jaw, "Dave was unhurt; but it broke the mule's leg."[23] "Kernel" Dave Day was informed that Churchill had "bribed her feminine foreman to answer him in her absence." The foreman, who signed herself "F. F.," promised to be "his uncompromising and relentless foe" and added, "Dave, we kick the beam at exactly 110; the broomstick is loaded; we have the Queen Bee shooting stick up our sleeve. A word to the wise is sufficient."[24]

Although Churchill maintained good relationships with many of her fellow editors, the Colorado Press Association refused to admit her in 1881. At the time, she wrote in the *Antelope* that she was glad the editors were afraid of her and that she would apply for membership every year to test their capacity for improvement.[25] However, she stated in her autobiography that she subsequently refused to have anything to do "with a class of men so much below par with the women of the country," even though the president of the association continued to send her its literature and one editor told her the blackballing had been "just for a joke."[26]

In a plea for subscribers, Churchill claimed to have done "as much to amuse and stir up the Western men as any ten journalists in the country" and suggested they show their appreciation by buying the paper. She also characterized the *Queen Bee* as the only real family paper published in the Rocky Mountain region and boasted that it had more than twice the circulation of any paper in Colorado or the five surrounding territories. Another reason for supporting the paper, at least in 1884, was that ladies did all its mechanical work, thus learning skills that would keep them from being "obliged to wash or keep boarders when they are called upon to support their families."[27]

Although the *Queen Bee* claimed a large circulation—larger than any other in the Rocky Mountain country—and the paper had a healthy number of ads over most of its life, it never supported its editor in extravagant style. In 1893 she complained that, although she had given the world's fair about a thousand dollars worth of advertising, she lacked the funds to travel to it. She suggested that society operated on the assumption that "woman is expected to work for every body and every thing and get no compensation."[28]

Perhaps the querulous tone of this complaint reflected Churchill's mood. Now close to sixty, she was producing a less lively and humorous paper, relying more and more on patent content. However, approval of woman suffrage by Colorado voters in November lifted her spirits. She wrote that she received the news in Council Bluffs, Iowa, and that a poetic medley came to her with her first outburst of joy. A few lines demonstrate her jubilation, her poetic style, and her still-active sense of humor:

Hail Colorado, happy land
Where buckwheat cakes are mixed with sand,
   And now the day is drawing near,
For woman's kingdom never fear. . . .
   I feel like singing all the time,
My tears are wiped away,
   For I am a citizen now;
I'll sing it every day.
   When the storms of life are raging,
Tempests wild on sea or land,
   I will seek a refuge
In Colorado land.[29]

Her enthusiasm for the adoption of suffrage, for which she took considerable credit, may have given Churchill energy to keep the paper going for two more years. An unsigned note held her up to the men of Colorado as "an example of perseverance, patience, endurance and general determination not surpassed in the history of the holy martyrs."[30] She now proposed toasting those men rather than roasting them, as she had done in the past.[31] She hailed the appearance of *The Woman Voter*, produced by the Woman's Club of Denver. When people asked why she continued the *Queen Bee* now that suffrage had been adopted, she replied cryptically, "Why do not the men stop publishing their papers every time they carry a point? Just to make fools ask questions would be a very good answer, only that Solomon says answer not a fool according to his follies."[32]

Churchill continued during the final years of the paper to speak out against abuses, like bad treatment of the Ute Indians on their Colorado reservation, and to support those with whom she agreed. In 1894 she sought the Populist party's nomination for state superintendent of public instruction. Failing to obtain it, she blamed the Roman Catholics for the party's problems and shifted her allegiance temporarily to the Prohibition ticket. One of her final travel reports came from Yellowstone Park, where she had gone with friends and family members, including her seven-year-old granddaughter.

In the number for September 4, 1895, she announced that the *Queen Bee* would not appear for some weeks, the office having been shut down for "repairs and different arrangements," explaining further that "the introduction of machinery in printing and the general cheapening of literature has made some changes imperatively necessary." That number is the last that survives in complete form. Two torn pages of a later, undated number exist, with a letter "To Our Readers" on page 1 referring to a lapse in publication of several months and indicating that the paper will be an educator upon various subjects and not a regular newspaper with dates and volume numbers. It concludes with an appropriate epitaph, "The paper is here to help straighten up a defective civilization."

Fourteen years after Churchill discontinued regular publication of the *Queen Bee*, she published her autobiography, *Active Footsteps*, with a dedication that read, "To the railroad men of the west this little volume is dedicated by the author, a friend of the workingmen the world over."[33] In the preface, she explained that the work would be written in the third person "that, as much as possible, the ego might be hidden."[34] Whatever else Churchill accomplished in the book, however, she failed to hide her ego. She combined original material with writings reprinted from her papers and emphasized her accomplishments throughout. She also included a description of herself:

> Mrs. Churchill is in height five feet and four inches; bust measure, thirty-two inches; waist, twenty-nine. Rather small hands and feet. Fair skin, with very red lips, but little color in face. Rare white hands. Very brown hair, one of the light nut brown shades, not very abundant; study ever caused it to fall. Eyes an intellectual gray, with drooping lids. Nose rather small, known as a fine nose. Lips full, with strong teeth, . . . Chin large enough for firmness, with genial expression and pleasant smile. . . . Great animation in countenance when talking. Her chief attraction. Constitution rather light; health seldom perfect. A student by mental temperament. Not mathematical nor mechanical, but an abstract reasoner. Order of brain, statesmanship, philosophical and poetical. Not really great in anything but perseverance, firmness and self-respect. . . . Naturally peaceable in disposition. . . . Temperament, emotional, sympathies easily excited. Has a strong sense of self-preservation. . . . Early in life was dubbed "strong minded." . . . Was distinguished for speeches remarkable. Was never popular; there was nothing in it, for this individuality. Had a remarkable musical voice, for strength and sweetness. A memory that few could equal in the way of events of general importance and statistics, but could not remember the component parts of sour milk griddle cakes, until age developed stronger will power.[35]

Churchill lived to be ninety-two years old, but no record remains of her activities after the 1890s. An obituary in January 1926 stated that she published the *Queen Bee* until shortly before her death, so perhaps she continued to produce occasional numbers. It also hailed her as a pioneer woman suffrage leader and reported that she died at the home of her sister in Colorado Springs after being bedfast for a year.[36] She may have moved from Denver to Colorado Springs some years earlier, for she published her autobiography there.

It is tempting to speculate that Churchill might have met Rowena Granice Steele, an editor in California's San Joaquin Valley during the years that Caroline traveled in that state, although no evidence of such a meeting exists. They could have discussed the vicissitudes of travel and journalism, in which both had been engaged, and shared ideas about the woman question.

Rowena Granice Steele was born Rowena Grannis in Goshen, New York, in 1824. She moved with her parents to New York City in 1830 and, at twenty, married Thomas N. Claughley, proprietor of a furniture business. By 1853, when Thomas departed for California, she had borne two sons and had been working for a year as the starring actress of several plays in P. T. Barnum's American Museum, using the stage name Rowena Granice. In 1856 Barnum sold out, and Granice traveled to San Francisco, although it is uncertain whether she ever rejoined her husband.[37] She changed the names of her sons from that of their father to her own, due to "domestic trouble of a sad and sorrowful nature."[38]

When she made her theatrical debut in San Francisco, the *Daily Alta California* commented favorably:

> Miss Granice made her debut at the Union last evening, and appeared in the "Dumb Girl of Oran" and in the "Yankee Housemaid," to which she sustained the Yankee character of "Jemima Sunflower" very admirably. This is the line of characters in which she excels, and which will secure for her in San Francisco crowded houses.[39]

Granice soon capitalized upon her success by opening a combined theatre and bar, the "Gaieties, Temple of Mirth and Song," one of many "bit" theatres in San Francisco, so called because of their 12½-cent admission price. Critical reaction was not uniformly positive. Thaddeus K. Kenderdine, writing of his travels in California, described the thirty-four-year-old actress leaning from a balcony "like another Juliet, or rather like the grandmother of that interesting young woman, although on her face paint, powder and paste had done their work, until she looked like a flamboyant fright: an exemplification of the conflict we are warring with time, . . ."

However, he admitted that Miss Rowena had been "enterprising, if old and faded," for "she had managed her 'Gaieties' until it was at the head of its class."[40]

After the Gaieties closed in 1856, Granice continued to perform in San Francisco and Sacramento and managed theatres in Sacramento as well. She settled there in 1857, supporting herself and her sons by writing and performing parlor entertainments consisting of readings and songs. When she wasn't traveling, she wrote sketches, poems, and stories for magazines and newspapers. In 1858 she published a collection of her stories called *The family gem*, recruiting her sons to help her sell it door-to-door in the mining towns near Sacramento.

It was also in 1858 that the *Daily Alta California* reported the existence of a marriage certificate for Granice and J. P. Adams, a "well-known comedian," although only a few weeks earlier the paper had published a notice signed "T. Claughley" that forbade anyone to credit his wife, Rowena Granice, on his account.[41] And the following year, on the occasion of a legal battle between Rowena and Thomas over ownership of the reopened Gaieties, another newspaper account referred to "Mr. Claughley, the husband (as it is stated) of Miss Rowena Granice," who had nailed shut the doors of the theatre, only to have Granice break them open with a hatchet.[42] She won the legal case, but the new Gaieties proved unprofitable and closed after six months. Claughley died of tuberculosis in June 1860. That same year Granice completed a short novel called *Victims of Fate*, thus becoming California's first woman novelist.

In 1861 she married Robert Johnson Steele, editor and publisher of the *Democratic Signal* in Auburn, California, but that paper soon expired, in spite of a change of name to *States Rights Journal*. Robert Steele probably worked for its successor, the *Union Advocate*, which printed his wife's novel, *Leonnie St. James; or, The suicide's curse!*, in 1862.

She bore a third son in 1863, after the family had moved to Snelling, the county seat of Merced County, to start the county's first paper, the *Merced Banner*. The family worked together to publish the first number, which appeared on July 5, 1862.[43] A "Salutatory" on page 1 expressed the conviction that the resources of Merced County were sufficient to support a paper and that the people desired one, then went on to sing the praises of the area. The *Banner* contained reports of political, church, and camp meetings; letters from political candidates seeking support; local news stories; birth, death, and marriage notices; articles praising the county and, in particular, the enormous beets and potatoes it produced; and social notes.

Rowena Granice Steele served as assistant editor and "plied the pen and scissors in the interest of her department," writing domestic stories and pleasant locals.[44] For the first number, she must have written the account of the July 4 ball, describing, among others, Miss Malinda Brown, who "looked pretty and fascinating; dress, white tarlaton, several tucks trimmed with white satin ribbon," and Miss Mary Fitzhugh, who "looked and moved like a sylph; her roguish eyes and silvery laugh made more than *one* of the opposite sex sigh and inwardly wish that he was the chosen one of her heart."

Political controversies became so unpleasant that the assistant editor withdrew her name from the masthead of the paper, but she continued to write for it. The *Banner* supported the Democratic party, sympathized with the cause of the South in the Civil War, and criticized the military for the arbitrary arrest and jailing of dissenters. It probably was such criticism that led a band of armed men, assumed to be an unruly U.S. Cavalry company, to raid the paper's office in 1864, scattering type, breaking up the press, and upsetting a stove so that the office caught fire. Rowena and her sons put out the fire, volunteers gathered to sort the type and mend the press, and the next week a small edition of the paper appeared. However, Robert sold the *Banner* a few weeks later.

Dogged by a reputation for disloyalty, Robert Steele had trouble finding another job. He worked as a typesetter and occasional editor on various papers while his wife continued to tour the mining towns with her parlor entertainments. Their flavor can be imagined on the basis of an ad in the first number of the *Banner*, which referred to an upcoming program as a "chaste and versatile Dramatic Entertainment," in which she would be assisted by her sons. It would consist of "Readings, Recitations, Songs, Funny Scenes, and Dances." She realized enough profit from such presentations to purchase a home.

In 1868 the Steeles returned to journalism in Snelling, taking over the *Weekly Merced Herald*, a descendant of the *Banner*, but abandoned it a year later to found the *San Joaquin Valley Argus*. Rowena took an active role in producing it, and the paper prospered. Shortly after transfer of the county seat to Merced at the end of 1872, Robert moved the *Argus* there, after having sent his stepson, Harry Granice, to test the waters by publishing the short-lived *Merced People*. With a Democratic paper, the

Merced Tribune, already in place, the *Argus* shifted its support to the new Independent, or People's, party and, in keeping with journalistic practice of the time, the two papers attacked each other bitterly. Their animosity led, in 1874, to the death of the *Tribune*'s editor.

The *Argus* had published Rowena Granice Steele's new temperance novel, *Dell Dart; or, Within the meshes*, a story about alcohol's ruination of a beautiful, wealthy woman. The author promoted it as she traveled to give temperance lectures. According to an account in the *Daily Alta California*, Editor Edward Madden of the *Tribune* commented on a notice in the Vallejo *Chronicle* that she had canvassed for her book there, after the Steeles' *Argus* had disparaged a young lady to whom he was attached. He wrote, "If any family desires to be posted in the life of a female in a house of ill fame they can ascertain all the knowledge in that line they desire by a perusal of the publication referred to. The authoress evidently knows whereof she speaks."[45]

This proved to be too much for Harry Granice, and, after having asked in vain for a retraction, he shot and killed the opposition editor. Rowena raised a large defense fund and secured expert legal help for Harry. Eventually the state supreme court freed him on a technicality, but only after he had been convicted twice of murder.[46]

A mob looking for Harry on the night of the murder ruined the *Argus* office and the paper was suspended for three months, later reappearing in a smaller size and with a lower price. A year later, the local constable attached all assets of the *Argus*—fraudulently, according to Rowena Granice Steele—on the pretense that it was owned by someone else. The constable, also a partner in the competing *Merced Express*, held the *Argus* for a year.

During 1877 Robert's health failed and Rowena's second son died. Still, she determined to resume publication of the paper, and in January 1878 she revived it, listing herself as editor and publisher and sending it to San Francisco to be printed until she regained control of the paper's confiscated equipment. As she put it three years later, "In the midst of winter, with no press, no type, and no money, the resolution to republish the *Argus* was formed, and by a woman."[47]

As editor she continued to support woman suffrage and temperance, as well as various philanthropic causes. For example, she raised money through the paper in 1884 to send a mentally handicapped child to a home in San Francisco, and listed names of contributors. Initially, she campaigned for the Workingmen's party, but later became a Republican. A series on public schools praised the progressive spirit of the county, and articles on "The Girls of Merced" and "The Boys of Merced" lauded the intelligence and ambition of the younger generation, praising the girls for having found other occupations "quite as respectable and honorable as that of school teaching," including work on the *Argus*.[48]

Along with local news, travelogues, exchanges, miscellaneous articles, poetry, and some patent material, the editor ran her own serialized fiction. She reprinted *Leonnie St. James* and wrote new works with titles like *The Village Mystery; or, George Manley's Vow, Why He Never Married*, and *The Fate of a Heartless Woman*. The latter she discontinued after receiving complaints from townspeople that the initials of her fictitious characters were the same as those of some local citizens.

In May 1879, an editorial announced that Robert Steele had recovered his health and would again take over as publisher and editor. However, his physical condition remained unstable, and his wife's stamp on the paper stayed, even though the masthead usually listed her only as associate editor. The Steeles began publishing a daily *Argus*, in addition to the weekly, in 1885.

Robert Steele died in January 1890, and Rowena Granice Steele again listed herself as editor and proprietor until her son, Lee R. Steele, took over the paper during the summer. She continued to write for it. They sold it in November, and it merged with the competing *Herald* to form the *Merced County Sun*. Both of Rowena's sons pursued publishing careers, at least for a time.

After her retirement from the *Argus*, she continued to write for newspapers and work for temperance and suffrage. An 1892 biographical sketch listed her as editor and proprietor of the Lodi *Budget*, of which no copies survive.[49] In 1893 her son Lee published her final novel, *Weak or wicked? A romance*. She died at the age of seventy-six, on February 7, 1901. Her favorite tribute might well have been that published in a sketch in the *History of Merced County*:

> She has been an active worker in the temperance cause, and a leader in the woman's suffrage movement in the State, but, in contradiction to the popular idea on the domesticity of such women, her home at Merced, under her own personal supervision and care, is said to be an ideal of neatness, comfort and beauty.[50]

The *San Francisco Chronicle* evaluated Marietta Lizzie Beers Stow more equivocally in a 1902 obituary, calling her "one of the strongest advocates of woman suffrage and a philanthropist in her way."[51] Marietta Beers was born in Webster, New York, possibly in 1830. At least, a biographical sketch published in 1890 celebrated her sixtieth birthday.[52] However, another obituary claimed she was sixty-five years, three months, and twelve days old at the time of her death in December 1902,[53] which would have made 1837 the year of her birth.

Her parents moved to Ohio when she was two years old and farmed there, as they had in New York. The biographical sketch states that, owing to the distance from school and her mother's ill health, she first learned the alphabet at the age of nine. She could cook, housekeep, sew, knit, wash, iron, spin, and weave before she could read. But once she started attending school she progressed so rapidly that she became a "schoolmarm" at fifteen, with a salary of one dollar a week and "board around." She finished her schooling at Baldwin Institute and Oberlin College.

At nineteen Beers married a Cleveland merchant named Bell, but within five years death claimed both her husband and a three-year-old son. At that point, she moved to New York City and took up humanitarian work, serving as an officer in an association for the protection of shop girls. In 1859 she made her debut as a lecturer, speaking throughout the East on such topics as "Woman's Capabilities and Duties" and presenting patriotic and humorous readings.[54] The biographical sketch quoted the Boston *Post* to the effect that she was one of the best public readers ever to entertain a Boston audience. During the Civil War, proceeds of her entertainments and lectures went to aid disabled Union soldiers and to establish a national home for destitute orphan daughters of those who had died.

Although pledges for the home totaled more than $50,000, she actually collected only the $8,000 subscribed in San Francisco and other California cities in 1865. This she turned over to San Francisco hardware merchant Joseph W. Stow, a widower from Vermont, who became "first her treasurer and then her treasure," as the biographical sketch put it. She married him in 1866, in the meantime having abandoned the idea of the national home because individual states had taken up the task of caring for orphans. She put the money into a Ladies Protection and Relief Society Home in San Francisco.

Her suffrage work began in earnest when she joined the California Woman's State Suffrage Association shortly after its organization in 1869. She considered herself to have been the association's second president, although unrecognized as such in official histories. She wrote that she had accepted the position against her husband's wishes and had held it for three months, actively soliciting funds until other members set what she considered a premature date for a state convention, intending to use the money she had gathered to finance it. She resigned but later rejoined the association with the hope that she could work through it to reform the probate laws and solicit members' support for her campaign in 1880 as the Greenback party's nominee for San Francisco school director, a post for which she ran again in 1882.[55]

In this capacity, she called what the biographical sketch characterized as "the first mass meeting ever held by women" and converted the porch of her house into a polling booth. "Several hundred women cast their *first* votes," the sketch reported, "and no pots went unboiled, no stockings unmended, and the cradle kept rocking to the tune of a new lullaby."

During these years a "trinity of calamities" befell her.[56] First, a male practitioner of medicine accidentally poisoned her, and treatment cost $10,000. Then her husband's death of tuberculosis in 1874, while she was traveling in Europe, led to the loss of $200,000 worth of community property at the hands of the probate court. Finally, she spent a night in prison in February 1881, because she refused to resurface the street in front of her home, which she claimed was already in perfect repair. She saw herself as the victim of an attempt by the street superintendent to test an ordinance that he knew was unconstitutional. She sued the city but collected nothing, even having to pay court costs of $52.

Her problems with the courts inspired her to become a writer. In 1876 she wrote a book called *Probate Confiscation*, with the subtitle "Unjust laws which govern woman." It went through at least four editions and led to two other works, "Equal-rights marriage property act and comparative law" and *Probate chaff; or, Beautiful probate; or, Three years probating in San Francisco*, subtitled "A modern drama, showing the merry side of a dark picture." An ad quoted a *Boston Globe* reference praising the latter as "A bright, witty book,"[57] and a circular referred to another book by Stow, *Little Etta's Frontier Life*,[58] an account of her early years apparently published some time before 1877 and later serialized in her paper. She also drafted legislation to protect the rights of widows and orphans and traveled east to encourage its introduction at state and federal levels and to lecture in support of the bill and of her books.[59]

The main purpose of the circular, dated January 7, 1877, that referred to *Little Etta's Frontier Life*, was to announce a campaign to raise $25,000 for the establishment of horticultural colleges for women, with proceeds from Stow's lectures, readings, and book sales to constitute seed money. Her plan was to open a school in the spring of 1880, letting students' labor pay for their expenses. She saw horticulture as a vocation admirably suited to women, having observed during a trip to Europe in 1874 that it was largely in their hands there. With fewer men marrying, she wrote, women needed to enlarge their field of labor beyond domestic employment, and gardening would get them out in the fresh air and sunshine. They had plenty of strength for it, although some claimed otherwise. In fact, it would be less hard on them than toiling with a needle. However, the horticultural colleges apparently never materialized, even though Stow promoted them on an 1877 trip to the East which she devoted primarily to the cause of probate reform.

In 1880, in San Francisco, Stow founded an organization with broader aims—the California Woman's Social Science Association. In fact, its goals were so broad as to be all encompassing:

> To suggest and develop plans for the advancement of industrial, educational, social, philanthropic and moral interests; to learn how to live pure and healthful lives; how to make beautiful, hygienic single and associate homes; how to prepare simple unadulterated food and drink; how to cleanse the home of tobacco, whisky and drugs; how to live five times the period of growth; how to clothe every part of the body so that circulation will be unimpeded; how to conserve time for study and amusements; how to progress without robbing the brain or purse of another; how to master the science of childbearing and rearing and the immutable laws of heredity; how to worship the *true* God.[60]

Perhaps worshiping the true God could be accomplished by joining the First Independent Church of San Francisco, founded in June 1881, and other reforms could be advanced by supporting the Woman's Independent Political party, founded in August. Calling members of her newest organization the Social Science Sisterhood, Stow gave them a trademark—clasped hands—and a badge consisting of a scarlet ribbon with S.S.S. and a flower embroidered on it.

In support of the Social Science Association and her other interests, Stow founded the *Woman's Herald of Industry and Social Science Cooperator* in September 1881. An eight-page monthly, its motto—"There is Nothing which the Human Mind can Conceive which it may not Execute"—was an apt description of Stow's attitude. Page 1 of the first number listed seven reasons for publishing the paper, including the promotion of birth control and the prevention of crime. The sixth reason incorporated several of the editor's pet causes:

> To lay bare the mischief resulting from a purely masculine form of government in Church and State; the dangers of monopolies; to demonstrate the great and growing necessity of a union of the producing classes through co-operation; to show that California is the paradise of woman's out-of-door industries.

The seventh reason was to seek amendment of inheritance laws so that women would be equal with men, a cause for which, she wrote, she had traveled the country.

Much of the *Herald*'s content concerned the Social Science Sisterhood and its activities. Stow encouraged use of its lecture bureau, which would furnish not only lecturers but also readers, concert singers, and dramatic performers. She reported meetings and activities and advertised a raffle of a diamond brooch and earrings for which she had paid $600 in Paris, proceeds of which would cancel the mortgage on the College of Industry housed in her San Francisco mansion, the sole property she had been able to save from the probate court. In January 1883, the Social Science Association went national, with Stow as president and S. Gertrude Smyth, her younger sister, as vice president. Several members of her family had moved to the San Francisco Bay area by this time. Gertrude also had assumed associate editorship of the *Herald*. Later that year the paper announced the first grand triennial conclave of the Social Science Sisterhood of America and International Dress Reform Exhibition to be held in San Francisco on September 4. Stow offered a prize for the most handsome design for a woman's costume.

To foster industrial education, she included in the *Herald* information on such topics as beekeeping and the culture of silk, roses, and tea. Health articles explored such subjects as the prospects for curing the lame, halt, and blind by the use of electricity, and a continuing column advocated temperance. During 1884, page 7 became the *Joyful News Co-operator*, organ of the Association of Brotherly Co-operators founded in March 1883, listing Isaac B. Rumford and Sara W. Rumford as editors. The paper also published a serial story for children. Every number contained women's rights and suffrage material, with Stow at one point inviting the suffragists to hold their meetings in the College of Industry.

She referred to the possibility of forming a woman's anti-monopoly league at the same time she reported formation of the First Independent church and the Woman's Independent Political party. The anti-monopoly league apparently never materialized, and Stow had little further to say about the church or the party. When she ran for governor of California in 1882 as an independent, the *Herald* served as a campaign vehicle, publishing her campaign pledges. She promised to give women the ballot, make honesty profitable, season law with justice, put a snaffle bit in the mouth of monopoly, stamp prohibition upon the escutcheon of state, abolish probate courts, and "retire" the Chinese—whatever that may have meant. Possibly with tongue in cheek, she claimed not only that women make better rulers than men but that, since she was the first woman to seek the governorship, the code of chivalry should compel men to grant it to her.[61]

Such mild levity paled in comparison with the ridicule of her candidacy by the mainstream press. The *San Francisco Chronicle* poked fun not only at her aspirations, but also at her spelling. Under the headline "Mrs. Stow's Ambition, She Will Run for Governor on a Misspelled Platform," the paper called her candidacy a little-known but "appalling" fact and her platform "a blood-curdling document," concluding with a list of misspelled words from "literary gems, evidently written by herself."[62] The *Daily Alta California* reported a party meeting where "the stage was adorned. Three bunches of dahlias and two pickle jars of evergreens set off two American flags and Mrs. Stow." The article quoted the candidate as saying, "I'll never lay down the sword and the battle-axe until we win this fight," and a headline writer twisted this statement slightly for a subhead: "Mrs. Marietta L. Stow is on the warpath again, and has proclaimed herself as the battle-axe of female liberty."[63] Even other feminists, including Abigail Scott Duniway, editor of *The New Northwest* in Portland, chided her for making herself an irresistible target of derision.[64] But Stow campaigned actively, even suspending the paper during November and December while she worked to win votes.

Her forays into campaign politics apparently whetted her appetite; in 1884 she ran for the vice presidency of the United States. The adventure began when Belva Lockwood, political activist and first woman lawyer admitted to practice before the United States Supreme Court, failed to win acceptance of an equal rights plank in the Republican party platform. In spite of this deficiency, suffrage leaders Susan B. Anthony and Elizabeth Cady Stanton urged women to support Republican candidate James G. Blaine. Lockwood, chagrined, sent a letter to Stow, suggesting that women run for office even though they could not vote; "It was time they had their own party, their own platform, and their own nominees," she wrote.[65]

The letter from Lockwood, who had helped Stow five years earlier to introduce her Equal Rights Marriage Property Act in Congress, provided the editor with the inspiration to try her hand once more at organizing a political campaign, and she called a convention in August 1884 at which members of the new National Equal Rights party nominated Belva Lockwood as their candidate for president. They chose Clemence S. Lozier, M.D., to run for vice president but she declined, and Stow agreed to a draft. The party platform, along with generalities like equal justice to all, education, and peace, included such specifics as veterans' benefits, civil service reform, and uniform laws on marriage, divorce, and property.[66]

Lockwood staged a ratification rally at a Maryland farmstead, and Stow turned her paper into a party organ called *National Equal Rights*, datelined San Francisco and Washington, D.C., and added Lockwood's name as co-editor. Undaunted by the ridicule of the press and the disapproval of suffrage leaders who advocated working within the established political system and suggested that Stow had engineered the nomination for her own promotion,[67] the candidates waged a brief but vigorous campaign. Their ticket received more than four thousand votes in the six states of California, Illinois, Maryland, Michigan, New Hampshire, and New York, plus additional votes that had been left uncounted or assigned to majority candidates, the women claimed. Lockwood petitioned Congress to credit her party with its earned votes, plus the electoral vote of Indiana, whose delegates had first voted for Grover Cleveland but then had changed their minds.[68]

Stow announced in *National Equal Rights* that she would spend all her energies for the next four years to increase support for the Equal Rights party, looking toward the election of 1888. However, a food reform column in the January 1885 number of the paper mentioned her as vice president of the Pacific Food Reform Society, so she must not have abandoned completely her other interests. The next month's number is the final one to survive, although the biographical sketch mentioned earlier stated that "Marietta forged her thunder-bolts at home and fired them through the paper, while Belva forged and fired on the wing—in her famous four-year's campaign lecture tour throughout the United States."

Members of the Equal Rights party chose Alfred H. Love, president of the American branch of the Universal Peace Union, as Belva Lockwood's running mate in 1888, but he declined to run for office in a country whose constitution recognized war. Press accounts made no mention of Marietta Stow. Perhaps her Woman's Business College, founded after the 1884 election, demanded her full attention.

In May 1889 Stow and Gertrude Smyth again joined forces, starting a quarterly called *Frolic* in Oakland. They dedicated the magazine "to long life, health and beauty; to patriotism, progress and play."[69] "Frolicking is the key note of long life, therefore we must all be frolickers," they wrote.[70]

Frolic formed part of a larger scheme that included Frolic Clubs and Frolic Temples—playhouses and gymnasiums for women and children. The sixteen-page publication promoted health, beauty, and long life, and ran news of women's accomplishments, instructions for playing games, travel sketches, poetry, and advertisements for everything from Radam's Microbe Killer to pianos. A handwritten note in the margin of a page that contains a poem titled "Turned Sixty" says that it was written by Marietta Stow on her birthday. One verse follows:

> To-day life's sky bends warm and bright,
> And every cloud is out of sight;
> The ripened grain is fair to see,
> And years are full of majesty,
> When each is set with "deeds well done,"
> At midday or at setting sun—
> Turned sixty.[71]

Frolic lasted just a year. Although a notice in the final number of the first volume stated that the second would be issued from the "Marietta Playhouse" with some months to elapse before the move could be completed,[72] a note on another page reported that Stow, "preening her wings for flight," had decided to resume traveling.[73]

The Marietta Playhouse was not the editors' only enthusiasm. On the first page of the same number that announced Stow's departure, they called on every woman in the republic to begin to make ready "*at once*" for a world's fair to be held in New York City, or its environs, in 1892. The Woman's Relief Corps, which they also supported and which received a special page in each number, would "show the world what patriotism means under a republican form of government."

Stow's final project may have been the Birdie Bell Republic, an Oakland kindergarten named after her son, whose nickname had been Birdie. There she sought to instruct children in methods of government by teaching them to govern themselves. Friends held her funeral there in December 1902, after cremation of her body. A birth year of either 1830 or 1837 would mean she had not attained the hundred years of life for which she had encouraged participants in her Frolic Clubs to hope, nor did she find her final resting place in a "Sacred Grove," which she had suggested as a name for sites that would provide scientific disposal of the dead.

During her last years she suffered from cancer, and an Oakland obituary reported that she had attempted suicide two months before her death by saving morphine prescribed to relieve her pain and taking it in a rented room at San Francisco's Palace Hotel. A note left in Oakland enabled rescuers to reach her before the drug could take effect. Friends accompanying her back to Oakland prevented her from jumping off the ferry boat in a second suicide attempt.[74] She had ridden many hobby horses and, as the *Frolic* biographical sketch stated, they had always been first-class racers, "ridden with whip and spur in the interest of her own sex."

And so the editors who attracted public attention with unconventional activities and behaved in ways seen as eccentric in the context of their times add vivid patches to the group portrait of early women editors of the West that this book presents. They held strong opinions and had confidence not only in the validity of their views but also in themselves as persons and as proponents of a better way. Caroline Nichols Churchill and Marietta Beers Stow used their papers as vehicles to promote their ideas and, in Stow's case, the organizations they spawned. Rowena Granice Steele found journalism an outlet for her literary aspirations, as well as a means of earning a living. Caroline Churchill's publications seem to have been her sole means of financial support.

At the same time these editors pursued uncommon goals, they held their periodicals to the patterns of the day. In content, Steele's papers typified the small-town weeklies of the latter half of the nineteenth century, and Churchill and Stow also used common types of content, even though the subject matter of their articles and editorials often differed from that of their more conventional colleagues. Apparently they realized, by instinct or observation, that they at least must present their papers in a form acceptable to a general readership in order to attract both the audience and the advertising that would help to keep their papers alive.

CHAPTER 8

Doctors and Editors

It is a practical Health Journal, teaching how to live when well so as to keep well; how to nurse the sick; how to make good blood, bright eyes, strong nerves, clear heads and good memories.[1]

—Woman's Pacific Coast Journal

 The field of medicine changed dramatically during the latter half of the nineteenth century. In the early part of the century, most members of the medical establishment had practiced what came to be known as heroic medicine, after Oliver Wendell Holmes gave it that label in derision. It included purging, bleeding, and administering large doses of drugs. Diagnosis was rudimentary, and few effective medicines were available. The practice of medicine required neither a medical degree nor a license. Thomsonian practitioners obtained licenses to use the methods and herbal medicines of Samuel Thomson by purchasing his book for twenty dollars.

Given the uncertain state of orthodox medicine, it hardly seems surprising that patients lost confidence and turned to a proliferation of medical sects. In the words of one historian:

As medical science searched for better methods and procedures, the public wandered amid an endless list of *pathies,* the claims of which rivaled the eschatological dreams of the era's religious and political leaders. The spirit of heresy was rampant and worshipers gathered before the newer medical shrines in search of cures.[2]

To the *pathies*—hydropathy, vitapathy, osteopathy, isopathy, homeopathy, phrenopathy, electropathy—could be added magnetic healing, physiomedicalism, sun therapy, chrono-thermalism, Thomsonism, Grahamism, eclectic medicine, and Christian Science.

By the turn of the century, conventional medical theory had undergone many changes. The work of Louis Pasteur led to recognition of a relationship between micro-organisms and disease. Robert Koch's discoveries paved the way for the development of vaccines. Diagnostic methods became more sophisticated and doctors began to specialize. Surgical innovations accompanied the use of anesthesia. Educational practices underwent reform, and hospitals began to take a central role in caring for the sick. Still, medical science in the United States lagged far behind that in Europe, and advances filtered down to everyday practice slowly.[3] Only toward the end of the century did the average citizen begin to benefit from the new discoveries and techniques.

Part of the credit for the modernization of medical treatment must go to the editors whose periodicals spread word of innovations. As early as 1829, health magazines began to be published. In fact, the aims of the *Journal of Health*, founded that year by an association of physicians in Philadelphia, resembled those of periodicals published in the West fifty years later. In presenting "plain precepts, in easy style and language, for the regulation of all the physical agents necessary to health," it advocated fresh air, good food, exercise, healthful clothing, proper correlation of mind and body, and abstinence from tobacco and liquor.[4]

Along with the periodicals designed to aid readers in making themselves more healthy came those directed toward medical practitioners, which contained more specialized and technical information. Of these, the two oldest were the *American Journal of the Medical Sciences* and the *Boston Medical and Surgical Journal*, both begun at about the same time as the *Journal of Health*. Most states and many large cities had their journals for physicians. Periodicals for the various medical specialties also appeared.

The *pathies,* too, had their journals. Between 1850 and 1865 at least seventeen of them promoted homeopathy, a system based on the use of small quantities of remedies that, in large quantities, produced the same effects as the disease being treated. The hydropaths, who advocated the therapeutic use of water, had the *Water-Cure Journal*, the *Water-Cure Monthly*, and the *Water-Cure World*. The *Osteopath*, a Los Angeles monthly, had a woman editor from 1896 to 1899. It circulated among osteopaths, who practiced manipulative techniques to correct bodily abnormalities thought to cause disease.

Disenchantment with conventional medicine led both to enthusiasm for the heretical movements and their publications, and to an avid concern with health that fueled interest in health magazines of all kinds. Probably a thousand journals in medicine and related fields appeared between 1885 and 1905, many of which depended on patent medicine advertising. A history of the American Medical Association refers to the middle 1890s as "the days of competitive journalism in American medicine," in which "the battle raged continuously."[5] Health also played a prominent part in popular general magazines.

This chapter will look at three women editors of two western health periodicals. All had studied medicine; two had medical degrees. All hoped to guide their readers to the happiness that would accompany better health. Carrie Fisher Young started the monthly *Woman's Pacific Coast Journal* in May 1870, as a general periodical with a major emphasis on health. She supported women not only in the title and content of the *Journal*, but through having it printed by the female members of the Women's Cooperative Printing Union, whom she praised as publishers of an entire number when a recruiting trip for the International Order of Good Templars took her to Nevada. When she changed the magazine's name to *Pacific Journal of Health* at the beginning of 1872, she changed its motto from "In the Interest of Women and Children" to "Devoted to Health, Temperance, Literature and Labor Interests." She attributed the new cover design inaugurated at the same time to Crane & Curtis, the only lady engravers in San Francisco.

Young wrote in the first number that she had started fighting intemperance and slavery when still a young girl. She was born in New York State, probably in 1828. Her health and strength failed, but, she continued, "we were yet in the work when slavery—the giant wrong—went down. . . . Now, after years of rest and recuperation, years of sweet home love-life, we are, with fresh vigor and renewed youth, again in the field."[6] Later she reprinted a letter published in a New York periodical, *Laws of Life*, that described her as a worker for the public for at least twenty years. She had traveled through Ohio lecturing on temperance, the letter said, had taken treatment at "Our Home on the Hillside" after her health failed, and then had gone west to engage in fruit culture for a number of years. During that time she wrote letters published in the *New York Tribune* and lectured for many months on the Pacific Coast before moving there to start her journal.[7]

Her lecture tours continued after she became an editor. The *Journal* quoted a Portland paper which had reported attendance of twelve hundred persons at her lecture there, along with a description of her from an Oregon City publication: "She is a plain-looking woman, and speaks with very little hesitancy and considerable ardor. Her arguments are forcible, and at times she is eloquent."[8]

Young announced in her paper that she was available to lecture, "teaching physiology and the laws of life and health, as applied to women and children," and she stressed temperance as a prime law of life and health. One of the fillers she used in the *Journal* pointed out that "Alcohol is found in nothing that has life. It is the product of death and decomposition. It is not in animals nor in grains until they are dead and rotting." She reprinted articles from other publications that supported temperance, as well as writing her own, and reported such signs of progress as the signing of a temperance pledge by the entire junior class of Princeton College.[9]

Like other editors who supported suffrage, Young had no trouble reconciling the ideal of "sweet home love-life" with the crusade for women's rights. She wrote that her title was editor: "We protest against being called an *editress,* or a *lecturess,* and object to having it said of us that because we are a *hard workeress,* we are a hearty *eateress,* and a sound *sleeperess.*"[10] She spoke out for suffrage and for education of women, even suggesting that husbands help out with housework. She claimed to have been "a *help make* as well as a help spend" all the years of her married life, and she taught her children self-reliance, which she considered good for them. In September 1872, she turned over to them the editing of "Children's Cosy Corner," a continuing feature.

The editor gave a straightforward answer to a couple who wrote her a letter about problems of incompatibility:

> *John and Alice*—Nonsense! Don't talk of incompatibility. Any husband and wife can find points of incompatibility if they look for them; and if they nurture them, they will grow to huge barriers. You each think too much upon the other's failings, and your own perfections. Reverse it, thinking upon your own failings, and your companion's excellencies.[11]

In the second number of the *Journal*, Young began an account of her family's journey from Idaho to California. In a wagon driven by her thirteen-year-old daughter, she, her husband, and her son left Idaho in November 1869. W. J. Young probably was her second husband, for her son used a different last name. They forded the Boise River through floating slush-ice, talking of "apples, and grapes, and sunshine, and the chances for papa to get well and strong." Crossing snowy mountains, the family had to abandon its wagon and ride two mules to shelter in a deserted cabin. The next morning they sent the thirteen-year-old back for their other mules and the wagon full of frozen food.[12]

Later, Young wrote that she had three motives in coming to California: First, she sought the even temperature of the coast—"absolutely necessary to the health of one of the family." Second, she expected "the free use of the luscious fruits, as necessary to health as change of climate." Third, she wanted the advantages of the free schools for her children.[13]

The editor gave no indication in early numbers of the *Journal* that her husband was a doctor, but toward the end of 1870 she began referring to him as Dr. W. J. Young, telling readers that in her absence they could transact *Journal* business with him at the office he shared with another doctor. How W. J. Young came by the title of doctor is problematical. Perhaps, like many others, he simply adopted it. However, his wife took care not to offend proponents of orthodox medicine unnecessarily. Under the heading of "Professional Courtesy," she rejected a letter denouncing the medical profession, explaining that it used its methods and "we use ours," but all sought to cure. "Who knows so much or so little as to presume to say that either is, for all cases, the best?"[14]

The following February, Young responded to a reader's question as to how she could travel and lecture so frequently and still edit a paper by recognizing her husband's contributions:

> In the literary work of the paper I am assisted by my husband, Dr. Wm. J. Young. The *Journal* is our joint production. The editorial correspondence is my own. The articles on Maternity and Care of Children are his; but, through the whole, our thoughts are so blended, and, in many instances, our *composition* is so mingled that we can only say, *it is ours*.[15]

When she changed the name of the publication in January 1872, she began listing both herself and her husband as editors.

Content changed only slightly. It continued to range widely, including articles on such diverse subjects as silk growing and California lakes, but focused most frequently on health advice. Young warned readers against fashionable clothing styles that were more injurious "than the hardships of poverty and neglect,"[16] told them how to soothe cross babies, and advised them to eat more fruit and take less medicine. The "Children's Cosy Corner" featured items designed to be read by or to children. She also included a series of letters to her daughter, who had left home to attend school. One of these explained how to avoid colds: "Whenever it is necessary for you to sit in a draft of cold air, face it. Like other evils, it is little to be feared if you look it fairly in the face." Daily cold baths would be helpful, too.[17]

The cold bath idea may have been a forerunner of the establishment by the Youngs in 1872 of the "Nicasio Water-Cure," in Marin County's Nicasio Valley, where patients would be "treated hygienically, and without the use of medicine, by careful attendants, under the direction of skillful physicians."[18] Related articles treated such subjects as "Baths and How to Take Them."[19] The Youngs apparently had joined the followers of hydropathy, imported from Germany during the 1840s. It advocated exercise, good hygiene, natural foods, avoidance of drugs, and, most importantly, use of various types of waters, both internally and for therapeutic baths. The Youngs also sympathized with homeopathy, another German import, which encouraged the use of only small doses of selected medicines. They started a "Homeopathic Department" in the *Journal* in 1872.

In 1871 Young had begun including the initials "M.D." after her name in ads for the *Journal*, so presumably she and her husband would be the "physicians" directing the water-cure. In fact, she assured readers in September 1872 that she would be in attendance, "for consultation and examination of patients."[20]

An ad that continued through much of 1871 made grandiose claims for the *Journal*:

> It is a practical Health Journal, teaching how to live when well so as to keep well; how to nurse the sick; how to make good blood, bright eyes, strong nerves, clear heads and good memories.
>
> It tells how to live hygienically and economically.
>
> It teaches how to preserve your teeth; how to clear a sallow complexion and a billious skin; how to cure chills, rheumatism, and cold feet; how to

dress babies; how to straighten crooked shoulders and make narrow chests broad.

How married people can live together happily.

In a serial story it illustrates what temperaments should be united in marriage to insure happiness, and give to children long life and power to resist disease.

Even such promises apparently did not attract enough readers to keep the *Journal* going. The opening of the water-cure coincided with the closing of the magazine. The final surviving number is for September 1872, although nothing in it alludes to the *Journal*'s demise. The *Union List of Serials* notes that it merged into *Science of Health*, a New York periodical that had started publication in July. In 1876 *Science of Health* merged with the *Phrenological Journal*. The fate of the Nicasio Water-Cure is uncertain, but Young returned to journalism for three years during the 1880s, again promoting healthful living, with *Life Crystals*, a monthly she published and edited in Oakland from 1882 to 1885, with her son, Robert E. Bush, as associate editor and business manager.

According to a newspaper obituary, Young obtained a degree from the Oakland College of Medicine in 1884, having studied earlier "in eastern medical colleges, at a time when women were not graduated to practice." She then practiced in Berkeley for many years. At some point, perhaps between the *Journal* and *Life Crystals*, she may have lived in Arizona; the obituary reported that her husband died there. It also mentioned her son as a civil engineer, but said nothing of her daughter. It emphasized her contributions to the cause of woman suffrage and her leadership in the fight to make the new University of California co-educational. Young became paralyzed in 1897 and died in 1911 at the age of eighty-three.[21]

Toward the end of the nineteenth century, the revolution in medical practice had quickened. During the 1880s the idea of vaccination spread through the country. Koch had isolated the microbes of tuberculosis and Asiatic cholera, and Friedrich Loeffler had discovered the diphtheria bacillus. Researchers realized that insects might be agents of infection. Physicians began operating successfully on the abdomen. Between 1890 and 1900 the U.S. mortality rate would fall nearly 10 percent and the average age at death would rise from thirty-one to thirty-five.[22]

In Utah, Mormon church president Brigham Young had overcome his aversion to doctors to the extent of sending Mormon men and women east to obtain medical training in the late 1860s and the 1870s. Three graduates of Philadelphia colleges—a husband and two of his "plural wives"—decided in 1888 that the Mormons needed a medical journal and started the *Salt Lake Sanitarian*. At that time Milford Bard Shipp, called Bard by his friends, was fifty-two, Ellis Reynolds Shipp was forty-one, and Margaret (Maggie) Curtis Shipp was thirty-eight. Like Carrie Fisher Young, they hoped to provide information that would improve the health and lives of their readers. Like the Youngs, they worked together to produce a publication. There the similarities ended.

Ellis Reynolds was born on January 10, 1847, in Iowa. In 1852 her family moved to Utah, and when she was fourteen her mother died. She lived with her grandparents for some time before being invited in 1865 to stay at Brigham Young's Salt Lake City residence and attend school with his children. Reynolds married Milford Bard Shipp in 1866, against the church president's wishes. Young probably considered Shipp a bad risk, since his two earlier marriages had ended unhappily, but Ellis Reynolds was undaunted. When she and two friends saw him at the theatre, and the friends said "he was *unkind*" to the wife who recently had left him, Reynolds did not believe it. Late in life, she wrote this eulogy: "The honored husband and father, after years of faithful, loving kindness and leadership in Gospel truths, passed beyond on the 15th day of March 1918. Yes, he was mortal, but at heart ever true to his convictions of right."[23]

Bard Shipp was helping his father with a hat and shoe store in Salt Lake City when the marriage took place, but the couple soon moved to central Utah to manage a new branch store in a small community there. It floundered, and they returned to Salt Lake to face financial problems and the acquisition of three more wives for Bard. The first of these was Margaret Curtis, whom he married in 1868. She had been born on December 17, 1849, in St. Louis and was another convert to Mormonism.

In 1869 Brigham Young began sending Mormons east to study medicine, more to ensure that his people would have physicians of their own faith than from any enthusiasm for the medical profession. The first of several women among the Mormon students went east in 1873. In 1875 Maggie Shipp followed, leaving two children in the care of her sister wives. However, she became extremely homesick and stayed for only a month of studies at the Woman's Medical College of Pennsylvania. Ellis Shipp took her place, having decided after the deaths of two of her children that her life's work would be caring for the sick. She left her three surviving children in Salt Lake City with her sister wives and Bard, who provided her with news and small amounts of money.

The stay in Philadelphia was grueling physically and emotionally, as well as financially. By 1876 Ellis and Bard decided she needed a rest, so she returned home for the summer, going back to school in the fall pregnant and penniless. She took in dressmaking to supplement the money she received from home. In May 1877 she gave birth to a baby girl and took care of her while preparing for final examinations and completing hospital work. She received her medical degree in March 1878, then practiced in Utah for a decade before returning to the East in 1887 for postgraduate work in Philadelphia and New York.

After Ellis returned to Salt Lake, Maggie gave Philadelphia another try, receiving her degree in 1883. In the meantime, Bard apparently concluded that medicine was the family vocation. He had studied law while Ellis Shipp was away, but he abandoned it and obtained his medical degree from Jefferson Medical College of Philadelphia the same year Maggie Shipp received hers. One of his daughters wrote that he never really intended to practice: "His purpose in going to a medical college was to better prepare himself to write and edit a health magazine for the people that they might better understand first aid, home nursing and sanitation." He did not open a medical office, but sometimes diagnosed and prescribed for his friends and acquaintances.[24]

Ellis and Maggie Shipp specialized in obstetrics, as did most women doctors of the time. In 1878 Ellis opened a School of Obstetrics and Nursing in which she and Maggie taught. Both women were heavily involved with the Deseret Hospital, operated by the women's organization of the Mormon church between 1882 and 1890.

Bard Shipp's health magazine was the *Salt Lake Sanitarian*, and he probably assumed major responsibility for it from the beginning, although the eight numbers of the first volume, issued monthly and dated April through December 1888, listed the Drs. Shipp as editors, and all three contributed regularly to its content.

Perhaps all three cooperated on the magazine's first editorial, in which they expressed their intention to cultivate an understanding of physiological laws and discuss care of the sick and treatment of disease. They assured readers that they were "tied to no exclusive dogmas," but would "endeavor to advance only such principles as are established in the light of science and have the sanction of professional authority." Ellis Shipp, who wrote poetry that was published in the Mormon women's periodical and in a book, may have been responsible for the flight of fancy that began and ended the editorial with marine metaphors: "It is with no little apprehension that we launch the *Sanitarian* upon an untried sea. . . . The aspirations of the *Sanitarian* will be to serve as a beacon light to warn the frail barks freighted with human lives of the shoals and snags that abound in the stream of time."[25]

The editors kept their promise to discuss prevention and treatment of disease. Most articles and editorials dealt in one way or another with these topics, treating special diseases and medical problems, health of children, use of medicines and other therapies, practices of healthful living, sanitation, or nutrition. Both Ellis and Bard wrote regular columns. In addition, the *Sanitarian* used fillers: humorous anecdotes, bits of miscellaneous information, or brief snippets of medical advice.

About two-thirds of the articles were reprints, most from professional medical periodicals. If nothing else, the list of forty-five publications from which the editors borrowed indicates their wide exposure to the medical literature and their conformity to standard journalistic practice of their day. Like other periodicals, the *Sanitarian* no doubt had a long lineup of exchange publications, all of which the editors considered fair game. They ranged widely and passed on whatever seemed of value to them.

In original articles and columns, the editors warned against excessive use of medicines, suggested treatments for specific medical problems, urged readers to improve sanitation in and around their homes, and advised them to get plenty of fresh air, sleep, and sunshine. Perhaps the two women editors contributed to the *Sanitarian*'s emphasis on the health of women and children. The unnamed author of "Physical Training for Women" assured those who might think that "the worst obstacle in the way of the enthusiast for physical training among women is the morbid dread that bodily development may be attained at the expense of those delicate personal charms which we all admire in women" that "this is the greatest nonsense on record."[26]

The *Sanitarian* also joined the battle against unhealthy clothing. It reprinted "A Scientific Attack on the Corset," which provided the following list of symptoms from which corset wearers could expect to suffer:

Local inflammation of the liver, gallstones and bilary colic, wandering liver, protuberant abdomen and enteroptosis, prolapse and flexious of the womb, lateral curvatures of the spine, anaemia and chlorosis, dyspepsia, diminished lung capacity and oxygen starvation, intercostal neuralgia, weak eyes and Bright's Disease.[27]

The column by Ellis Shipp, "Mothers' Methods," started in the third number and ran for six months. It told expectant and nursing mothers to leave tea, coffee, and beer alone, in line with Mormon church practice. It also explained first aid for bleeding, choking, and foreign bodies in the ear or nose; approvingly quoted Alexander Pope to the effect that two years old is two years too late to begin training a child; assured mothers that no one is more qualified to understand the ailments of infancy than an observing and intelligent mother; and urged mothers to educate themselves in physiology, hygiene, and nursing. Maggie Shipp wrote no regular column for the publication, but contributed articles during its first year on such subjects as "Nurses," "Cholera Infantum" (or "Summer Complaint"), "The Skin—Construction and Care," and "Confidence Between Mother and Daughter."

Bard Shipp began the second volume of the *Sanitarian* in April 1889, as sole editor, after only nine numbers of volume I, blaming his "incarceration in the pen" for the failure of the periodical to catch up with its numbering.[28] He had served a ten-week sentence for "unlawful cohabitation," the standard charge on which federal authorities prosecuted Mormon polygamists.

His editorial also recognized the difficulty of terminology in one of that number's articles and admitted to criticism "that some of the pieces that have appeared in the *Sanitarian* carried such a scientific diction that they were better suited to the professional than to the general readers." However, the editor suggested, it was best to let the authorities speak for themselves, and readers could solve the problem with the help of "a little 'dictionary light,'" which would "bring astonishing relief," and the rewards would be well worth the effort.

The increasing difficulty of articles in professional medical journals reflected the continuing professionalization of medicine. Soon such periodicals would be completely unintelligible to the general public, and doctors with medical degrees would frown on publications that advocated self-help and popularized scientific findings. Widespread free exchange of publications, with assumed permission to reprint articles, would be discontinued.

Only eight numbers of the *Sanitarian* came out between June 1889 and January 1891, the date of the final number. Bard Shipp explained in October 1890 that

> during the winter months of last year's volume we published the lectures of Drs. Shipp, instead of the regular issues of the *Sanitarian* proper. The past summer we have been engaged traveling through the settlements and cities of this and adjacent territories, lecturing on the subject of sanitation, and in consequence did not commence the third volume until now, October.[29]

Readers received no explanation for its demise in the pages of the *Sanitarian*, and Salt Lake City newspapers published no farewells. A 1978 article suggests that "Feuds between Maggie and Milford, who were eventually divorced, may have been the cause of its demise."[30] A more likely explanation would seem to be the magazine's excessive reliance on long, often technical reprints. Readers might not have shared the editors' enthusiasm for scientific phraseology, even if they agreed that the *Sanitarian* brought "some of the best products found in our medical literature upon topics that are of common interest and can be utilized in domestic practice."[31] This promised reward probably seemed insufficient recompense for the effort of reading with dictionary in hand.

After their journalistic venture ended, Ellis and Maggie Shipp continued lecturing, teaching, and maintaining their private practices. Someone estimated that Ellis Shipp delivered more than five thousand babies.[32] Of the ten she bore, only half survived infancy. She traveled to Michigan in 1893 for a final year of medical study. She also maintained her literary interests, serving as an officer of the Utah Woman's Press Club and the Reaper's Club, a Salt Lake literary group. She worked as a member of the General Board of the Mormon women's organization, the Relief Society, from 1898 to 1907. She died on January 31, 1939.

Maggie Shipp had nine children. She married Brigham R. Roberts, a Mormon church official, after her divorce from Bard Shipp, partially retiring from the involvement in public activities that had characterized her life up to that time. She died on March 16, 1926, in Brooklyn, New York, where Roberts was presiding over a church mission.

Both the Shipps and the Youngs undoubtedly saw their publications primarily as vehicles toward the advancement of broad medical and social aims. The editors held strong convictions about how to improve the health of the general populace and hoped with their periodicals to reach a wider audience than they could educate in person. They represented two of the many threads in the fabric of medical journalism of their time, the Youngs operating on the fringes of the medical establishment but leavening their predilection for health fads with a strong measure of common sense, the Shipps firmly in the mainstream of the infant science of medicine but preceding its full professionalization.

They illustrate, as well, two of the myriad of different divisions of responsibility in which women editors functioned. Carrie Fisher Young apparently started out as working editor of her *Journal*, then recruited her husband to assist with the paper as she became increasingly involved in lecturing and organizing for temperance. The guiding spirit behind the *Sanitarian*, on the other hand, seems to have been Bard Shipp, who recruited his wives to write for the publication and probably to perform other editorial functions as well.

The women's contributions to the health of their readers differed as much as their publications. If Young's reliance on hydropathy turned out to be misdirected, she at least warned readers of the dangers of over-medication and overindulgence and urged them to reap the benefits of healthful food and fresh air. The Shipps added an opportunity for readers to acquaint themselves with the latest thinking from a variety of health disciplines. Both publications provided for their readers one more window on the diversities of the contemporary medical scene and provided information which readers could use to make more intelligent choices from the array of medical options offered them.

CHAPTER 9

Literary Ladies

Almost the last thing I did before turning the business over to Mr. Wild-man was to pay a dressmaker's bill for Miss Shinn. Her salary had always been magnificent—payable in stock—but the coin she drew was little. Still it had been recorded in the elder day that Anton Roman had gone out of the magazine with a new suit of clothes to pay for his years of work, and I was determined that Miss Shinn should have at least as much as that to show.[1]

—*Charles S. Greene of* The Overland Monthly

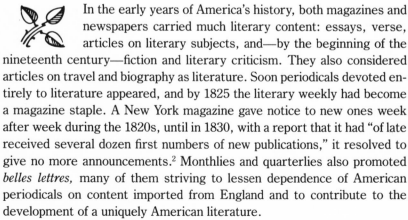 In the early years of America's history, both magazines and newspapers carried much literary content: essays, verse, articles on literary subjects, and—by the beginning of the nineteenth century—fiction and literary criticism. They also considered articles on travel and biography as literature. Soon periodicals devoted entirely to literature appeared, and by 1825 the literary weekly had become a magazine staple. A New York magazine gave notice to new ones week after week during the 1820s, until in 1830, with a report that it had "of late received several dozen first numbers of new publications," it resolved to give no more announcements.[2] Monthlies and quarterlies also promoted *belles lettres,* many of them striving to lessen dependence of American periodicals on content imported from England and to contribute to the development of a uniquely American literature.

As the population moved westward, magazine publishers had to contend with the literary dominance of the East, even as the easterners had struggled to escape the overwhelming influence of England. Each successive frontier made an effort to create a culture of its own, and editors often sought material by western writers on western themes. They also hoped "to bring the gentle charm of the arts into their brash and exuberant communities and so leaven the loaf of commercialism," although "their forty-eight-page idealism usually starved to death in a dozen or two numbers."[3] San Francisco, as the cultural center of the Far West, came early to the periodical scene, its *Golden Era* appearing in 1852 as the first distinctly literary publication of the Pacific Coast.

If content of the earliest literary periodicals resembled that of newspapers, the literary magazines of the nineteenth century can be distinguished from general magazines only with difficulty. Like *The Hesperian* (the literary publication for women discussed in chapter 2), they contained much miscellaneous content that seems to the modern reader to have little relationship to literature. Along with fiction, poetry, reviews, and essays on literary topics, came articles about philosophy, education, politics, science, and history, as well as humor and specialized content for particular audiences.

Women played a major role in the world of the literary magazines, although this was the one journalistic area where their participation attracted frequent criticism. The "damned mob of scribbling women," as Nathaniel Hawthorne called them,[4] came in for derogatory comments about their sentimentality and banality. However, much nineteenth-century fiction and poetry by men could be charged with the same sins. Perhaps the large number of women who wrote material with literary pretensions constituted a threat that literary men did not perceive in the smaller inroads made by women into other fields of periodical publishing.

Milicent Washburn Shinn was a San Francisco editor who came in for her share of criticism during the eleven years she guided *The Overland Monthly*. The fact that this periodical in its first incarnation had been edited by Bret Harte and had attracted most of the literary luminaries of the West Coast as contributors did not help. Shinn's age when she began her editorship, twenty-five, no doubt combined with her sex to make her even more suspect.

One of the few native westerners treated in the pages of this book, she was born on April 15, 1858, in the rural community of Niles, now part of Fremont, California, where her father farmed and ran a tree nursery. The third of four children, she attended local public schools and the Oakland High School before entering the University of California at Berkeley.

The poet Edward Rowland Sill, who taught her both in high school and at the university, became an important influence in her life and steered her toward a literary career. She left the university for two years to teach school, returning to finish her studies and receive a degree in 1880. Even before that time she did some editing for the *Commercial Herald* of San Francisco and, with the encouragement of her poet mentor, wrote prose and poetry for *The Californian*, a literary magazine founded in 1880 to replace the defunct *Overland Monthly*.

The *Overland* had been founded in 1868 and suspended in 1876. A publisher who sold it in 1869 agreed to a stipulation that he would not publish a magazine for the next ten years. At the end of that time, he tried to repeat his former success with a new magazine called *The Californian*. The economic climate had changed, however, and financial problems led him to sell out the same year. After several changes in ownership and the acquisition of permission to use the *Overland* name, *The Californian* in January 1883 became *The Overland Monthly*, with twenty-three-year-old Lemuel Warren Cheney as publisher and Milicent Shinn as editor. Edward Rowland Sill had suggested her for the position when the new publisher sought his advice. She had begun to help with editorial chores even before the name change. The publisher intended to act as business manager, but he soon sold out, and Shinn was left to run the *Overland* with the help of an assistant editor, Charles Samuel Greene, who also served as business manager beginning about 1892.

As the introductory quotation to this chapter implies, the financial rewards for the editor proved small. She wrote in a letter that from the first it was virtually a "life-and-death struggle to get each number out," particularly since she was "unacquainted with moneyed men, and obliged to . . . make their acquaintance, one by one, with due dignity and propriety, and influential introductions."[5] Her assistant editor recalled—perhaps referring to the years from 1885 to 1890 when Milicent's older brother, Charles Howard Shinn, held the position of business manager, or perhaps to his own managership—that "many a time the editor shivered in her office while the manager went out on the street with blood in his eye to compel somebody to pay a three-dollar subscription, so there could be a sack of coal and some postage stamps bought."[6]

This must have been especially discouraging for Shinn, who had not sought the editorship and had serious reservations about taking it. She admitted in letters that she had "never had the passion" for the literary life and that, as far as the editorship went, "I did not take hold of it with the least idea of ever becoming responsible editor. I should as soon have expected to take command of an army."[7]

The unenthusiastic reception of the new *Overland* and its editor in some quarters must have added to her doubts. An article in a competing magazine stated,

> The *Overland* lacks something very needful to a magazine—it lacks an editor. We find fault with the present editor, she is a woman, not a strong robust woman, but a lady with a delicate constitution and a poetic mind, a valuable assistant to any venture, but a hindrance to success, alone. We admit that a lady could control successfully a weekly paper, but it is not possible for the female mind to grasp and control the sphere of a literary monthly that depends upon its editorial ability for success. We simply laugh at the attempts of the feminine mind to cope with the masculine in the prescribed sphere of masculinity. The *Overland*, with an editress, will be a failure.[8]

Ambrose Bierce, the vitriolic writer and editor who admitted that he intended "to purify journalism in this town by instructing such writers as it is worth while to instruct, and assassinating those that it is not,"[9] wrote of Shinn's work as "the unrewarded labor of a misguided young girl-editor who has no true friend to dissuade her" and referred to the magazine as the "Warmed-overland Monthly" or the "Shinnplaster."[10]

But Shinn persevered, having written in the first number under her editorship that, even though the odds were against her, "There is often more hope of success for an enterprise that starts against the odds than for one that starts with them; for it argues that there was great reason for the undertaking, great courage, and much determination." She went on to state that her aim for the magazine was to make it as good as the best magazine in America.[11] While it never attained that eminence, it still could be characterized by a magazine historian seventy-five years later as "the most important magazine of the Pacific Coast" during the period of her editorship.[12]

The magazine had the motto "Devoted to the Development of the Country," but Shinn did not explain exactly what sort of development or which country the motto meant. Although the *Overland* attracted some contributors from the East, its flavor remained distinctly western. While avoiding boosterism, it printed many articles about western people and places and used mostly western writers. It intended to interpret California to the rest of the world and the rest of the world to California, but it emphasized the former.[13]

Shinn wrote that the *Overland* had four purposes: To publish the best literary and intellectual work of the Pacific region, to maintain an open forum for discussion of questions concerning it, to bring to it the best of the world, and to present a picture of its natural aspects and daily life. The descriptive material would cover not just the Pacific states, but also the Mexican and South American West, British Columbia and Alaska, China, Japan, and the Pacific islands, she explained.[14]

Its content consisted of fiction, articles, editorial comment, letters to the editor, poetry, and book reviews. Popular subjects included travel, history, natural history, education, literature, agriculture and industry, and public policy. In a western vein, Shinn included pieces on such topics as the West's Indian peoples, visits to scenic spots, the Chinese labor situation, and problems facing California's big trees. The ecological articles may have reflected the interests of her brother, who left the magazine for a long career in the forest service.

The magazine received more poetry than anything else, and it published two or three poems in each number. "Few people print a hundred poems without including two or three that can be commended," Shinn wrote in discussing the *Overland*'s reviews of books of poetry, "and it has been our practice always to give the versifier credit for such, however hopeless the rest of his volume might be."[15] The same policy held for poetry accepted for publication; it included works by many unknowns. First in frequency came poems about nature, followed by those devoted to love and death, the treatment unremittingly serious.

The magazine received almost as many short stories as poems from its contributors. In fact, the short story as a literary form probably owed its development to the literary periodical, and the first *Overland Monthly*, with the works of Bret Harte, contributed significantly to the genre. No such literary notable graced the pages of the second *Overland*.

Shinn's name appeared only occasionally as an author, with the magazine not even listing an editor or editorial staff. But she probably wrote under pseudonyms as well, and she undoubtedly produced most of the unsigned editorial items collected in sections called "Current Comment" and "Etc.," as well as many of the book reviews, another magazine suggesting "it would seem that her critical instinct is more highly developed than her creative."[16] Over the years of her editorship she signed her name to only thirty-nine contributions.[17]

These ran the gamut of the kinds of material published in the *Overland*. A reminiscence, which may have been fictionalized, told the story of a courageous country woman, dying of cancer but determined to keep her family together. Shinn wrote that she had met the woman while teaching school. An article on women school directors offered a history of efforts to open such positions to women, commended their success, and praised local women who had organized to support women candidates in a recent election. A two-part article titled "Poverty and Charity in San Francisco" reported on the extent of poverty and the organizations working to relieve it, with results of a survey made in cooperation with the Pacific Assocation of Collegiate Alumnae—a group of which Shinn was a founding member, president, and secretary, and which evolved into a chapter of the American Association of University Women. Only the Boston and New York branches preceded the one in San Francisco.[18]

If Shinn had a pet topic it was education. She saw it as a means of improving both the individual and society. Her idealism came through clearly in a commencement address she delivered at the University of California:

> The good of education I find not in any power to reveal to the initiated a secret door to happiness . . . but in its help toward making available to all, more and more, and in higher and higher forms, those same old sources of happiness which the patriarchs had; in defining the desires and increasing the capacity for happiness; in removing both, for one's self and for others, those obstacles to it, set up by ignorance and shallowness.[19]

The *Overland* used illustrations sparingly during the 1880s. Mostly woodcuts, they might depict scenery referred to in articles or embellish the borders of a page of poetry. A vignette of a bear decorated the cover. In 1887 the magazine began occasional use of halftones, the first on the Pacific Coast to do so, according to Charles Greene. The quality of illustrations improved sufficiently to win a medal at the World's Columbian Exposition in 1893.

Advertisements appeared both before and after the editorial portion of the magazine with separate page numbering. They ran from 21 to 43 pages and came mostly from San Francisco firms. The editorial text usually filled 112 pages. Circulation reached a high of about twelve thousand in 1890, after which it declined. In 1892 the publisher reduced the subscription price from four dollars a year to three dollars in an effort to give circulation a boost, but this proved futile, although the *Overland* continued to provide its readers with "a literary possession of honest and earnest spirit, pure taste, disinterested patriotism, and very creditable literary quality," as it claimed in 1884.[20]

Shinn resigned from the editorship in March 1894, when a new owner took over. Between then and 1935, when it finally expired, the magazine had fifteen editors and co-editors and gradually popularized its content to attract a wider audience. In 1923 it absorbed *Out West Magazine* of Los Angeles and moved there in 1931. Perhaps Shinn had the *Overland* in mind when she wrote a poem with these lines:

> Only by slow-wrought heapings-up of toil
>   Comes strength to move the world one inch the higher;
> Only by countless drops on rocky soil,
>   This world is chiseled nearer man's desire.[21]

In 1890 her brother's wife bore a baby girl, and Shinn immediately began keeping a detailed daily record of the child's physical and mental development after the pattern of a German work which had been translated the year before. At that time she entered the University of California again briefly, as a graduate student, and returned to school full time after leaving the *Overland*. She became California's first woman Ph.D. in 1898, and the university published the second part of her dissertation on the sensory development of infants. Her work received favorable attention, and she published a popularized version of it in 1900 as *The Biography of a Baby*, but she did not continue her research or writing, choosing instead to retire to the family ranch at Niles and spend the rest of her life there.

She tutored her brother's children and joined such organizations as the Save-the-Redwoods League, the League of Nations Association, and the American Eugenics Society. She continued her work with the Association of Collegiate Alumnae and her support of woman suffrage. A list of her hobbies indicated that her interests remained catholic: crossword puzzles and word games, education, genetics, abolition of war, reading, and gardening.[22] An active outdoors enthusiast in her younger years, she became increasingly frail and died of heart disease on August 13, 1940, at the age of eighty-two.

A biographical sketch from the period of her editorship described her thus:

With a masculine grip and force of intellect which command respect, she discusses social and political problems, has her say on art, finance and religion, urges the material development of the coast, and illumines all she touches with an art that springs only from keen insight and thorough mastery of the subject in hand. . . . There is probably no woman writer in California today, and few of the other sex, who are her superiors in purely intellectual force.[23]

No one described Madge Hilyard Morris Wagner in terms of her intellectual force. Her friends used terms like "originality," "suppressed fire," and "eloquence."[24] Ambrose Bierce and other critics probably saw her as a prime example of the horde of sentimental women writers they so abhorred. She considered herself first of all a poet, although she started her literary career as a newspaper reporter, and it seems unlikely that she would have found herself in the position of editing a literary magazine if her husband had not been its owner.

The year and even the place of her birth are uncertain. Apparently she was born as her parents traveled by covered wagon to California—in Iowa, or Oregon, or somewhere in between. In any event, she arrived in California, perhaps in the 1850s, as a very young child and grew up to make it her home. Little information about her life before the early 1880s has been found. She married a man by the name of Morris and bore two daughters before her husband died. The elder child died of consumption about 1882.

By this time Madge Hilyard Morris had settled in San Jose and obtained a job with the San Jose *Mercury*, doing general reporting and feature writing. She covered meetings of the state legislature in Sacramento, and her daughter later wrote that she became the first woman court reporter in California.[25] Another editor from San Jose, Carrie Stevens Walter, described her as

a frail little woman, working beyond her physical strength to win bread for herself and two children. . . . Night after night, almost until the very coming of the death angel, did the 'little mother' ply her pencil . . . to supply medicines and luxuries for the precious child.[26]

The same editor also recounted the occasion of an invitation to Morris to write a poem for San Jose's July 4 celebration in 1882. Morris had doubts about the poem, according to Walter, to whom she showed it with the comment, "Of course it isn't fit to be read. How *can* I write poetry now?" Walter, struck by the work's beauty, reassured her. However, the committee in charge of the celebration neglected to send a carriage for the "local elocutionist" who was to read the poem, and so it was published in the *Mercury*, instead.

Another writer claimed that Morris's fame dated to the time when the *Mercury*'s editor ordered her, half in jest, to go to the top of the city's 180-foot electric tower and write a poem about the panorama to be seen from that dangerous height. Taking him seriously, Morris had herself hauled up in a large bucket, run with a windlass, that ordinarily took electricians to inspect the lanterns at the top of the tower.

She called her first volume of published poetry *Carmel*. Another, titled *Debris*, followed in 1881. She also wrote for San Francisco periodicals and thus met the editor of *The Golden Era*, Harr Wagner. He had come to California from Pennsylvania and bought the venerable *Golden Era* in 1882, establishing a magazine- and book-publishing business that he maintained until his death in 1936. The *Golden Era* Company published *Poems*, by Madge Morris, in 1885.

The original owners of *The Golden Era* had founded it in 1852 as a weekly. While they made it a literary magazine of sorts, it contained a great deal of general news and attracted readers and advertisers with content of popular appeal. After they sold it in 1860 it became more literary. Harr Wagner struggled to make it into a paying proposition. In January 1886, he transformed it into a monthly, "as a drowning man catches at a straw," and contracted with the well-known poet Joaquin Miller to edit it. This required considerable persuasive skill because the poet had a conviction that any periodical with which he established a close connection was bound to die.[27] *The Golden Era* proved no exception, but it did survive his editorship by several years.

The same year that the magazine became a monthly, when both probably were about thirty years old, Madge Morris became the wife of Harr Wagner and an even more frequent contributor to his magazine. She may have done more than simply contribute, although she had Wagner's daughter, as well as her own, to take care of, in addition to chores she performed for *The Golden Era* and writing she did for an eastern magazine syndicate. She made a fast friend of Joaquin Miller, who praised her work lavishly.

In 1887 Wagner decided to move his struggling magazine to San Diego, where a burgeoning population had led city officials to offer him a subsidy of $5,000 if he would make his San Francisco publication into a San Diego one. He used the bonus to pay off old debts. It looked for a while as though the *Era* would prosper in its new location, but San Diego's boom did not last and, by the time he installed his wife and C. S. Sprecher as editors in 1891, the magazine had entered its final downward spiral.

The Golden Era in 1891 offered a varied menu of articles, fiction, and poetry, with attractive illustrations. It had begun its San Diego tenure with many features promoting that area, and vestiges of boosterism continued to appear, as in June 1891, when the magazine ran photographs of Orange County's exhibits, all constructed of oranges, at a Chicago carnival. Joaquin Miller still contributed poetry, and so did Wagner. She also wrote most of the material for a regular "Youth's Department." An "Educational Department" reflected Harr Wagner's interests, "The Editor's Office" provided opportunity for brief comments on many topics, and "'This' Department" offered a miscellany of humor and information. Other continuing columns discussed the content of current magazines and gave the publisher a chance to commend advertisers and announce community events. The *Era* continued its tradition of encouraging young writers.

Acquaintances and interviewers described Madge Wagner as shy, retiring, and self-effacing. Those qualities could not have been particularly useful for the editor of a struggling literary magazine. One of the *Era*'s original founders wrote that

> it was a great paper, and, if the same policy had been continued, it would be a great paper today. But I will tell you where we made the mistake, and that was when we let the women write for it. Yes, they killed it—they literally killed it with their namby-pamby school-girl trash.[28]

Of course, the policy had changed well before Harr Wagner took over the magazine, and the *Era* used no more women writers than most other literary periodicals of the time. Placing the blame for its demise on its women writers reflects the prejudice against them in certain masculine literary circles more than it explains the decline of the *Era*. Changing tastes in literature no doubt contributed to its problems, but, in fact, the majority of readers responded much more readily to "namby-pamby school-girl trash" than to less accessible styles of writing.

Harr Wagner, who had taught school as a teenager and had served as superintendent of schools for San Diego County after his arrival there, finally gave up the battle to keep the *Era* alive in 1893, replacing it with *The Western Journal of Education* in 1895. That publication proved more successful. It was the official organ of the State Department of Education until his death forty years later.

Wagner continued her career as a poet and wrote prose as well, including a novel called *The Titled Plebian*, which filled an entire number of *The Golden Era* in 1890. The Harr Wagner Publishing Company issued *The Lure of the Desert Land, and Other Poems* in 1917 and *The Autobiography of a Tame Coyote* in 1921. Some of her poetry was set to music.

The one occasion when she stepped into the limelight occurred at about the same time that her editorship ended, after a man visiting the Liberty Bell in Philadelphia's Independence Hall saw a copy of her old July 4 poem, "Liberty's Bell," tacked up there and decided that a new bell should be made for the 1893 Chicago Exposition. Backed by the Daughters of the American Revolution and state governors, he spearheaded a drive that brought 250,000 historic metal relics—mostly medals and coins—to be melted and cast into a new bell.

Wagner and her daughter traveled to Chicago, where a reception at the exposition honored her and provided the opportunity for her daughter to read the seventy-eight-line poem, which told the story of a far-off land where the people gathered their relics to make a wonderful bell, rung only upon the birth or death of a king. But a tyrant became king, and the bell never sounded, until finally the people joined to throw off their shackles and ring it as a symbol of liberty, which it remained to the American colonists, who somehow also heard it ring, and to future generations. The final lines follow:

> While dear is the name of child, mother or wife,
> Or sweet to a soul is the measure of life,
> America's sons will to battle prepare
> When its tones of alarm ring aloud in the air;
> For Liberty's goddess holds in her white hand
> The cord of the bell that swings over our land.[29]

San Diego presented Wagner with a key to the city when she returned from Philadelphia, and a reporter for *The Morning Call* interviewed her during the convention of the Pacific Coast Women's Press Association in San Francisco at which she was honored a short time later. She said that she "really couldn't talk about herself," then added, "If my daughter were only with me, she would talk for me. She is my Aaron, you see, and I am lost without her."[30] When asked about her plans for future literary work, she replied that before making any she had to take care of her health, which had been very poor, although it was improving, and her weight had risen to 100 pounds. The interviewer concluded with the comment that "the world needs just such bright, sweet, lovable women as is Mrs. Wagner to bring sunshine into its dark places."

Wagner's quest for health took her into the Colorado desert, where she continued to write. One of her best-known poems, published by *Lippincott's Magazine* of Philadelphia, grew out of her experience there. "To the Colorado Desert" inspired Joaquin Miller's most extravagant praise of her:

> Not since I can remember have I heard a voice so true as this. It is like the sublime and solemn bass of St. John. It is even John the Baptist crying in the wilderness. Indeed, I doubt if you will find anything more . . . fearfully sublime this side of Job, than this one lone, lorn cry from the desert.[31]

Miller contrasted this poem, which had "lengthwise sun-dried shapes with feet and hands" dying, their "thirsty mouths pressed on the sweltering sands," with "Rocking the Baby," a poem by Wagner that thousands of schoolchildren learned, according to the *San Francisco Chronicle*.[32] He wrote:

> Here are the two extremes of song, the solitude, nakedness, desolation, mystery and awful death and dearth of the boundless desert, and the crooning cradle song, . . . Madge Morris Wagner has pictured life and death. You can hear the mother rocking, rocking. You can see the dead men lying in the sands . . . as you rarely see shapes in any song.[33]

Wagner's health remained poor, but she lived until February 28, 1924. She died at Montara, a San Mateo County community developed by her husband that later failed. Her obituary in the *San Francisco Chronicle* called her "one of California's foremost poets for the past half century."[34]

Madge Hilyard Wagner and Milicent Washburn Shinn both wrote poetry, fiction, and expository prose, and both edited literary periodicals, but beyond that and the fact that both bore the brunt of attacks by Ambrose Bierce, their similarities were few. They worked in California, which reflects that state's position as a center of population and culture in the nineteenth-century West. It had five identifiable literary periodicals edited by women, Colorado had one, other states none.

This modest total reflects not a lack of interest in literature, but rather the blurred boundaries between categories of publications. Many more editors no doubt would have called their periodicals "literary," although they included content that seems decidedly nonliterary to today's reader or had purposes other than the cultivation and dissemination of fine writing. Some not primarily literary, like the *Medico-Literary Journal* edited in San Francisco by Mrs. M. P. Sawtelle from 1878 to 1886, claimed devotion to literature even in their titles.

The women who edited literary periodicals of general circulation faced the prejudice of male writers who assumed women to be incapable of literary excellence, in addition to the normal struggles of the editorial life. Men like Ambrose Bierce considered women's efforts inferior by definition and took delight in criticizing them. Shinn retired early from the fray, but Wagner apparently received enough positive responses to keep her writing for the rest of her life.

As editors, they found an outlet for their own works but also, and more importantly, provided a showcase for the writing of other women. Unlike many male editors of their times, they offered opportunities for publication to established and unknown authors of both sexes.

CHAPTER 10

A Miscellany

Since this mortal is of the weaker sex, it is with no little trepidation that I take up the new work. . . . Newspaper business is entirely to my liking and I hope to succeed by patient work and unfailing energy.[1]
—Annie H. Martin

 With that modest introduction, Annie Hudnall Martin assumed the editorial reins of the Carson City, Nevada, *Daily Morning News* in 1892. At thirty-five, she had taught in the public schools of Carson City for thirteen years, but was ready to move on to a new career. Martin had her experience as a teacher in common with several of the editors described in earlier chapters. She, like many others, also wrote well, read widely, participated in community affairs, sought to improve the lot of humanity, and remained an editor for only a few years.

However, she differed from most of her sister editors in several respects. She moved to Carson City with her family as a child and remained there. She never married. She opposed woman suffrage. For the final twenty years of her life she worked at the United States Mint, the first woman to be placed in charge of a government mint or assay office.

Like all of the editors, Martin must be considered as an individual before she can be placed in the context of a group portrait. This chapter presents brief sketches of several editors, including Martin, all of whom had some characteristics in common, but each of whom combined the common and the uncommon into a unique whole. Their ideas and experiences help to round out the portrait this book paints, illuminating in one way or another its shadowy edges.

Biographical works have been published about only one of the editors described here. Availability of the papers of Charlotte Perkins Gilman at the Schlesinger Library of Radcliffe College led to a revival of interest in her as a seminal feminist thinker and to articles and books about her life, including her year and a half as editor of a San Francisco periodical. More commonly, the researcher faces a void. The stories of women like Martha A. Hayes or Mrs. A. L. McGinnis, both of whom edited weeklies in New Mexico toward the end of the nineteenth century, will be told only after patient searching through local records and histories, and perhaps not even careful combing through county archives will turn up substantial information about their lives.

The earliest of the editors discussed in this chapter joined her husband to follow the railroad to the state of Washington. In fact, the Northern Pacific actually may have owned their paper, the Kalama *Beacon*, or at least held a mortgage on it.[2] Mr. and Mrs. M. H. Money certainly supported the railroad editorially, and for a time their newspaper featured a locomotive on its nameplate. They started the paper a year after the railroad established its construction headquarters at Kalama and wrote in their first number, on May 19, 1871, that "the great and important enterprise inaugurated and already in rapid process of construction by the North Pacific Railroad Company, will receive from us the attention the magnitude of the undertaking demands." This statement followed shortly after another that promised the paper would take "an independent position upon all public questions, exercising impartial criticism toward men and measures, so far as they may affect the material interests of the community."[3]

The Moneys divided the labor of producing their weekly. M. H. Money did the printing and M. L. Money, as she referred to herself on the paper's masthead, the writing. They had come to Washington from Jefferson, Iowa, where they had published the Jefferson *Era*. M. L. Money had been "universally conceded to be one of the best paragraphists in the State, and to rank with the best female writers in the West," according to a report from the *Iowa State Register* that she quoted in the first number of the *Beacon*.[4] The Moneys boosted the territory of Washington, the new town of Kalama, and the railroad, taking an optimistic view of prospects for development. The first page of each number featured a column called

"Town and County," in which M. L. Money demonstrated her talent for producing "well-written, spicy locals."[5]

By 1873 the railroad terminus had moved to Tacoma, and the Moneys wrote of plans to open a print shop there and start a new weekly, *The Northern Pacific Head Light*, implying that they would continue to operate the *Beacon* as well, but by the end of that year it was appearing only twice a month, and the masthead listed no publishers or editors. The last surviving number dates from February 10, 1874. In Tacoma, the Moneys established connections with several existing newspapers and then went on to bring out another paper of their own, the *North Pacific Times*, in 1878. It died the following year, and a rival editor rejoiced at its demise, claiming that the Oregon Steam Navigation Company, the Northern Pacific Railway, and the Tacoma Land Company "infused the first filthy breath of life into the disreputable sheet which has succumbed to its own rottenness."[6]

The Moneys announced at the end of 1879 that they would try again with a paper to be called *North Pacific Coast*, but no copies of it survive, if indeed the *Coast* ever saw the light of day. The couple ran a job-printing business and stationery store along with their newspaper business, and M. L. Money also established an exotic bird business, trading with sailors who frequented the port. She attained notoriety by walking to work with a live parrot perched on her head.[7] She must have found that attention more satisfying than the opprobrium heaped upon her as a hireling of the Northern Pacific, for she apparently abandoned journalism for good. She and her husband provide an example both of the mobility of early editors, probably more common among men than among women, and of financial sponsorship by powerful interests seeking a newspaper voice to support their views.

Legh R. Freeman and his three successive wives depended less directly than the Moneys upon railroad financial support in their editorial endeavors, but Legh and his brother Frederick had moved their newspaper with the Union Pacific from Fort Kearney, Nebraska, to Bear River City, Wyoming, between 1865 and 1868, earning the nickname "press on wheels," and Legh continued to look for railroad towns after he married in 1869 and made his wife his editorial partner, eventually settling in Washington only a few years after the Moneys ended their newspaper careers there.

Ada Virginia Miller was born in 1844 at Strasburg, Virginia, the daughter of an apothecary. She studied German, piano, art, and needlework, and she taught fourteen students during the final year of the Civil War. Subsequently, she became the assistant to the principal of the Strasburg Academy and wrote articles for a newspaper at neighboring Winchester. She also translated a German folktale for publication. Her father took her hunting and fishing, so she could handle a shotgun as well as a pen. She demonstrated both skill and spunk in driving Yankee soldiers out of the family garden.[8]

She probably met Legh Freeman while he was in the army during the Civil War, before he took up journalism and made a name for himself writing as "General Horatio Vattel, Lightning Scout of the Mountains." A year after a mob destroyed his press at Bear River City, Wyoming, in 1869, he returned to Virginia in the character of the flamboyant general for a lecture tour. He married Miller, lost money on the Chicago stock market, and moved back west to Rock Springs, Wyoming, where he planned to mine coal and sell it to the railroad. When this scheme proved less than lucrative, he turned again to journalism, sending his wife to Utah to announce plans for publication of a paper in Ogden, another location on the Union Pacific line.

She produced the first number of the *Ogden Freeman* on June 18, 1875. The following month a Salt Lake City paper quoted her in the following note:

> The editress of the Ogden *Freeman* says: "Be it recorded as part of the history of Utah, that a Virginia born and bred lady, came into Utah unacquainted with a single soul, and, within a period of six weeks, organized, established, and conducted the Ogden *Freeman*, took charge of two infant sons, and gave birth to a third, and in that time was never censured because her endeavors to assist her husband did not accord with 'notions.'"[9]

After he moved to Ogden, Legh Freeman continued to leave much of the day-to-day work of the paper with his wife, as he traveled to seek subscribers and advertisers. When he stayed in Ogden and wrote for the *Freeman*, he made enemies by publishing extreme attacks on individuals, groups, and organizations. A writer for the *Salt Lake Tribune* suggested that he "had better retire again to his coal mines and leave the editorial department to his estimible lady, taking warning by the fate of his former paper, The Frontier Index."[10] Ada Freeman bore a fourth son in 1877, but continued to work on the paper.

Numerous altercations, both verbal and physical, led Legh Freeman to announce in May 1879 that a branch of the Ogden paper would be published in Butte, Montana, at the terminus of the Utah and Northern Railroad. He moved there, ordered the *Freeman* discontinued, and, in August, sent for his family. In Ogden, Ada Freeman supervised loading of the printing equipment into two covered wagons for the trip and set out. She drove the first wagon, a printer the second. A rough road in southwestern Montana dislodged a shotgun hanging in her wagon; it fell into the spokes of a front wheel and discharged a load of bird shot into Ada Freeman's hip. Six days later, on August 22, she died. Legh Freeman wrote an obituary and published it in his new paper, named the *Frontier Index* after his earlier publishing ventures:

> She was one of the noblest women on earth. During the most excruciating suffering she was joyous to the last, and when informed that she must die, said: "Well, I am prepared for death. Tell my children to be good, and meet me in heaven." . . . As joint editor of *The Ogden Freeman*, she performed good work in Utah, and even the Mormons regretted her departure.[11]

While in Montana, Freeman learned of the Northern Pacific's plan for a new town in Washington to be called Yakima City and moved there in 1884 to help found the *Washington Farmer*, a publication that combined community and agricultural news. Freeman immediately embroiled both himself and the paper in controversy, but he took time out in 1886 to travel back to Virginia and acquire a new wife.

Freeman's sister, who taught in a boys' school at Cuthbert, Georgia, had written him about a close friend, Janie Nicholas Ward, an instructor of mathematics at a women's college there. Freeman began corresponding with Ward, and a romance soon developed. Their wedding took place June 10 in the Cuthbert home of Freeman's brother. Legh was 43, Janie 30.

Back in North Yakima, where Legh Freeman had arranged living quarters at the back of his print shop, Janie Freeman immediately began helping with publication of the *Washington Farmer*. She also cared for Legh's three sons and contributed money, perhaps saved during her years as a teacher, toward acquisition of North Yakima real estate. In 1888, "from her own separate funds and estate," she purchased an acre of property for $100 and a month later paid $225 to the Northern Pacific for a lot next to the printing office.[12]

The Freemans sold these and other properties a year later, when Legh decided to follow the Northern Pacific once more and moved his family and the *Washington Farmer* to Puget Sound in response to a gift of property from landowners on Fidalgo Island. There, Janie gave birth to a son in 1890 and a daughter in 1894, the year that marked the family's return to North Yakima, where they sought to keep the paper going by subsisting on butter, vegetables, and fruit traded by farmers for subscriptions. They obtained firewood the same way, and merchants traded clothing and flour for advertising. Late in 1897 Janie Freeman contracted "typhoid malaria" and died on November 2, a month before her forty-second birthday. Shortly after her death, Legh Freeman presented to the city library several hundred books that may well have belonged to her.

Meanwhile, Freeman's son Miller had established a successful publication in Seattle, and Freeman joined him as a partner in 1899. Difficulties arose almost immediately, leading to legal actions, and Freeman returned to North Yakima to start yet another publication, *Northwest Farm and Home*. Even before Freeman left for Seattle, a writer for the *Yakima Epigram* had asked, "Who will be the lucky girl [filling] the need for a lady editor [?]"[13] Freeman found her on a trip to St. Paul, corresponded with her, and married her on July 11, 1900.

Sources disagree as to the birthdate of Mary Rose Genevieve Whitaker, but she was in her mid-thirties when she and Legh married. He was fifty-seven. Mary had received a degree from the commercial department of the University of Minnesota and also held a teaching certificate. She worked in a wholesale produce commission firm before her marriage. A Roman Catholic, Mary became an active member of the St. Joseph parish in North Yakima.

She also maintained a high level of activity in the *Farm and Home* printing office. Freeman installed her as associate editor, which allowed him to travel widely in the interest of the paper—and of his continuing wanderlust. He made a trip in 1901 to bring his two young children back from Georgia, where they had lived with their grandparents. In 1902 he spent two months on Puget Sound and in British Columbia.

Freeman's daughter, Varinia, recalled that Mary Freeman enjoyed working in the printing office "tremendously," being particularly fond of talking with the visitors who frequented the plant. Varinia said that Legh and Mary "did a great deal of joking," and she remembers that "pleasant and uplifting conversation at the dining table was the rule." This disagrees to some extent with the memories of her stepbrothers, who saw their father as strict and stern, and of a woman friend of Mary's, who claimed that she saw Legh slap Mary in the face.[14]

Upon Legh's death in 1915 of Bright's disease, Mary and Varinia inherited *Northwest Farm and Home*, no copies of which have survived. They kept it going until Mary's death of pneumonia in 1917. Varinia moved to Seattle, where her stepbrother Miller employed her. To the end of his life, Legh Freeman maintained the flamboyant persona of Horatio Vattel. His three wives and his daughter, joined by his sons only until they grew old enough to leave home, made it possible for him to do so.

Another woman who helped make her husband's career possible was Josephine Brawley Hughes. The accomplishments of Louis C. Hughes, who established a long-lived, financially successful newspaper and served as governor of Arizona, exemplified the kind of economic and political influence which Legh Freeman sought but never achieved.

Born in rural Pennsylvania in 1839, Elizabeth Josephine Brawley attended schools near the family farm and then enrolled in Edinboro State Normal School, from which she obtained a teaching credential. At Edinboro she met Louis Hughes, a law student who had been wounded in the Civil War, and married him in 1868, after she had left Edinboro to begin teaching. Hughes continued his studies, at the same time becoming deeply involved in movements for labor and social reform. His health failed in 1871, and his doctor suggested that he move to a warmer climate and cut back on his activities. Since Hughes had a brother in Tucson, Arizona, the couple decided they would try to establish themselves there.

However, they had little money, and so Hughes left his wife, by then pregnant, with her parents while he opened a law office in Tucson. He saved most of his earnings for a year in order to bring Josephine and their infant daughter to join him in 1872. The journey involved traveling by train to San Francisco, then by boat to San Diego, and finally by stage to Tucson —a five-hundred-mile, day-and-night journey so rough that at one point the baby bounced out of the coach, landing unscathed on soft sand.[15]

Josephine Brawley Hughes might have been a model for the image of western woman as civilizer. She sent east for candle molds and made candles to replace the usual household light source—rags burning in saucers of grease. She obtained a flock of chickens to combat the insects. She introduced board floors, carpets, and screens for windows and doors. She had a cistern dug for storing rainwater.[16]

In 1873 she opened the first public school in Arizona, a school for girls, and became the territory's first public school teacher, serving until women recruited elsewhere could complete the long trip to Tucson. Finding no Protestant church in the predominantly Catholic town, she turned to the Presbyterian church's board of missions after her own Methodist church provided little encouragement and saw to the establishment of the community's first Protestant church. Later, she helped organize and maintain a Methodist church. A strong advocate of temperance, she succeeded in bringing Frances E. Willard, president of the Woman's Christian Temperance Union, to Tucson to organize a territorial WCTU, with herself as president. Finding the path to temperance blocked by the ballots of men who profited from saloons and gambling halls, she turned to the campaign for woman suffrage, convinced that only by winning the vote could women succeed in reforming the social order. She persuaded a national suffrage organizer to come to Arizona and set up a territorial organization, again serving as president. In 1875 she traveled to Philadelphia as Arizona commissioner to the women's department of the Centennial Exposition.

Meanwhile, Louis Hughes had decided that Tucson needed a second newspaper, one that would counteract the solid Republican sentiments of the *Tucson Citizen*. He had written in the East for a Pittsburgh labor newspaper, and that experience had given him the confidence to gather financial support and found, in 1877, the *Arizona Weekly Star*. Although the paper's masthead did not name her, his wife apparently served as business manager, bookkeeper, and circulation director. She also had added a son to the family by this time. In 1879 the Hugheses started the *Arizona Daily Star*, the territory's first daily, and published both daily and weekly editions of the paper for many years.

The *Star* proved an outspoken opponent of the saloon, the gambling hall, the Republicans, and other influences which the owners considered detrimental to the best interests of Arizona. They refused advertising for gaming or drinking establishments and for alcoholic beverages and eventually saw laws passed that closed business establishments on Sunday, banned gambling, and closed the state's saloons. Josephine Hughes played a major part in the formation of editorial policy, according to a reporter hired by her in 1887 as a member of the paper's staff.[17]

Hughes achieved success in politics, as well as in journalism, working for the fledgling Democratic party of Arizona and serving successively as probate judge, superintendent of schools, and county attorney. In 1893 he was named territorial governor. The *Star* for April 11 contained four columns of congratulatory letters to the new governor and his wife, with an introductory note referring to his absence and thanking well-wishers on behalf of the governor and Mrs. Hughes. In fact, nearly half of the correspondents addressed their letters directly to Mrs. Hughes.

During the three years of Hughes's governorship, Josephine Hughes superintended both the business and editorial sides, continuing to produce a lively and readable publication. She hired an editor, who stayed until the fall of 1894, listing his name on the paper's masthead but never her own. The *Star* emphasized news, carrying national and regional stories obtained through a wire service, along with local notes. It included reports about women and their activities, the WCTU, and Tucson's churches, but gave them no special prominence.

Editorials, usually brief, concentrated mainly on political and civic issues. The paper provided no bylines for its editorials, but it is tempting to conclude that Josephine Hughes, thinking back on her own experience, might have written the following strong statement on suffrage:

> We have pioneer women in Arizona who for a quarter of a century have given their best life to the building of schools, churches and social institutions for the benefit of this territory—who came to Arizona in the pride of useful womanhood and who are now wearing the snow white locks. They ask for justice and fair dealing, and the democratic principles of our government demand equal rights and privileges of citizenship, irrespective of sex.[18]

Despite strong support from both the governor and the *Star*, a suffrage measure failed in 1895. Suffrage went down to defeat again in successive legislatures. Hughes had come into conflict with the Cleveland administration in 1896, and the secretary of the interior asked for his resignation. He resumed supervision of the *Star* and continued its crusades.

The Hugheses' daughter became the first woman instructor at the University of Arizona; their son became a state senator. In 1912, as his mother watched, he introduced the bill that would finally give Arizona's women the right to vote. Louis Hughes died in 1915, their son in 1921, and Josephine Hughes moved to Hermosa Beach, California, where her daughter lived. Complications from a broken leg took her life on April 22, 1926, at the age of eighty-eight. The Methodist church and the WCTU conducted joint burial rites at Tucson's Evergreen Cemetery.

Shortly after Josephine's death, Arizona's governor unveiled a memorial plaque to her in the rotunda of the state capitol:

In Memorium
E. JOSEPHINE BRAWLEY HUGHES
Wife of
GOVERNOR L. C. HUGHES
and Mother of
HON. JOHN T. HUGHES

*   *   *

Mother of Methodism
Founder of W.C.T.U.
and Founder of the First Daily Newspaper in Arizona

*   *   *

Born at Meadville, Pa., Dec. 22, 1839
Died April 22, 1926

In spite of such recognition, Louis Hughes, like Legh Freeman and other publisher husbands, overshadowed his wife during the years that both worked on their newspaper. Some of the women editors, however, were overshadowed by more prominent women. Catherine Amanda Scott Coburn, younger sister of Oregon's noted editor and suffragist, Abigail Scott Duniway, makes a good case in point. While Abigail attained more notoriety, Catharine worked in journalism for a longer time and gained more respect from fellow journalists for her professional skills.

Catharine Scott was born in 1839, five years after her sister Abigail, in Illinois. She moved west with her parents, sisters, and brothers in 1852. At seventeen or eighteen years of age, she married John R. Coburn, a carpenter and builder, and lived with him at Canemah, Oregon, until his death eleven years later, in 1868. By this time she had four daughters. Like other women who eventually became editors, including her sister, she turned to teaching as a means of financial support.

In 1874, however, Abigail Scott Duniway apparently decided she needed help with *The New Northwest*, and Catharine abandoned her six-year teaching career to become associate editor in June of that year. She already had written occasional pieces for the paper, and Abigail welcomed her editorially by calling her "a far better writer than ourself." The editor also took advantage of the opportunity to solicit subscribers by telling readers that Catharine's salary "for the support of herself and her fatherless family *must* come from week to week through your subscriptions." [19]

A reader agreed in 1877 that Coburn was "a much better and more finished writer" than Duniway, who replied that she wrote for only two reasons, to pass on her knowledge and experience and because it paid, adding, "It floats Mrs. Coburn's admirable and carefully written editorials."[20] However, in 1879 Coburn left *The New Northwest*, with no editorial explanation. Perhaps the paper simply did not pay enough to support both women and their families.

Coburn then "took charge" of the Portland *Daily Bee*, "a journal of force and influence in its time," according to one source.[21] Apparently she moved from the *Bee* to the *Oregonian*, of which her brother, Harvey W. Scott, was the editor, for city directories list her as news editress in 1881 and assistant editor in 1882.

From 1883 to 1888, she edited the *Evening Telegram*, another Portland daily, but finally settled at the *Oregonian*, where she remained as associate editor until shortly before her death on May 27, 1913, of a cerebral embolism. Only one of her four daughters survived her.

A newspaper historian called her writing "smooth and pleasant" and suggested that, while the men on the paper supplied strength, she added "a graceful touch" to the paper. He offered as an example a quotation from an editorial she wrote about the poet Joaquin Miller:

> The songs of a lyric poet record the moments when his life, after hours or days of smoldering, breaks into clear flame. The long stretches of existence for all men are a moving slumber; the senses are dull; the passions sleep. But every man wakens now and then from the lethargy of the soul which we call "routine"; the "crowded hour of glorious life" comes flaming; for most of us it passes with no record but regret; the lyric poet makes it eternal in his song.[22]

In addition to editing and writing for newspapers, Coburn participated actively in the First Unitarian Church, worked at the Portland Baby Home, and served as president of the Portland Woman's Union. Thus, she combined her thirty-nine-year professional career in journalism with civic and religious service, like other women editors. An obituary in the *Oregonian* called her an authority on Oregon history and pioneers, with a special interest in political economy and sociology. Her editorials, it said, "were marked by originality of thought, freshness of vision and keen sympathy."[23]

A contemporary of Coburn's with a different editorial vision was Lucy A. Rose Mallory, founder and editor of a spiritualist monthly called *The World's Advance-Thought*. The town of Roseburg, Oregon, had been named after her father, and she was born there February 14, 1846. Her mother died giving birth to her, and her father remarried fifteen months later. She later wrote that her stepmother treated her and her sister with "unbelievable cruelty" and threatened to kill their father if the children told him. Her childhood playmate, an Umpqua Indian boy she characterized as "a mystic and philosopher," taught her a love of nature and a knowledge of woodcraft.[24] A biographical sketch in *American Women* covered her early years in one sentence, "Though reared among Indians and surrounded constantly in early life by the wildest aspects of nature, she was always a vegetarian."[25]

She became a dreamer, living in a world of her own. At twelve years of age she had a vivid dream of the man she would marry. The next morning she saw him on the porch of her father's hotel. His name was Rufus Mallory, and he had arrived the night before, having heard that the district needed a schoolteacher. The school board hired him, and Lucy became one of his pupils. After her father left to spend a year in Washington, D.C., conditions at home deteriorated. The sympathetic schoolteacher decided his student had reached a marriageable age, and the local justice of the peace married them on June 24, 1860. The bride was fourteen, the groom twenty-nine.

Rufus Mallory, who had studied law while teaching school, began to practice in 1860, and the governor appointed him district attorney in 1862. That same year voters elected him to the state legislature, and the couple moved to Salem shortly before the birth of their only child, a son. Five years later, Lucy accompanied him to Washington after his election to Congress. He did not seek re-election, returning to Salem when his term ended in 1869. However, his political career continued. He served as speaker of the Oregon House of Representatives in 1872, as U.S. district attorney from 1874 to 1882, and as a delegate to Republican national conventions in 1868 and 1888.

In the meantime, Lucy Mallory had decided that her life's work would be to stimulate thought and to make the world a better and happier place.[26] She volunteered in 1874, "in the face of sneers and ridicule," to teach forty-five black and mulatto children whom the state schools refused to admit. No other instructor could be found, even though a public fund provided a salary. However, her example proved contagious, and three years later the public schools admitted her pupils with little opposition.[27]

In 1886, with the salary money she had saved from her teaching days and probably with financial support from her husband, Mallory founded two monthly papers in one, *The World's Advance-Thought* and *The Universal Republic*. Calling them the "Companion-Papers," she devoted eight pages to each and bound them together, making little distinction in their content. Judge H. N. Maguire assisted her for the first five years, then moved to Springfield, Oregon, to promote settlement there, at the World's Advance-Thought Colony Grounds. Mallory's office occupied a house next to the Mallory Hotel. In the basement she set up a free reading room. She also gave spiritualistic readings in the house, according to an obituary,[28] and held weekly meetings there to forward the cause of advanced thought. Not only did she write articles for the paper, she also set type.

With such slogans as "The Unity of Humanity is the Millennium of Peace" and "Love Is the Way, the Truth and the Life," Mallory used the paper to support a miscellaneous array of causes, including the initiative and referendum, woman suffrage, proportional representation, international peace and a league of nations, spiritualism, and, as one account put it, "many progressive measures then considered radical."[29]

One of her pet projects was "Whole-World Soul-Communion." Each month she published a timetable, so that like-minded persons around the globe could concentrate their psychic energy simultaneously on the accomplishment of worthy goals, like defeating a project to use taxes for building military fortifications or promoting schemes to build irrigation projects in the West. More fundamental were the seven essential principles of a complete reform movement: universal equality of the sexes, universal vegetarianism, a universal language, universal money, universal peace, universal cooperation, and universal love, which "includes all the others and all there is."[30]

Mallory remained optimistic about the eventual success of her ideas:

> All religious, political, commercial and social movements will become more and more inclusive in character, until the countries of the world will become one Universal Republic, its parts indissoluble in the bonds of amity and peace, and holding within its unlimited embrace happy, peaceful and contented populaces.[31]

Although newspaper directories report that its circulation never exceeded three thousand, the authors of *American Women* suggest that the influence of *The World's Advance-Thought* went beyond what that number might indicate, for its readers included "advanced thinkers and workers in every portion of the civilized world," Count Leo Tolstoi of Russia among them.[32] The magazine regularly published contributions from foreign readers, and a newspaper account stated, "Her pronounced views on many world problems, and particularly upon international peace, gained for her an audience in every country of the old world, and brought to her desk letters from many famous men and women, who discussed with her the questions she raised."[33]

The World's Advance-Thought survived until 1918. Mallory's husband had left her a large estate upon his death in 1914, and she continued her magazine and her crusades. After her son died in 1917, she moved to San Jose, California, to be near friends. She survived a brain concussion suffered in 1919 when a train struck the automobile in which she was taking a daily outing. She died a year later, in September 1920.

Rarely did the women editors have such prominent husbands as Rufus Mallory or Louis Hughes, although most of them were married for at least some part of their lives. A Nevada editor, one of the few who never married, used journalism as one of several occupations with which she supported herself over her seventy-one years.

Annie Hudnall Martin was born on February 1, 1857, in Memphis, Missouri. She went to Nevada six years later. One source states that distant relatives, living in Carson City, adopted her.[34] After completing her education there, she taught in the city's elementary schools for thirteen years, acquiring a lifelong interest in the problems and possibilities of education.

In the spring of 1892 she bought the *Carson Daily Morning News*, whose former owner had brought it to the highest circulation in the state, according to his "Valedictory." He told readers that Martin, a longtime resident and popular teacher in the public schools, needed no introduction and called her "a young lady of great natural gifts and rare acquirements," even "genius." Responding to his comments, Martin wrote a "Salutatory" that included the quotation introducing this chapter. She also stated that the politics of the paper would be "thoroughly and distinctly Republican."[35] Later, looking back on her assumption of the editorship, she wrote, "May 17, 1892, we dropped the rattan and the primer, left the schoolroom, and boldly (though blindly) jumped over into the next field—the field of journalism."[36]

Martin continued the paper as a four-page morning daily, heavy on advertising. Over the three and a half years of her editorship, the *News* averaged six to seven columns of news in a total of twenty-four columns.

Local news came primarily in the form of brief notes under headings like "Jottings" and "All Sorts." Expanded articles covered theater presentations, court news, weddings and funerals of note, school graduations and prizes, legislative sessions, and sports competitions. Editorials often were reprints from other Republican papers. The editor wrote perhaps a third of them.

On several occasions she had to remind readers that she did, indeed, write them herself. Or perhaps she intended the reminders more for competing editors than for readers. Only a month after she took over the paper she pointed out that she was sole owner and proprietor and solely responsible for the paper's "utterances and policy." She did not receive one hundred dollars a month or any other sum as compensation or salary, she wrote, apparently responding to a published accusation.[37] Two years later she scolded the *Reno Journal* for referring to "Editor Coffin of the Carson News." She found it puzzling that anyone should think Mr. Coffin had anything to do with the editorial department of her paper, when he had not even visited the office for several months. She continued:

> Of course it is not an easy matter for a woman uneducated in politics to cope successfully with men who have been in the harness for a quarter of a century, or more, but we beg Mr. Journal that you will in the future place the blame where it belongs, on our shoulders.[38]

Perhaps Coffin had something to do with the job-printing establishment that operated in conjunction with the paper.

Although disclaiming political expertise, Martin argued the Republican point of view frequently and forcibly. At the same time, she printed news of other parties' conventions and published their platforms. More restrained than many editors of the time, she still managed occasionally to "stir up the hornet's nest," as she put it in commenting on references to the *News* as the "petticoat paper" or the "Sunday School journal."[39]

She also gave fair coverage to the woman question, although she treated it infrequently. Martin opposed woman suffrage. She reprinted articles to the effect that women owed their first loyalty to their children and should not squander their energies on activities outside the home. She even wrote that she would "gladly relinquish the political column of this paper just as soon as our finances will warrant the hiring of a political editor."[40] She referred approvingly to a successful woman who got tired of having a fuss made about her accomplishments.[41]

However, she picked up an item about three young ladies who took charge of a "combined harvester" and handled the big machine creditably, heading the story "The New Woman in Nevada" and commending their demonstration of competence.[42] She also reprinted a favorable report of her own professional ability from *The Journalist* of New York: "Miss Annie Martin, of the Carson News, is probably the only woman publishing a daily paper on the Pacific Coast. She is quiet, modest, unassuming and a 'worker from the word go.' "[43] And she regularly announced suffrage speakers and meetings, sometimes commenting on the oratorical skills of the national suffrage leaders who came to Nevada.

Martin apparently never made enough money to hire a political editor. In fact, she gave up the paper entirely in October 1895. She had increased circulation and maintained advertising, but the general depression, she wrote, had kept her from prosperity. She liked many things about being an editor, others she parted from "without a sigh." She took pride in having kept the *News* going for forty-two months, after detractors had predicted when she bought it that she would not last for six.

Several years later, Martin returned to the *News* as city editor and bookkeeper, after having managed a dry goods store for four years and a stationery store for three. In 1908 she found her final career, with the United States Mint in Carson City. She began working there as a clerk, became chief clerk in 1913, and in 1921 was appointed assayer in charge, or superintendent—the first woman to supervise a U.S. mint. She held that position until her death of an apoplectic stroke on February 19, 1928.

Obituaries spoke of her support for amateur theatricals, which included playing the organ for the Carson City opera company; her arranging of entertainments for Nevada prison inmates; her facility for remembering names; and her affiliation with the Presbyterian church, where she served as organist for forty years. During her funeral, the organ remained closed, and the flag over the mint flew at half mast.[44]

Annie Martin worked her way up to a governmental position of authority. Perhaps her lifelong support of the Republican party had something to do with it, too. One of the few women editors whom voters elected to public office was Grace Espy Patton Cowles[45] of Colorado. Her work as editor of a magazine for women gave her the recognition she needed to launch a successful campaign for the position of state superintendent of public instruction.

Grace Espy Patton was born in Hartstown, Pennsylvania, on October 5,

1866. Her family moved to Colorado when she was ten and settled in Fort Collins, where her father became mayor. She enrolled at the State Agricultural College in 1880, graduating with a B.S. degree in 1885 and an M.S. two years later. She held a faculty appointment in the College and Preparatory Department from 1885 to 1890 and taught courses in English and stenography from 1890 to 1896, serving as president of the alumni association and at the same time pursuing a variety of literary and political interests.

She wrote for newspapers in Fort Collins and Denver, as well as for the Chicago *Tribune*, and in March 1894 she began publication of a fifty-page monthly magazine, *The Tourney*. She intended it to focus on "the intellectual energy of the West in general, and of Colorado in particular, upon the questions of the day, and to promote an independent public opinion thereon."[46] It carried articles with titles like "The Science of Money," "The Graded School System," and "Strikes in Our Railroad System," and featured contributions from readers in a section called "The Tilt Yard." Many articles centered on questions related to women's rights. For example, one written by a fellow woman professor at the college declared that men's training, not their inherent ability, led them to do a large share of the world's thinking and argued that women needed expanded opportunities for intellectual training.[47]

At the beginning of 1895, Patton moved the magazine to Denver under a new name, *The Colorado Woman*. Its scope, she announced, would include "ALL WOMAN'S WORK: Literary, Educational, Political, Philanthropic, and Scientific subjects will be treated in a catholic and ethical spirit."[48] She also published separately a novelette she had written for *The Tourney*, called *The Chalchihuitl*. This fable told the story of an Indian princess who sought enlightenment in the company of a noble prince and found it in the divinity of nature. An article in the magazine made a similar point, as it described a "Wise Physician" who declared that the ailing world "needs pure air, warm sunlight, wholesome surroundings, and less medicine. It needs better company, more purity of purpose and a higher aim on the part of its whirling aspirants for fame."[49]

By appealing to Colorado's women voters, who had gained the franchise in 1893, Patton gained recognition and influence, lecturing frequently and winning the post of president of the Colorado Woman's Democratic Club. She gave up her magazine in November 1895, after making it a weekly in July, perhaps to enter politics. The Democrats nominated her as their candidate for state superintendent of public instruction in 1896, two years after Caroline Nichols Churchill's unsuccessful bid for the post, even though she would not reach the required thirty years of age until a month before the election. Opponents, citing her petite stature and girlish appearance, claimed that she was too young and inexperienced for the office. But "the little professor," as she came to be known, proved a formidable campaigner and scored a decisive victory.[50]

As superintendent, she worked to establish kindergartens, libraries, and manual training programs and to raise qualification standards for teachers. Her political position brought responsibilities in the state teachers' association and on the board of trustees of the state normal school, along with the presidency of the state board of education. She also served as auditor for the Colorado Woman's Suffrage Association and represented that organization at a national suffrage convention in 1898 as a featured speaker.

She married Lt. Warren Hayden Cowles, an army officer appointed in 1889 to establish a department of military science at the State Agricultural College, on April 9, 1898. Perhaps she elected to retreat from the statewide arena of public office and journalism and join her husband as he traveled to new assignments; her name disappears from Colorado sources after 1898.

At the same time that women in Colorado began to exercise their right to vote, women in Hawaii joined the campaign for Hawaiian independence. Among them was Emma Aima Nawahi, who, with her husband, Joseph Kahooluhi Nawahi-o-Kalaniopuu, founded a weekly newspaper in Honolulu in 1895 as a successor to other patriot papers with which he had been associated. He served briefly as minister of foreign affairs in one of Queen Liliuokalani's last cabinets, and his wife was a lady-in-waiting to the queen.[51] Although the Nawahis sometimes criticized Hawaiian royalty, their paper remained committed to Hawaiian institutions and culture.

Aima Aii, daughter of a Hawaiian chiefess and a pioneer Chinese sugar miller, was born September 28, 1854, in Hilo, but settled in Honolulu after her marriage in 1881. Her husband, brought up by early Hilo missionaries, had taught school, practiced law, and served in the Hawaiian legislature for several terms between 1872 and 1892. The couple named their new publication *Ke Aloha Aina* (The Patriot). Joseph died in 1896 on a trip to California, but Emma continued to publish the paper, principally in Hawaiian, until at least 1908. One source reported that she sold it in 1910.[52] She was listed as editor, along with Joseph's nephew Edward Like, from 1896 to 1899. For a time in 1903 one of her two surviving sons assisted Like. Two other sons died as children.

Under Emma Nawahi, the paper printed news from home and abroad, serial fiction, editorials, and advertisements. It supported home rule after the United States annexed Hawaii in 1898, thereby making independence a lost cause. It survived until 1920.

After her retirement from journalism, Nawahi remained active in social and civic organizations. A biographical sketch lists her affiliations: Daughters of Hawaii, the Kaahumanu Society, Hale O-na Alii, Hilo Woman's Club, the Haili church, and the American Red Cross.[53] She died in December 1935.

In contrast to the relatively scant information about Nawahi are the articles and books about the life and thought of Charlotte Perkins Gilman. Although few of them concern her two years as editor for the paper of the Pacific Coast Women's Press Association, she gained the experience and confidence there that enabled her to return to the East and to proceed with her career as a writer and reformer.

Charlotte Anna Perkins was born July 3, 1860, in Hartford, Connecticut. Her autobiography, *The Living of Charlotte Perkins Gilman*, written mostly in the 1920s but published posthumously, tells the story of a precocious and headstrong child in a fatherless home. In 1884 she married Charles Walter Stetson, an aspiring artist. Difficulties leading to depression and despair began almost immediately, continuing through the birth of a daughter in 1885 and a move in 1887 to Pasadena, California, where efforts at reconciliation proved unsuccessful.

After a final separation from Stetson in 1890, Charlotte Perkins Stetson (as she called herself at that time) embarked on a campaign to improve society. In that "first year of freedom," as she called it, she wrote thirty-three short articles, twenty-three poems, and ten verses for children.[54] She also wrote plays and acted in them. Developing an enthusiasm for Edward Bellamy's Nationalism, she began to lecture successfully to Nationalist clubs. However, none of these activities brought much income.

Hoping that a move to Northern California would improve her prospects, she resettled in Oakland in 1891, living with Adeline E. Knapp, a reporter for the *San Francisco Call*. Stetson's daughter and her ailing mother joined them. Perhaps Knapp had something to do with a *Call* article describing the leaders of the Pacific Coast Women's Press Association and calling Stetson "keen, witty, satirical, well read, thoughtful, generous and frank." [55] In 1892 the *New England Magazine* published her most famous story, "The Yellow Wall-paper," which described the mental and emotional deterioration of a wife unable to meet her husband's and society's expectations. Her first book, a collection of verse titled *In This Our World*, came out in 1893.

Stetson became president of the press association and, in September 1893, took over editorship of its *Bulletin*, a monthly publication intended for members. While the *Bulletin* published news of association activities and interests, it also included literary and dramatic reviews, poetry, columns on education and reform, and news of the suffrage and labor movements. In November the editor changed its name to *The Impress*, in line with plans for its expansion. An announcement stated that, as a sixteen-page weekly, the paper would

> remain a review and grow to be a much more thorough and exhaustive one; space will be given to other arts than literature; all the best things in the current life of the world will be kept in view, and the women of this coast will find their best interests constantly advanced by an organ of their own. While not devoted to any special reform, *The Impress* will advocate all truly progressive measures, and holds that none are more so than the movement for "The New Education," and for nobler and freer art.[56]

Having sent her daughter east to live with her former husband and his new wife, Stetson moved to San Francisco and recruited a group of friends to assist her with the new magazine, which would have its headquarters, along with the Women's Press Association, in the house she shared with Helen Campbell, her associate editor. To the content of *The Bulletin* she added two pages on "The Art of Living," written by Campbell and including recipes and advice on household management; a series of "Every-Day Ethical Problems," for which readers suggested answers; commentary on selected local and national news; and passages written in imitation of the works of noted authors, with readers invited to guess the authors' identities. She contributed a poem to each issue, and she remained on sufficiently good terms with Charles Stetson, even after their divorce became final in 1894, to have him design illustrated titles for the columns. Among the many favorable notices from other periodicals that appeared in *The Impress* was one from the Springfield, Massachusetts, *Republican* that called it "clever, upright and bright." [57]

However, it failed to become profitable and ceased publication after twenty weeks, in February 1895, in spite of a favorable reception by literary critics and the local press. Although no explanation of its demise appeared in the paper, Stetson attributed its lack of support to her own notoriety as a divorced woman and unnatural mother, and later in 1895 she left California. Her experience as a writer, editor, lecturer, and reformer had laid the foundation for her subsequent career.

After five years of an itinerant life of lecturing and writing, including a short term as a contributing editor of *The American Fabian*, she married Houghton Gilman, a New York patent attorney, and settled in New York. As one biographer put it, she became "a respected authority on issues as narrow as the housefly menace and as trivial as public gum-chewing, and as broad and weighty as race and war."[58] She wrote books that attracted favorable attention and wide audiences, including *Women and Economics* and *The Home*, and had articles published in both popular and specialized periodicals. From 1909 to 1916 she returned to magazine editing with the monthly *Forerunner*, which she wrote, edited, and published almost single-handedly. In it she serialized her novel, *Herland*.

After 1916 she lived in semi-retirement, moving to Connecticut and producing one more book, *His Religion and Hers*. In 1934, ill with cancer and mourning her husband, who had died in May of that year, she returned once more to Pasadena, where her daughter lived. On August 17, 1935, she took her own life by covering her face with cloths soaked in chloroform. She left a note excerpted from her memoirs that read, "Human life consists in mutual service. . . . But when all usefulness is over, when one is assured of unavoidable and imminent death, it is the simplest of human rights to choose a quick and easy death in place of a slow and horrible one."[59]

Charlotte Perkins Gilman (the name she used during most of her professional life) had been virtually forgotten by the time of her death, but since the feminist revival of the 1960s her works have risen to prominence, and scholars have credited her with anticipating present-day struggles for the social and economic emancipation of women. Her work as a San Francisco editor helped her to clarify and articulate her ideas and aspirations and presaged the themes of the major works that followed.

In contrast to Gilman, about whom so much information is available, stand two New Mexico editors, much more typical of the majority of women editors, who, pending further investigation, remain only names listed on newspaper mastheads or in periodical directories. Martha A. Hayes and Mrs. A. L. McGinnis edited New Mexico weekly newspapers in the late 1880s and 1890s.

Hayes appeared on the journalistic scene in November 1889, when she assumed the editorship of the *Golden Nine* in San Pedro, apparently staying on until the paper moved to Albuquerque a year later. The paper's four pages contained standard material: local news, many articles and features reprinted from other publications, stories boosting the area and particularly its mineral potential, humor, poetry, and advertising. A departure from the standard occurred in the 1889 Thanksgiving number, when a poem about a turkey appeared with type set in a turkey shape.

The paper listed no editor during the period of Hayes's affiliation with it, although a note directed that correspondence should be sent to M. Hayes. She may have moved on to a career in business education after she left the editorship; a note in the paper on October 19, 1890, advertised a shorthand and typing course offered for fifty dollars by M. A. Hayes, P.O. Box 175, Albuquerque.

The name of New Mexico's other woman editor, Mrs. A. L. McGinnis, comes up in connection with two weekly newspapers, the *New Mexico Interpreter* of White Oaks and *The Lincoln Independent*. She edited the *Interpreter* from March to November 1891, at which time it evolved into a paper called *Old Abe Eagle*. In the paper's eight pages, she offered the same sort of content that Hayes used in the *Golden Nine*, adding occasional fiction and legal notices. She referred to the *Interpreter* as the "official paper of the county" and as the county's only Democratic paper, and also advertised her plant's job-printing capabilities.

After a Christmas Eve fire destroyed her home, the editor moved to Lincoln, where she took over the *Independent* in January 1892, listing herself as editor and publisher and promising that the paper would tell the truth and work for the interests of town and county, traveling on "in the same sober job-trot which has hitherto characterized it, undisturbed by the evanescent booms of younger and more bustling towns, waiting for the good time coming with serenity and equanimity."[60] Later she explained to readers that the printshop's owner, James J. Dolan, had agreed to turn printshop and profits over to her in return for her resumption of the paper.[61]

However, James Dolan, a staunch Republican, soon decided that the paper should reflect his political orientation. In April he renamed it *The Lincoln Republican* and assumed the editorship. McGinnis continued to contribute local items and commentary, with her name appearing on page 4 as local editor and publisher. She reported in September that she had traveled to Albuquerque to attend an organizational meeting of the Woman's New Mexico Press and Literary Association.

Perhaps because of the widespread defeat of Republican candidates—including himself—in the November elections, the owner decided to discontinue the paper, the last number appearing in January 1893. Like Martha Hayes, McGinnis must have turned to other work at that time.

Perhaps an ambitious researcher will succeed in finding additional information about these two women, providing a more complete picture of their lives and careers, so that they can be added to the ranks of the editors whose ideas and activities can be followed to some extent, bringing them into focus as individuals with unique attributes. Others, who have left neither biographical traces nor copies of their publications, will remain only names on lists.

CHAPTER 11

Group Portrait

The woman journalist was then [sixteen years ago] a decided oddity of jour-nalism. Today the decided oddity in journalism is the newspaper office that does not include anywhere from three to half a dozen women in its editorial and reportorial force. And who in this year of 1889 thinks of women as being in any way out of place in the ranks of newspaper workers? . . . I am prouder of my profession on this ground than on any other—that it has been the pio-neer of all professions in opening the door of opportunity wider for women . . . What the press does today the people will do tomorrow.[1]

—Boston newspaperman quoted in
the Queen Bee *by Caroline Nichols Churchill*

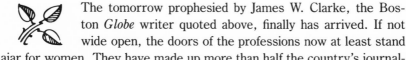 The tomorrow prophesied by James W. Clarke, the Bos-ton *Globe* writer quoted above, finally has arrived. If not wide open, the doors of the professions now at least stand ajar for women. They have made up more than half the country's journal-ism students since 1977. They move into newspaper offices in increasing numbers, comprising about 35 percent of newsroom workers by 1987.[2] Journalism as a profession deserves credit, along with the women who tested its hospitality, for leading the way in accepting them into its ranks.

However, women editors remain relatively rare. In fact, they comprise only 17 percent of today's managing editor positions. The total for daily papers, at 13 percent, is even smaller. None holds the title of editor in chief, while 5 percent of the executive editors, 10 percent of the editors, and 13 percent of the senior editors are women. In terms of relative numbers, the group portrait of women editors at the end of the twentieth century may not differ greatly from that of one hundred years ago.

The women editors' minority status—at 1 to 2 percent of the total—is one characteristic that helps define the outlines of the portrait painted in this book. Others might be their middle-class origins, their comparatively high educational levels, their tendency to carry responsibility for their publications by themselves, their preference for small-town weeklies, and their brief journalistic careers.

For most of them, journalism constituted one phase of a work life comprised of multiple pursuits carried on before and after their editorial careers, or sometimes simultaneously with them. Like today's professional women, they juggled demands of family and civic responsibilities with the complex tasks of their professional lives. Often, they recruited family members to assist them in putting out their papers. In a few cases, they held the publications in trust until children, usually sons, could take over or until fathers or husbands could resume interrupted supervision.

Carrie Fisher Young, who practiced medicine along with journalism, illustrates an editor with a dual career. Another was Mary Hayes-Chynoweth, who founded a church as well as a periodical. Maude Hulbert Horn exemplified many women editors who managed to combine journalism with running family businesses, serving their communities, and fulfilling family responsibilities.

A substantial number of women editors made journalism a stepping-stone to achievement in other fields. As periodical editors, they gained experience and confidence that served them in good stead when they moved into politics, literature, education, or social reform movements. Marietta Beers Stow gave up her paper to run for vice president of the United States. Charlotte Perkins Gilman went on to write scholarly sociological works. Grace Espy Patton won election as a state superintendent of public instruction.

In some cases, of course, the publications served as adjuncts to the women's larger interests, a means of promoting organizations or ideas, or both. Agnes Leonard Hill aspired to be an arbiter of Denver society. Jennie Anderson Froiseth began the *Anti-Polygamy Standard* as the organ of her Woman's National Anti-Polygamy Society. The suffragists founded publications to promote their campaign for the right to vote. Often the periodicals provided financial support for their editors, as well as vehicles for expressing their opinions.

A search for patterns proves difficult. What begins as a set of generalizations soon deteriorates into a list of differences. The experiences of the western editors support what a historian wrote about the West as a whole: "Simplicity, alas, is the one quality that cannot be found in the actual story of the American West."[3] As the group portrait develops, few patterns emerge. In age, in family situation, in type and purpose of their publications, the editors show far more differences than similarities. They ranged from the youthful Lula Greene Richards, who founded the *Woman's Exponent* at twenty-three, to her successor, Emmeline B. Wells, who held onto it until she was eighty-six; from the unmarried Huntington sisters to the Shipp sister wives; from Madge Morris Wagner fostering culture in a San Francisco literary monthly to Ada Chase Merritt earning a living by detailing the comings and goings of her small-town neighbors each week.

Examples can be drawn from the list of women editors to support almost any interpretation of women's place in the West. To illustrate traditional histories that either ignored women or dubbed them sunbonneted civilizers, one might look again to Maude Hulbert Horn, who ran her weekly paper for many years but remained virtually invisible to later generations because the paper listed first her father and then her husband as editors, or to Rowena Granice Steele, who sought to civilize the frontier with theatrical tours to California mining towns. Even Marietta Beers Stow, notorious for her zeal in unconventional causes, ended a long career by nurturing children at her Birdie Bell kindergarten.

Examples also substantiate the views of more recent writers, some of whom stress western women's autonomy, others their dependence. Of course, the editors were more likely to be emancipated, although they might not have thought of themselves in that way, than downtrodden. They liked the West and often used the opportunities it offered them to chart unconventional courses. They found they could develop their ideas and talents there. Charlotte Perkins Gilman found her voice as a feminist philosopher; Catherine Scott Coburn supported herself and four children. On the other hand, Legh Freeman left each of his three wives at home to care for papers and progeny while he ranged the frontier in pursuit of fame and fortune.

The various women editors' conduct of their journalistic careers also supports any number of historians' widely divergent views of what early western editors were like. Although less migratory than many male editors, the women often joined their masculine counterparts in boosting the communities where they settled. Even Ada Chase Merritt, who later chided a competing Salmon City editor for his exaggeration of the value of mining claims in the area, began her paper with a promise to awaken interest both at home and abroad to the "boundless mineral, stock raising, agricultural and other material resources of our county."[4]

Certainly the women sought the amenities of civilization that would accompany development, and often they led the way in supporting schools and churches, both in their papers and through community organizations. Josephine Brawley Hughes opened Arizona's first public school, saw to the establishment of Tucson's first Protestant church, and brought Frances E. Willard to town to establish a branch of the Woman's Christian Temperance Union, over which Hughes presided.

In line with another stereotype, the women editors generally brought little capital to their publications. Carrie Fisher Young started the *Woman's Pacific Coast Journal* only six months after a wagon trip from Idaho with two children and an ailing husband. Caroline Nichols Churchill used the proceeds from sale of her books to found *The Colorado Antelope* and then kept it going by soliciting subscriptions and contributions throughout Colorado and surrounding states. And after they started their papers, they struggled to stay in business. Editors—both men and women—commonly published pleas for new subscribers and tried to persuade old ones to keep up to date on payments.

The women editors of Nevada illustrate both the complexity of a group portrait and the difficulty of making it complete. They work well as a microcosm of the group as a whole. Because a superior bibliographic work, *The Newspapers of Nevada*,[5] identifies virtually all the state's editors, one may assume with some confidence that the list of women is complete. In addition, their number, at ten, is small enough to make a detailed examination possible. Like other areas, Nevada had women publishers who owned papers without editing them, but this study investigates only those who appear to have had a hand in the editing.

However, looking into available information soon leads to the conclusion that few details are available about the lives of at least half of the women who edited Nevada publications between 1874 and 1900. No copies survive of four of their nine publications. Only mentions in other publications substantiate their existence. Sometimes these offer tantalizing glimpses of the personalities and predilections of the editors; more often they provide only a name and a date.

The first woman on the Nevada journalistic scene edited a publication that hardly qualified as a periodical. *The Golden Echo,* a four-page literary paper sold to benefit St. Patrick's Church, apparently came out only once, in October 1874, during a fair at the Miner's Union Hall in Gold Hill. Its editor, Mary Atkinson, filled more than half of its columns with poetry. Her life apart from her literary interests remains a mystery.

In 1879 two more ephemeral publications appeared briefly. One represents what probably was a large group of manuscript papers, very few of which survive. Nancy Hill and a group of her friends founded the *Mottsville Star* as a weekly. They wrote it out by hand and distributed copies of perhaps two or three numbers. By that time the drudgery of producing the paper must have outweighed the novelty, despite the recognition of bona fide newspaper editors, one of whom called it "a spicy little sheet."[6] Vienna Dollarhide, a primary teacher in Austin, started *Spark of Genius* as a juvenile monthly. Other editors commented favorably on it, too, but even though it demonstrated the "literary genius of the youthful climbers of the ladder of learning," it soon disappeared.[7]

Also in 1879, Nellie Verrill Mighels took over the daily *Nevada Appeal* of Carson City after the death of her husband, Henry R. Mighels. The founders of the paper had hired him as its first editor in 1865, and he soon bought into it. New owners changed its name and its politics in 1870, but Mighels obtained backing to revive it in 1872 and became sole proprietor in 1878. In August 1866 he married Nellie Verrill, a native of Greenwood, Maine, where Henry's father was a physician. Born September 10, 1844, she set out for the West and her wedding at the age of twenty-two, traveling by steamer from New York to Panama, across the isthmus on a narrow-gauge railroad, to San Francisco by steamer, and from Sacramento to Carson City by stagecoach. Mighels arranged for the Nevada state treasurer, who had been in the East on business, to accompany her. The marriage took place in Sacramento.

Mighels made his wife, according to an obituary, "his partner and confidential adviser in all his affairs, whether of politics or of business."[8] He taught her to set type, to take notes for stories, and to manage the business of the paper. Mighels's political activities between 1868 and 1878 included service in the Nevada state senate, a term as speaker of the state assembly, and an unsuccessful campaign for the post of lieutenant governor, but then he became ill with cancer. His wife cared for him, their four children who survived childhood, and her two younger sisters. She also set the type for his editorials in their home office while he was ill.

After her husband's death, Nellie Mighels continued to list his name on the paper's masthead as its founder, with her name beneath as proprietor. She evidently took an active role in running the paper because she listed no other editor. Her daughter credited her with "a good business head" and stated that "there wasn't much she didn't know or understand about the newspaper."[9] In 1877 she had covered the sessions of the Nevada legislature for both the *Appeal* and a paper in Virginia City. She returned to the same duty in 1879, this time receiving one hundred dollars in gold from the legislature for her fine work.[10]

She hired Samuel P. Davis to assist her in November 1879 and married him the following July. His name appeared on the masthead as editor in October. She apparently left the running of the paper largely to Davis, but returned to newspaper reporting from time to time, even trying her hand at sports writing when she covered the 1897 Corbett-Fitzsimmons championship fight in Carson City for a Chicago paper, writing under a fictitious name to avoid embarrassment.

Davis, too, had political aspirations, winning an appointment as deputy secretary of state in 1895 and election to the post of state controller in 1898 and 1902. He lost that position in 1906 but, beginning in 1907, served as state industrial and publicity commissioner for four years. He also gained fame as a humorist, short story writer, poet, and historian. He and Nellie had two daughters.

Nellie Mighels Davis lived to be one hundred years old. Her family continued to be connected with the *Appeal*. A son, Henry R. Mighels, Jr., leased the paper from 1898 to 1906 and owned it from 1927 to 1933. Ida B. Mighels then took over and kept it until 1938.

The next woman to appear as an editor in Nevada was Mrs. G. R. Kemp. She started the *Halleck Gossip*, a monthly, at Fort Halleck in February 1885. The fort was abandoned the following year, so the *Gossip* ceased publication then, if not earlier. It is another publication of which no copies survive.

In 1888 Mrs. Margaret E. Latta joined the Reverend C. H. Gardner to produce *The Nevada Prohibitionist*, a four-page monthly that served as the official organ of the Woman's Christian Temperance Union of Nevada. The reverend started the reform organ as *The Bugle* in June 1888 in Genoa and affiliated it with the WCTU the next month, changing the paper's name and acquiring Latta, who held the office of WCTU editor and press secretary, as an associate. She lived in Carson City, twelve miles from Genoa, and apparently made her contribution to the *Prohibitionist* from there.

She may have had responsibility primarily for the "Department of the WCTU," which provided a page or so of news notes and editorial comment, along with a list of state officers, in each number. At least, her name appears only as the editor of that department in the one number of the publication extant, dated April 1, 1889. Reverend Gardner discontinued the *Prohibitionist* that summer and moved his press to Reno.

Annie H. Martin bought the *Daily Morning News* of Carson City in May 1892 and kept it until November 1895. The preceding chapter of this work tells her story.

Like the temperance movement, the woman suffrage movement had its published voice in Nevada. Frances A. Williamson and her daughter, Mary Laura Williamson, founded *The Nevada Citizen*, a four-page monthly, in March 1897, "to promote the advancement of women in the ethics of civil government, ordained in the Declaration of Independence and established by the Constitution of the United States."[11] Frances, first president of the two-year-old Nevada State Equal Suffrage Association, served as editor in chief, Mary as associate editor. They published the paper in Reno, where they had settled in 1896, perhaps seeing that city as a more likely headquarters than Austin, site of their first organizational effort in the suffrage cause, the founding in 1894 of the Lucy Stone Non-Partisan Equal Suffrage League.

The Williamsons published the paper at their own expense, according to the *History of Woman Suffrage*, and received a liberal patronage.[12] However, they had to contend with the same sort of ridicule directed at other suffrage editors. A poem in the *Eureka Weekly Sentinel* recognized Frances Williamson as a lecturer, writer, and president of seven clubs but concluded,

> Yet when she goes to bed at night,
>   She kneels beside it—not in prayer,
> But just to look beneath to see
>   If any horrid man is there.[13]

Business called the editors to Oakland, California, and they discontinued the paper when they left Nevada. Sources disagree as to whether that was one or two years after its founding. The two surviving numbers date from 1897.

Nevada's final woman editor of the nineteenth century took over *The Yerington Rustler* when her husband became ill early in 1899, after he spent the summer of 1898 in Alaska prospecting for gold. Mrs. Charles W. Patterson ran the weekly paper as "proprietor" for about a year. Because that title could refer to an editor, a publisher, or both, it is impossible to determine how much she had to do with the day-to-day operation of the *Rustler*. Several "Local News" mentions during 1899 refer to her taking her baby daughter on trips back and forth between Yerington and Gold Hill, where her mother lived, so she certainly did not spend all her time managing the paper. Her husband suspended the paper shortly after he resumed editorial duties and moved the printing plant to Lovelock to start a weekly there.

Thus, half the years from 1874 to 1900 saw women working as editors in Nevada, which had become a state in 1864 with a population of only 21,400, primarily due to its mineral riches and anti-slavery sentiment. Four were active during the 1870s, three during the 1880s, and four during the 1890s. This contrasts with the situation in other western states and territories, which tended to have a more steady increase in numbers of women editors. However, Nevada's population increased rapidly with the mining activity of the 1870s, reaching 62,266 in 1880 and then declining to 45,761 by 1890 and even lower, to 42,335, by 1900, so the number of women editors relative to the population as a whole actually grew.

Half of the women worked in Carson City, the state's capital, or Reno, its largest city, but the other five edited papers in scattered boomtowns, most likely because husbands or families had settled there. Half had been married and perhaps four still had husbands during their editorships, but this can be confirmed only for Mrs. Charles W. Patterson of *The Yerington Rustler*. Nellie Verrill Mighels inherited the *Nevada Appeal* upon the death of her husband.

Ages of the editors prove even more elusive than marital status, but most of them probably were in their thirties or forties at the time of their forays into journalism. Annie Martin, at thirty-five, could well stand as the median figure. Nellie Verrill Mighels was a thirty-four-year-old widow with four children. Frances Williamson had a daughter old enough to work with her. Mrs. C. W. Patterson traveled to her mother's with a young baby. Nancy Hill may have been the youngest of the group. One is tempted to imagine her and her friends as a group of teenagers gathering to write out a weekly report of the comings and goings of their small community.

The editors' working arrangements also illustrate their diversity. Nancy Hill put out her paper with the help of her friends. The Williamsons functioned as a mother-daughter team. Mrs. Patterson's husband may have advised her when she took over during his illness. Margaret Latta worked with an unrelated man. Five of the editors had no co-editors or partners.

Like their sister editors in other states and territories, the Nevada women remained editors only briefly, half of them for less than a year, four for one to two years, one—Annie Martin—for three and a half years. None of them appears to have edited more than one publication or to have produced other literary efforts.

Their papers make a nice sample of the various types of periodicals that women edited: two weekly newspapers, two daily newspapers, and five monthlies that probably would be considered magazines by modern readers. The monthlies represented the causes of suffrage and temperance, crusades in which women frequently participated and in which they gained communication and organizational skills. One offered literary content, and another sought to appeal to children. The aim of the monthly *Halleck Gossip* remains a mystery; we know only that a neighboring editor considered it "spicy."

The Nevada editors are representative both in what is known about them and in the fact that much is unknown—and likely unknowable. Still, it appears that they acted as women of their times. When they took or made an opportunity to play nontraditional roles, they could justify that action to themselves as part of their civilizing mission, if they ever stopped to think in such terms. Apparently, none of their male colleagues found them out of place, although their views on politics or suffrage might attract ridicule. In keeping with the spirit of the West, and of the successive frontiers that had led to it, they acted pragmatically, holding on to their feminine image while completing whatever tasks seemed likely to lead them to the goals they sought.

Western women in general did whatever was necessary to keep themselves and their families, when they had them, functioning. If that meant working on a farm or ranch alongside husband and children, obtaining a job for wages, heading a committee to find a preacher, running a household or a publication, they accepted that challenge. Society's prescriptions about what a woman might be and do, while given lip service, undoubtedly meant less to them than the realities of their immediate lives.

Women in the West filled many nontraditional roles. The editors provide one example of reaching out to new ways of thinking and behaving. Journalism proved to be a profession in which a woman could exert a civilizing influence, in line with traditional expectations, at the same time she demonstrated her skills in a public arena. She could lead a crusade or boost her community or publicize religious and educational activities. She could make editing a paper one aspect of wide involvement in public concerns.

The editors apparently liked the West. Many made a conscious choice to go there. Those who found themselves there as a result of someone else's choice made the best of it and acted to improve their own lives and the lives of others.

In a book titled *The Female Frontier*, a historian suggested that women's experience of the frontier differed markedly from men's. Their lives had a pervasive domestic orientation, while men's roles were much more varied. They stayed at home waiting, while men moved about the country.[14] Perhaps the editors, while rarely relinquishing domestic concerns, in some ways bridged the gap between the female frontier and the male, showing that gap not to be insurmountably wide nor deep. Most had a strong sense of their own worth. They were helping to build the West, and they knew it. They also built a bridge to the future.

The effort to construct a group portrait ends with a small tribute to the unnamed and unrecognized women who occupy its shadowy borders, a tribute that contains, appropriately, recognition both of their abilities and of their traditional role as women. It appeared in a note published by Annie Martin in the *Carson Daily Morning News* about a young lady who was running her father's paper without any assistance whatever while he served in the Nevada legislature. Annie identified her sister editor as the daughter of Senator Andrew Maute of Nye County, praised her for the manner in which she filled the position, and quoted an exchange from the *Walker Lake Bulletin* that referred to her: "If any newspaper man is in search of a really smart wife we would recommend him to look to Eastern Nevada."[15]

Appendix

The appendix includes the names of all women editors discovered in the course of research for this book. The entry for each editor lists, to the extent such information is available, the name of the publication(s) she edited, periodicity of the publication, the years of her editorship, joint editors, and a major location of the most complete run of copies or microforms. In many cases, standard indexes provide others. "Bancroft" refers to The Bancroft Library at the University of California, Berkeley. Other major repositories are the California State Library in Sacramento and the Huntington Library in San Marino, California. State historical societies and state university libraries, as well as state libraries and archives, also have significant holdings.

Alaska

No female editors located.

Arizona

Bagg, Katherine. *The Bug-Hunter* (monthly), Tombstone, 1891. Copies at The Arizona Historical Society, Ohio State Historical Society.

De Corella, Josefina Lindley. *La Sonora* (weekly), Tucson, 1879–80. Microfilm at UC Berkeley.

Dutton, Mrs. W. A. *Holbrook Press* (weekly), Holbrook, 1885. No copies located.

Hughes, E. Josephine Brawley. *Arizona Daily Star* (daily), Tucson, 1893–96. Microfilm at Tucson Public Library.

California

Armor, Alice L. *Orange Post* (weekly), Orange, 1893–1908. Copies at Kansas Historical Society.

Arnold, Nannie M. *Christian Workman* (monthly), Whittier and Berkeley, 1892–1903. Copies at Haverford College, Haverford, Pennsylvania.

Bentley, Mrs. George. *Azusa Valley News* (weekly), Azusa, 1890–91. Microfilm at UC Berkeley.

――――. *Valley News* (weekly), Burbank, 1895–96. With George Bentley. Microfilm at UC Berkeley.

――――. *San Pedro News* (weekly), San Pedro, 1897. With George Bentley. No copies located.

Bentley, Laura May. *Echo* (weekly), Glendora, 1893–94. Copies at Bancroft.

Biddle, Mrs. M. A. *Clipper* (weekly), San Diego, 1889–90. No copies located.

Bradford, Maria E. *The Pacific Monthly* (monthly), San Francisco and Pacific Grove, 1898. Copy at Bancroft.

Browne, Lida B. *Progress* (weekly), San Francisco, 1897–99. No copies located.

Browne, Mary Frank. *The Bulletin/The Pharos* (monthly), Oakland, 1885–91. Microfilm at Bancroft.

Burns, Mrs. Frank J. *Central California/San Miguel Messenger* (weekly), San Miguel, 1894–98. Microfilm at UC Berkeley.

Calhoun, Mrs. C. C. *The Pioneer* (weekly), San Francisco, 1873. Microfilm at UC Berkeley.

Case, Clara H. *Insurance Sun* (monthly), San Francisco, 1897–1907. No copies located.

Clarke, Sarah Moore. *The Contra Costa* (weekly), Oakland, 1854. Copy at State Library of Pennsylvania.

――――. *San Francisco Evening Journal* (daily), San Francisco, 1854–55. Copies at California State Library.

Cluff, Augusta De Force. *Valley Review/Cyclone* (weekly), Lodi, 1878–94. Copies at California State Library.

Conneau, Tillie. *Social Tidings* (weekly), Modesto, 1891–92. No copies located.

Conners, Mollie E. *Saturday Night* (weekly), Oakland, 1895–99. No copies located.

Cramer, Mrs. M. E. *Harmony* (monthly), San Francisco, 1888–96. Copies at California State Library.

Cranna, Mrs. William R. *Contra Costa News* (weekly), Martinez, 1884. No copies located.

Darmoore, Dora (Mrs. Boyer). *Homestead/Golden Dawn* (monthly), San Francisco and Oakland, 1874–78. With Ada Hutchins after 1875. Copy at Bancroft.

Day, Hermione Ball. *The Hesperian/The Pacific Monthly* (monthly), San Francisco, 1858–62. With Mrs. A. M. Schultz in 1858. Microfilm at Bancroft.

De Cuena, Laura M. *Revista Hispano-Americana* (monthly), San Francisco, 1896. No copies located.

De Jarnette, Mrs. A. K. *Report* (weekly), San Jose, 1893–95. No copies located.

De Mott, Mrs. William. *Oroville Mercury* (weekly), Oroville, 1882. Microfilm at California State Library.

Easton, Barbara. *Colton News* (semi-weekly), Colton, 1897. No copies located.

Eddy, C. E. *Alhambra Review* (weekly), Alhambra, 1891. With O. L. Eddy. Copies at Bancroft.

Eddy, O. L. *Southwest News* (weekly), Los Angeles, 1890–92. Copies at Kansas Historical Society.

——— . *Alhambra Review* (weekly), Alhambra, 1891. With C. E. Eddy. Copies at Bancroft.

Edmunds, Mrs. A. C. *Star of the Pacific* (monthly), Marysville and Sacramento, 1857–62. With A. C. Edmunds. No copies located.

Einfalt, Mrs. R. G. *Gilroy Telegram* (semi-weekly), Gilroy, 1896–99. No copies located.

Entler, Mrs. E. B. *Azusa Valley News* (weekly), Azusa, 1891. Microfilm at UC Berkeley.

Eyster, Nellie Blessing. *The Pacific Ensign* (weekly), San Francisco, 1897–98. Copies at office of Woman's Christian Temperance Union, Oakland.

Flesher, Helen Gregory. *Society* (monthly), San Francisco, 1897–99. No copies located.

Francis, Louise E. *Enterprise* (weekly), Castroville, 1891–92. Copy at Bancroft.

Friedlander, Alice G. *Student* (monthly), San Francisco, 1894–98. No copies located.

Fuller, Mrs. M. N. *Colusa Gazette* (weekly, daily), Colusa, 1893–1900. Copy at Bancroft.

Gallanar, Anna A. *Review* (weekly), Pacific Grove, 1892–1900. Copy at Bancroft.

Gift, Mrs. George W. *Napa County Reporter* (weekly), Napa, 1879–82. Microfilm at California State Library.

Gilman, Charlotte Perkins Stetson. *The Bulletin/The Impress* (monthly, weekly), San Francisco, 1893–95. Microfiche at Schlesinger Library, Radcliffe College.

Gordon, Laura De Force. *Daily Leader* (daily), Stockton and Sacramento, 1874–76. Microfilm at UC Berkeley.

——— . *Evening Democrat* (daily), Oakland, 1876–78. Microfilm at UC Berkeley.

Hall-Wood, Mrs. M. F. C. *Santa Barbara Daily Independent* (daily), Santa Barbara, 1889–92. Microfilm at University of Illinois.

Hasse, Elsa A. *Western Child Life* (quarterly), Los Angeles, 1896–1900. Copy at Bancroft.

Hayes-Chynoweth, Mary Folsom. *True Life* (semi-monthly), Eden Vale, 1894–1903. Copies at Bancroft.

Horn, Maude Hulbert. *The Gazette* (weekly), Georgetown, 1891–1924. Copies at California State Library.

Howe, Mrs. John F. *Telegraph* (weekly), Folsom, 1875–84. Microfilm at Bancroft.

Hoyt, Mary E. *Pacific Household Journal* (monthly), Los Angeles, 1892. No copies located.

Huston, Mrs. S. A. *Home Alliance* (weekly), Woodland, 1894–1908. No copies located.

Hutchins, Ada. *Golden Dawn* (monthly), San Francisco, 1876–78. With Dora Darmoore. Copy at Bancroft.

Isgrigg, Elizabeth. *Dunsmuir Herald* (weekly), Dunsmuir, 1896–99. Copies at Siskiyou County Courthouse.

Jackson, Roma T. *Santa Margarita Times* and *Templeton Times* (weeklies), Santa Margarita and Templeton, 1889–90. Copies at Bancroft.

———. *Coast Advocate* (weekly), Half Moon Bay, 1890–92. Copies at Stanford.

———. *Breeze* (daily), San Luis Obispo, 1895–99. No copies located.

———. *Oracle* (weekly), Arroyo Grande, 1898. No copies located.

Jones, Mrs. C. H. *Sabbath School Worker* (monthly), Oakland, 1891. With Mrs. J. F. Waggoner. No copies located.

King, Ada T. *Southwest News* (weekly), Los Angeles, 1893–95, 1897. Copies at Kansas Historical Society.

King, Lenora H. *Southwest News* (weekly), Los Angeles, 1895–96. No copies located.

Knapp, Adeline E. *Alameda County Express* (weekly), Irvington, 1889–90. Copies at Bancroft.

Laird, Jane. *Daily California Express* (daily), Marysville, 1857–60. With others. Copies at Marysville City Library.

Larkin, Polly. *Petalumian* (weekly), Petaluma, 1895–96. No copies located.

Lester, Lisle. *The Hesperian/The Pacific Monthly* (monthly), San Francisco, 1863–64. Microfilm at Bancroft.

Little, Alberta L. *Sabbath School Worker* (monthly), Oakland, 1898–1900. With M. H. Brown. No copies located.

Livernash, Lizzie A. *Healdsburg Enterprise* (weekly), Healdsburg, 1894–96. Microfilm at UC Berkeley.

Logan, Mrs. A. E. *News Letter* (monthly), Oakland, 1894–95. No copies located.

Lord, Mary Case. *The Pacific Ensign* (weekly), San Francisco, 1899–1902. Copies at office of Woman's Christian Temperance Union, Oakland.

Lynch, Belle. *Democratic Dispatch* (weekly), Ukiah, 1875–78. Microfilm at UC Berkeley.

———. *Our Paper* (weekly), Oakland, 1879. Copies at Bancroft.

MacDougal, Mrs. *Golden Gate* (periodicity unknown), Sacramento, 1864? No copies located.

McFarland, Mrs. Thad J. *Folsom Telegraph* (weekly), Folsom City, 1897–1902. Microfilm at Micro Photo Division, Bell & Howell Co.

McNeal, Mrs. L. E. *Political Age* (weekly), Port Kenyon, 1895–96. No copies located.

Marshall, Emma Seckle. *Pacific Household Journal* (monthly), Los Angeles, 1892–94. No copies located.

———. *Citizen* (weekly), East Los Angeles, 1892–94. Copies at Los Angeles Museum Library.

Moore, Audrey C. *Osteopath* (monthly), Los Angeles, 1896–99. Copies at New York Public Library.

Morse, Cora A. *Coming Light* (monthly), San Francisco, 1897–1900. With E. B. Payne, 1899–1900. Copies at Library of Congress.

Noel, Mrs. A. E. *Lower Lake Bulletin* (weekly), Lower Lake, 1892–1908. Microfilm at UC Berkeley.

North, Mrs. E. M. *The Searchlight* (monthly), San Francisco, 1896–1902. Copies at California State Library.

Off, Louise A. *New Californian* (monthly), San Francisco and Los Angeles, 1891–96. Copies at California State Library.

Ogle, Mrs. Van M. *Anderson Enterprise* (weekly), Anderson, 1887–88. Copies at Kansas Historical Society.

Oliver, Mrs. E. R. *The Pacific Churchman* (semi-monthly), San Francisco, 1899–1904. Copies at California State Library.

Olsen, Vesta J. *Sabbath School Worker* (monthly), Oakland, 1893–97. With F. M. Wilcox and M. H. Brown. No copies located.

Orcutt, Olive L. *Out of Doors for Women* (monthly), San Diego, 1893–96. Copies at Bancroft.

Owen, Mrs. J. J. *Le Petit Courier* (monthly), San Francisco, 1897. No copies located.

Patrick, Jennie E. *Illustrated Pacific States/Pacific Graphic* (monthly), San Francisco, 1895–96. With Frank I. Francoeur. Copies at Bancroft.

Pitts-Stevens, Emily. *California Weekly Mercury/The Pioneer* (weekly), San Francisco, 1869–73. Microfilm at UC Berkeley.

Reed, Amanda Slocum. *Common Sense* (weekly), San Francisco, 1874–75. With W. H. Slocum. Copies at Bancroft.

———. *Roll Call* (periodicity unknown), 1878? No copies located.

Reed, Mrs. C. N. *Gridley Herald* (weekly), Gridley, 1892. Microfilm at UC Berkeley.

Reed, Nellie. *Webster School Reporter* (monthly), Colusa, 1875. With E. E. Swiford. No copies located.

Remme, Mrs. S. *Yreka Tribune* (weekly), Yreka, 1884. No copies located.

Rice, Maggie C. *Household* (monthly), Los Angeles, 1895. No copies located.

Robertson, Jessie M. *Society* (monthly), San Francisco, 1896. No copies located.

Russell, Virginia F. *Index* (weekly), Santa Barbara, 1874–76. Microfilm at UC Berkeley.

Sawtelle, Mrs. M. P. *Medico-Literary Journal* (monthly), San Francisco, 1878–86. Copies at Bancroft.

Schenk, Elizabeth T. *The Hesperian/The Pacific Monthly* (monthly), San Francisco, 1862–63. Microfilm at Bancroft.

Schlesinger, Mrs. J. *Carrier Dove* (weekly), San Francisco, 1883–1900. Copies at Bancroft.

Schultz, Mrs. A. M. *The Hesperian/The Pacific Monthly* (monthly), San Francisco, 1858. With Hermione Ball Day. Microfilm at Bancroft.

Shattuck, Rena. *Petalumian* (weekly), Petaluma, 1897. No copies located.

Shinn, Milicent Washburn. *The Californian* (monthly), San Francisco, 1880–82. With others. Microfilm at UC Berkeley.

———. *The Overland Monthly* (monthly), San Francisco, 1883–93. Copies at many California libraries.

Smith, Mrs. R. S. *San Mateo County Times and Gazette* (weekly), Redwood City, 1888. With J. V. Swift. Copies at Bancroft.

Smyth, S. Gertrude. *Frolic* (quarterly), Oakland, 1889–90. With Marietta L. Beers Stow. Copies at Oakland Public Library.

Stanley, Otha L. *New Era* (weekly), Kelseyville, 1889–93. No copies located.

Steele, Rowena Granice. *San Joaquin Valley Argus* (weekly), Merced, 1878–90. Microfilm at UC Berkeley.

———. *Budget* (weekly), Lodi, 1892? No copies located.

Stevens, Alice J. *The Tidings* (periodicity unknown), Los Angeles, 1890s. No copies located.

Stickney, Gabriella T. *Southern California White Ribbon* (monthly), Los Angeles, 1895–96. No copies located.

Stow, Marietta L. Beers. *Woman's Herald of Industry and Social Science Co-operator/National Equal Rights* (monthly), San Francisco, 1881–84. Copies at California State Library.

———. *Frolic* (quarterly), Oakland, 1889–90. With S. Gertrude Smyth. Copies at Oakland Public Library.

Strong, Mrs. J. D. *The Hesperian/The Pacific Monthly* (monthly), San Francisco, 1863. With Rev. J. D. Strong. Microfilm at Bancroft.

Sturgeon, Inis. *West Side Index* (weekly), Newman, 1897–1900. No copies located.

Taylor, Juliette E. P. *Weekly Independent* (weekly), Santa Barbara, 1882. Microfilm at UC Berkeley.

Thrasher, Sarah Murray. *Golden Gate* (weekly), San Francisco, 1894–95. Copies at Bancroft.

————. *The Searchlight* (monthly), San Francisco, 1895. Copy at California State Library.

Tucke, Mercie A. *Pacific Methodist Collegian* (weekly), Santa Rosa, 1892. No copies located.

Van Pelt, Ada. *The Pacific Ensign* (weekly), San Francisco, 1891–97. Copies at office of Woman's Christian Temperance Union, Oakland.

Waggoner, Mrs. J. F. *Sabbath School Worker* (monthly), 1891–92. With Mrs. C. H. Jones. No copies located.

Wagner, Madge Morris. *The Golden Era* (weekly, monthly), 1891–93. With C. S. Sprecher. Microfilm at California State Library.

Walter, Carrie Stevens. *The Santa Clara* (monthly), San Jose, 1893–98. Copies at Stanford.

Weekes, Cora Anna. *The Athenaeum* (weekly), San Francisco, 1858. Copies at Bancroft.

Willis, Mrs. L. M. *Ledger* (weekly), Antioch, 1888–89. Microfilm at UC Berkeley.

Wilson, S. A. *Signal* (weekly), Santa Margarita, 1891. No copies located.

Winchester, Mrs. A. S. *Light for All* (monthly), San Francisco, 1882–84. With A. S. Winchester. Copies at Bancroft.

Winslow, Mrs. J. B. *San Gabriel Valley Vista* (weekly), Pasadena, 1892. No copies located.

Wright, Mrs. *Every Day Life* (periodicity unknown), San Francisco, 1867. Copy at Bancroft.

Young, Carrie F. *The Woman's Pacific Coast Journal/Pacific Journal of Health* (monthly), San Francisco, 1870–72. Microfilm at U.S. National Library of Medicine.

————. *Life Crystals* (monthly), Oakland, 1882–85. Copies at U.S. National Library of Medicine.

Colorado

Bay, Sadie. *Buena Vista Wasp* (weekly, semi-weekly), Buena Vista, 1885–87. Copies at Kansas Historical Society.

Boyd, Jennie F. *Arlington Blizzard* (weekly), Arlington, 1889–92. Copies at Bancroft.

Campbell, Della Kelsey. *Mascot* (weekly), Palmer, 1895–96. No copies located.

Cassidy, Ellen G. *Ridgway Populist* (weekly), Ridgway, 1894–1905. No copies located.

Chaddock, Mrs. M. C. *Pueblo Bon Ton* (weekly), Pueblo, 1895–96. No copies located.

————. *Pueblo Republican* (weekly), Pueblo, 1897. No copies located.

Child, Neva C. *Pueblo Ranch* (weekly), Pueblo, 1890–94. With R. A. Southworth, 1892. No copies located.

Churchill, Caroline Nichols. *The Colorado Antelope* (monthly), Denver, 1879–82. Microfilm at Colorado State Historical Society.

————. *Queen Bee* (weekly), Denver, 1882–95. Microfilm at Colorado State Historical Society.

Curtis, Emma G. *Royal Gorge* (weekly), Canon City, 1893–94. No copies located.

Darley, Mary C. *Pueblo Individual* (weekly), Pueblo, 1896–99. With Alex M. Darley. Copy at Yale.

Duffy, Mrs. C. E. *Montrose Recorder and Monument Recorder* (weekly), Montrose, 1890. No copies located.

Farley, Maud. *Pitkin Miner* (weekly), Pitkin, 1898. No copies located.

Foltz, Clara. *Mecca* (weekly), Denver, 1898–99. No copies located.

Fosdick, Jennie M. *Call* (weekly), Pueblo, 1898. No copies located.

Garmire, Mrs. T. B. *Harrisburg Pioneer* (weekly), Harrisburg, 1891–92. No copies located.

Gigliotti, Nicola. *Giustizia* (monthly), Denver, 1896–97. No copies located.

Hill, Agnes Leonard. *Western Society* (monthly), Denver, 1888–89. No copies located.

Hodges, Myrtle B. *Littleton Independent* (weekly), Littleton, 1890–91. Copies at office of publisher.

Hotz, Mary E. *Silver West* (weekly), Denver, 1895–97. With George J. Blakeley. No copies located.

Hubert, Loretta. *Greeley Herald* (weekly), Greeley, 1897–98. No copies located.

Hutchcraft, Emily G. *Kiowa County Leader* (weekly), Sheridan Lake, 1893–94. No copies located.

Johnson, Lillian Hartman. *Dolores News* (weekly), Rico, 1880–84. Microfilm at Colorado State Historical Society.

————. *Rico Record* (weekly), Rico, 1883–86. Copies at Kansas Historical Society.

Lawlor, Lula. *Trinidad Baptist* (monthly), Trinidad, 1890–92. No copies located.

Lease, Mrs. J. E. *Colorado Workman* (weekly), Pueblo, 1892. With E. S. Moore. No copies located.

Lee, Mary. *Jamestown Whim* (periodicity unknown), Jamestown, 1882–83. No copies located.

Leggett, Emma. *Kiowa County Press* (weekly), Eads, 1889–92. No copies located.

McMurtry, M. E. *Woman's World* (monthly), Denver, 1876. With Z. T. Spalding. No copies located.

Martin, Ida R. *News* (weekly), Manzanola, 1897–99. No copies located.

Metcalf, Mrs. M. A. *Lamar Sparks* (weekly), Lamar, 1887–88. Copies at Colorado State Historical Society.

Mills, Belle. *Berthoud Bulletin* (weekly), Berthoud, 1897–99. With J. Mack Mills. Microfilm at Colorado State Historical Society.

Patton, Grace Espy. *The Tourney/The Colorado Woman* (monthly), Fort Collins and Denver, 1894–95. Copies at Colorado State University, Denver Public Library.

Pearson, Anna G. *Royal Gorge* (weekly), Canon City, 1895. No copies located.

Phelps, Virginia F. *Colorado Women* (semi-monthly), Pueblo, 1897–98. No copies located.

Porter, Mrs. S. A. *Colorado Women* (semi-monthly), Pueblo, 1898–1902. No copies located.

Price, Mary E. *Sterling Democrat* (weekly), Sterling, 1897–1905. With C. T. Price. Microfilm at Colorado State Historical Society.

Pyles, Nellie. *Crystal Park Beacon* (weekly), Florissant, 1889–94. With T. B. Pyles. No copies located.

————. *El Paso County Democrat* (weekly), Colorado Springs, 1894–1905. With T. B. Pyles. Copies at Colorado State Historical Society.

Reed, Blanche. *Times* (weekly), Thurman, 1891–95. Copies at Bancroft.

Romney, Caroline W. *The Durango Record* (weekly, daily), Durango, 1880–81. Copies at Kansas Historical Society.

————. *Trinidad Review* (weekly), Trinidad, 1884. Copies at University of Colorado.

Roosa, Mrs. John. *Trinidad Review* (daily), Trinidad, 1883–85. Copies at University of Colorado.

Sherwin, Kate B. *Palmer Lake, Yesterday & Today* (weekly), Palmer Lake, 1898–1909. No copies located.

Spalding, Z. T. *Woman's World* (monthly), Denver, 1876. With M. E. McMurtry. No copies located.

Strong, Mary L. *Colorado Club Woman* (monthly), Pueblo, 1898–1902. No copies located.

Telford, Mary Jewett. *Colorado Farmer* (periodicity unknown), Denver, 1882–84. No copies located.

————. *The Challenge* (weekly, monthly), Denver, 1884–91. No copies located.

Wilson, Harriet E. *Castle Rock Mascot* (weekly), Castle Rock, 1898. No copies located.

Wise, Josephine L. *Crystal Silver Lance* (weekly), Crystal, 1892–97. Microfilm at Colorado State Historical Society.

Wood, Mary. *Pebbles Gathered by the Way* (monthly), Otis, 1890–93. No copies located.

Wright, Mattie B. *Elyria Journal* (weekly), Elyria, 1897–99. No copies located.

Hawaii

Nawahi, Emma Aima. *Ke Aloha Aina* (weekly), Honolulu, 1895–1910. Copies at Hawaii State Archives.

Wilcox, Theresa Cartwright. *The Liberal* (weekly), Honolulu, 1892–93. With Robert Wilcox. Microfilm at Hawaii State Archives.

————. *Aloha Aina Oiaio* (weekly), Honolulu, 1896–97. With Robert Wilcox. Microfilm at Hawaii State Archives.

Idaho

Butler, Isabelle. *The Ladies' Mite* (weekly), Idaho City, 1864. With Mrs. Rees. Copy at Idaho State Historical Society.

Graham, Mrs. *Bellevue Herald* (weekly), Bellevue, 1895. No copies located.

Merritt, Ada Chase. *Idaho Recorder* (weekly), Salmon, 1888–1906. Microfilm at Idaho State Historical Society.

Rees, Mrs. *The Ladies' Mite* (weekly), Idaho City, 1864. With Isabelle Butler. Copy at Idaho State Historical Society.

Montana

No female editors located.

Nevada

Atchison, Mary. *The Golden Echo* (periodicity unknown), Gold Hill, 1874. No copies located.

Dollarhide, Vienna. *Spark of Genius* (monthly), Austin, 1879. No copies located.

Hill, Nancy. *Mottsville Star* (weekly), Mottsville, 1879. No copies located.

Kemp, Mrs. G. R. *Halleck Gossip* (monthly), Fort Halleck, 1885. No copies located.

Latta, Mrs. M. E. *Nevada Prohibitionist* (monthly), Genoa, 1888–89. With Rev. C. H. Gardner. Copy at Nevada Historical Society.

Martin, Annie Hudnall. *Carson Daily Morning News* (daily), Carson City, 1892–95. Microfilm at Nevada State Library.

Mighels, Nellie Verrill. *Nevada Appeal* (daily), Carson City, 1879. Microfilm at Nevada State Library.

Patterson, Mrs. Charles W. *Yerington Rustler* (weekly), Yerington, 1899–1900. Copies at Nevada State Library.

Williamson, Mary L. *The Nevada Citizen* (monthly), Reno, 1897. With Frances A. Williamson. Copies at Nevada Historical Society.

Williamson, Frances A. *The Nevada Citizen* (monthly), Reno, 1897. With Mary L. Williamson. Copies at Nevada Historical Society.

New Mexico

Hayes, Martha A. *Golden Nine* (weekly), San Pedro and Albuquerque, 1889–91. Microfilm at Museum of New Mexico History.

McGinnis, Mrs. A. L. *Independent* (weekly), Lincoln, 1892–93. Microfilm at Lincoln County Courthouse, Carrizozo.

————. *New Mexico Interpreter* (weekly), White Oaks, 1891. Microfilm at Museum of New Mexico History.

Oregon

Brown, Mrs. L. L. *Rising Sun* (weekly), Portland, 1880s. No copies located.

Clark, Mrs. E. A. *Sheridan Courier* (weekly), Sheridan, 1891. No copies located.

Coburn, Catharine A. Scott. *Evening Telegram* (daily), Portland, 1883–88. Microfilm at Oregon Historical Society.

Douglas, Edith. *Dispatch* (weekly), Dufur, 1898–99. Microfilm at University of Oregon.

Duniway, Abigail Scott. *The New Northwest* (weekly), Portland, 1871–87. Microfilm at University of Oregon.

————. *The Coming Century* (monthly), Portland, 1891–92. Copies at University of Oregon.

————. *The Pacific Empire* (weekly), Portland, 1895–98. Copies at Oregon Historical Society.

Edmunds, Mrs. A. C. *Union Crusader* (periodicity unknown), Eugene, 1862–63. With Rev. A. C. Edmunds. No copies located.

Foster, Susie E. *Oregon White Ribbon* (monthly), Portland, 1894. With Anna Rankin Riggs. No copies located.

Fulton, Mrs. L. F. *Temperance Star* (weekly), Portland, 1884–85. No copies located.

Grace, Nellie R. *East Oregon Herald* (weekly), Harney, 1887. With D. L. Grace. No copies located.

————. *News* (weekly), Burns, 1894. No copies located.

Jones, Laura E. *North Douglas Watchman* (weekly), Drain, 1898–1900. Copies at Oregon Historical Society.

Koch, Anna. *Hjemmet* (monthly), Portland, 1896–1902. No copies located.

Mallory, Lucy A. Rose. *The World's Advance-Thought* (monthly), Portland, 1886–1918. Copies at Oregon Historical Society.

Nash, Mrs. L. A. *Oregon White Ribbon/Northwest White Ribboner* (monthly), Portland, 1892–98. With Anna Rankin Riggs. No copies located.

Riggs, Anna Rankin. *Oregon White Ribbon/Northwest White Ribboner* (monthly), Portland, 1892–1905. With Mrs. L. A. Nash, 1892–98; with Susie E. Foster, 1894. No copies located.

Smith, Amelia De F. *Pacific Good Fellow* (monthly), Portland, 1894–99. No copies located.

Strong, Caroline. *Oregon Christian Endeavor* (monthly), Portland, 1892–94. No copies located.

Turner, Mrs. L. F. *Star of the West* (weekly), Portland, 1875–76. No copies located.

Whiting, Abbie M. *Music Life* (monthly), Portland, 1896–97. No copies located.

Utah

Boan, Kate Jean. *The Uintah Pappoose* (weekly), Vernal, 1891–92. Microfilm at University of Utah.

DeWitt, Candace A. *Piute Pioneer* (weekly), Marysvale, 1896–98. No copies located.

Freeman, Ada Virginia Miller. *Ogden Freeman* (semi-weekly, weekly), Ogden, 1875–79. With Legh R. Freeman. Microfilm at UC Berkeley.

Froiseth, Jennie Anderson. *Anti-Polygamy Standard* (monthly), Salt Lake City, 1880–83. Microfilm at University of Utah.

Gates, Susa Young. *Young Woman's Journal* (monthly), Salt Lake City, 1889–1901. Copies at University of Utah.

Hemenway, Ireta Dixon. *Utah Valley Gazette* (weekly), Provo, 1887–90. With Charles Hemenway. Microfilm at University of Utah.

Henderson, Elizabeth S. Worthen. *Panguitch Progress* (weekly), Panguitch, 1898, 1901–04. No copies located.

Hilliard, Kate S. *Ogden Times* (periodicity unknown), Ogden, 1896. No copies located.

Richards, Lula Greene. *Woman's Exponent* (semi-monthly), Salt Lake City, 1872–77. Microfilm at University of Utah.

Sessions, Samantha. *Woods Cross Watchman* (weekly), Woods Cross, 1898. No copies located.

Shipp, Ellis Reynolds. *Salt Lake Sanitarian* (monthly), Salt Lake City, 1888–89. With Margaret Curtis and M. Bard Shipp. Copies at Mormon Church Historical Department.

Shipp, Margaret Curtis. *Salt Lake Sanitarian* (monthly), Salt Lake City, 1888–89. With Ellis Reynolds and M. Bard Shipp. Copies at Mormon Church Historical Department.

Smith, Eva B. *The Kaysville Eagle* (weekly), Kaysville, 1893. With W. E. Smith. Microfilm at University of Utah.

———. *American Fork World* (weekly), American Fork, 1896. With W. E. Smith. Microfilm at University of Utah.

———. *Box Elder County Herald* (weekly), Brigham City, 1891. With W. E. Smith. No copies located.

Wells, Emmeline B. *Woman's Exponent* (semi-monthly), Salt Lake City, 1877–1914. Microfilm at University of Utah.

Washington

Adams, Mrs. P. D. *North Yakima Signal* (weekly), North Yakima, 1883–87. With J. M. Adams. Copies at Washington State University.

Cates, Henrietta D. *Masonic Review* (monthly), Tacoma, 1898–1908. No copies located.

Eldredge, Nellie M. *Oracle* (weekly), Orting, 1895–1901. Copies at University of Washington.

French, Allison. *Orator/Outburst* (weekly), Spokane, 1895–98. No copies located.

Harsell, Agnes C. *Weekly Epigram/Yakima Epigram* (weekly), North Yakima, 1896–99. With J. T. Harsell. Microfilm at Washington State Library.

Hill, Mrs. Homer M. *The Washington Women* (weekly), Seattle, 1895. Copy at Washington State University.

Kellogg, Mrs. L. *Washington Progress* (periodicity unknown), Cheney, 1885. No copies located.

Kennedy, Julia E. *Pacific Boys and Girls* (monthly), Seattle, 1893–94. No copies located.

LeFevre, Ida. *The Alki* (semi-monthly), Puyallup, 1895. Copy at Washington State Historical Society.

———. *Citizen* (weekly), Puyallup, 1898–99. No copies located.

Money, M. L. *Beacon* (semi-weekly, weekly), Kalama, 1871–75. With M. H. Money. Microfilm at University of Washington.

Norton, B. A. *Roslyn News* (weekly), Roslyn, 1899. No copies located.

Peters, Laura E. Hall. *The Model Commonwealth* (weekly), Seattle and Port Angeles, 1886–95. Microfilm at Washington State Library.

Smart, Florence M. *Fremont Pioneer* (weekly), Seattle, 1895–98. No copies located.

Spencer, Mrs. F. J. *Sentinel* (weekly), Cheney, 1883–87. With F. J. Spencer. No copies located.

Weinhagen, Anna L. *Washington Staats-Zeitung* (weekly), Seattle, 1889–1902. With W. E. Stroetzel 1891–1902. Copy at Washington State University.

Wyoming

Chappell, Edith M. *Buffalo Bulletin* (weekly), Buffalo, 1897. Microfilm at Wyoming State Archives.

Merrell, Gertrude M. Huntington. *Platte Valley Lyre* (weekly), Saratoga, 1890–1902. Copies at University of Wyoming, Wyoming State Archives.

Parmelee, Mary M. *Buffalo Bulletin* (weekly), Buffalo, 1899. Microfilm at Wyoming State Archives.

Preston, Cora V. *Wind River Mountaineer* (weekly), Lander, 1899–1903. Copies at Lander Public Library.

Notes

Chapter 1: Introduction

1. Quoted in J. Cecil Alter, *Early Utah Journalism* (Salt Lake City: Utah State Historical Society, 1938), p. 117.

2. *Piute Pioneer*, March 26, 1898, p. 1.

3. Ibid.

4. "Candace A. Blakeslee," *Piute County News*, April 22, 1927, p. 1.

5. Ibid.

6. Both the total number and the percentages probably are low, partly because not all females listed can be recognized as such, but also because some publications did not appear in the directories and because some women performed the work of editor without having the title. The two major directories are George P. Rowell's *American Newspaper Directory*, first published in 1869, and N. W. Ayer's *Directory of Newspapers and Periodicals*, first published in 1880. They merged in 1910. Histories and bibliographies have been published for several of the western states, but most are limited to newspapers.

7. Edward C. Kemble, *A History of California Newspapers, 1846–1858* (Los Gatos, California: The Talisman Press, 1962, reprinted from an 1858 supplement to the Sacramento *Union*, edited and with a foreword by Helen Harding Bretnor), p. 223.

8. Quoted in Robert F. Karolevitz, *Newspapering in the Old West* (New York: Bonanza Books, 1965), p. 176.

9. For 1 percent of the women, length of editorship cannot be determined.

10. *Cheyenne Leader* and *Laramie Sentinel*, quoted in Elizabeth Keen, "Wyoming's Frontier Newspapers," M.A. thesis, University of Wyoming, 1956.

11. See Dee Brown, *The Gentle Tamers* (Lincoln: University of Nebraska Press, 1958), and William W. Fowler, *Woman on the American Frontier* (Hartford, Conn.: S. S. Scranton & Co., 1876).

12. Emerson Hough, *The Passing of the Frontier* (New Haven: Yale University Press, 1918), pp. 93, 94.

13. Cathy Luchetti, in collaboration with Carol Olwell, *Women of the West* (St. George, Utah: Antelope Island Press, 1982), p. 31.

14. Joanna L. Stratton, *Pioneer Women* (New York: Simon and Schuster, 1981), p. 58.

15. Elizabeth Fox-Genovese, "Placing Women's History in History," *New Left Review*, no. 133 (May–June 1982), p. 13.

16. Johnny Faragher and Christine Stansell, "Women and Their Families on the Overland Trail to California and Oregon," *Feminist Studies*, vol. 2, no. 2/3 (1975), pp. 150–66.

17. Julie Roy Jeffrey, *Frontier Women* (New York: Hill and Wang, 1979), p. 106.

18. Carl N. Degler, in Lillian Schlissel, *Women's Diaries of the Westward Journey* (New York: Schocken Books, 1982), p. 4.

19. Sandra L. Myres, *Westering Women and the Frontier Experience, 1800–1915* (Albuquerque: University of New Mexico Press, 1982), chaps. 6 and 9, pp. 141–66, 238–70.

20. Daniel J. Boorstin, *The Americans*, vol. II, *The National Experience* (New York: Random House, 1966), pp. 124, 127.

21. Barbara Cloud, "Establishing the Frontier Newspaper: A Study of Eight Western Territories," *Journalism Quarterly*, vol. 61, no. 4 (Winter 1984), pp. 805–11.

22. David Fridtjof Halaas, *Boom Town Newspapers: Journalism on the Rocky Mountain Mining Frontier, 1859–1881* (Albuquerque: University of New Mexico Press, 1981), pp. 2, 3.

23. William E. Huntzicker, "The Frontier Press, 1800–1900." Chap. 8 in W. David Sloan, James G. Stovall, and James D. Startt, eds., *The Media in America: A History* (Worthington, Ohio: Publishing Horizons, Inc., 1989), p. 182.

24. Jo Ann Schmitt, *Fighting Editors* (San Antonio: The Naylor Co., 1958), pp. xiv–xv.

25. John Myers Myers, *Print in a Wild Land* (Garden City, New York: Doubleday & Co., Inc., 1967), p. 4.

26. *Compendium of the Eleventh Census, 1890* (Washington, D.C.: Government Printing Office, 1897), part III, pp. 400–39, and *Population, Twelfth Census of the United States, 1900* (Washington, D.C.: United States Census Office, 1902), part II, pp. 510–49.

Chapter 2: By Women, For Women

1. Kemble, *History of California Newspapers*, p. 223.

2. Frank Luther Mott, *A History of American Magazines* (Cambridge: Harvard University Press, 1957), vol. I, p. 348.

3. Quotation and figures from ibid., vol. IV, p. 356.

4. Letter from Larry M. Odoms, Library Assistant, Oakland Public Library, January 24, 1985.

5. Kemble, *History of California Newspapers*, p. 331.

6. "Mother and Son," *San Francisco Chronicle*, December 6, 1879, p. 3.

7. "H. K. W. Clarke's Death," *San Francisco Chronicle*, May 21, 1878, p. 3. The story of H. K. W. Clarke's death and subsequent events is pieced together from

reports in the *San Francisco Chronicle* on May 21, 1878, December 6, 10, 12, 14, 17, 18, 20, 25, and 27, 1879, and January 8 and April 17, 1880; and in the *Daily Alta California* on May 21, 1878, December 12, 18, and 27, 1879, and April 17, 1880.

8. "Mother and Son," *Chronicle*.

9. Ibid.

10. "Mother and Son," *Daily Alta California*, December 12, 1879, p. 1.

11. "Death of Mrs. Sarah M. Clarke," ibid., April 17, 1880, p. 3.

12. Quoted in Mott, *History of Magazines*, vol. II, p. 117.

13. Hubert Howe Bancroft, *The Works of Hubert Howe Bancroft*, vol. XXXVIII, *Essays and Miscellany* (San Francisco: The History Company, 1890), p. 600.

14. Marion Tinling, "Hermione Day and the Hesperian," *California History*, vol. LIX, no. 4 (Winter 1980/81), pp. 282–89. This article contains all available biographical information about Hermione Day.

15. Franklin Henry Day, *Autobiography* (San Francisco: Eastman & Co., 1903), p. 6.

16. Tinling, "Hermione Day," p. 289.

17. Ella Sterling Cummins, "The Women Writers of California," in Mary Kavanaugh Oldham Eagle, *The Congress of Women* (Chicago: W. B. Conkey Co., 1894), vol. I, p. 185.

18. Lawrence Ferlinghetti and Nancy J. Peters, *Literary San Francisco* (San Francisco: City Light Books and Harper and Row, 1980), p. 27.

19. "Editor's Table," *The Hesperian*, February 1859, pp. 46–47.

20. "To the Women of California," ibid., May 1, 1858, p. 9.

21. John Bruce, *Gaudy Century* (New York: Random House, 1948), p. 105.

22. Doris West Bepler, "Descriptive Catalogue of Materials for Western History in California Magazines, 1854–1890," M.A. thesis, University of California, 1917, p. 46.

23. Quoted in ibid., p. 47.

24. "Editor's Table," *The Hesperian*, March 1859, p. 45, and April 1859, p. 92.

25. "Editor's Table," *The Pacific Monthly*, June 1863, pp. 90–91.

26. Cummins, "Women Writers," pp. 185–86.

27. Frances E. Willard and Mary A. Livermore, eds., *American Women* (New York: Mast, Crowell and Kirkpatrick, 1897), vol. I, p. 379.

28. "Mrs. Agnes Leonard Hill," *The Journalist*, January 26, 1889, p. 11.

29. Quoted in ibid.

30. "City and Vicinity," *Rocky Mountain News*, May 13, 1873, p. 4.

31. "In Memoriam," ibid., March 19, 1873, p. 4; and "City and Vicinity," February 7, 1877, p. 4.

32. Frank Hall, *History of the State of Colorado* (Chicago: Blakely Printing Co., 1895), vol. 4, pp. 81–82.

33. "Personal," *The Denver Daily Times*, April 16, 1881, p. 4. The *Dispatch* is mentioned in Willard and Livermore, *American Women*, vol. I, and in "Mrs. Agnes Leonard Hill," *The Journalist*.

34. Untitled note, *The Daily News*, March 1, 1881, p. 3; and "Mrs. Hill's Lectures," *The Denver Republican*, March 30, 1881, p. 8.

35. Untitled note, *The Queen Bee*, April 13, 1887, p. 1.

36. Mott, *History of Magazines*, vol. III, p. 308.

37. "Mrs. Agnes Leonard Hill," *The Journalist*.

38. Willard and Livermore, *American Women*, vol. I, p. 379.
39. Agnes Leonard Hill, *The Colorado Blue Book* (Denver: James R. Ives & Co., 1892).
40. Agnes Leonard Hill, "Hints on How to Talk" (Chicago: R. R. Donnelley & Sons, 1891), unpaged preface.
41. Agnes Leonard Hill, *Social Questions* (Denver: The Chain & Hardy Co., 1893), unpaged preface.
42. Agnes Leonard Hill, *"Said Confidentially"* (Denver: The Smith-Brooks Printing Co., 1902), unpaged preface.
43. Eugene Parsons, "Colorado Literature," chap. 42 in Wilbur Fisk Stone, ed., *History of Colorado* (Chicago: The S. J. Clarke Publishing Co., 1918), vol. I, p. 885.

Chapter 3: Small-Town Businesswomen

1. Untitled note in "Local Intelligence," *The Idaho Recorder*, January 15, 1890, p. 3.
2. S. N. D. North, *History and Present Condition of the Newspaper and Periodical Press of the United States*, vol. 8 of the Tenth Census, 1880 (Washington, D.C.: U.S. Government Printing Office, 1884), p. 59.
3. Ibid., pp. 186–91.
4. Myron K. Jordan, "The Golden Age of the Press Revisited," paper presented at the West Coast Journalism Historians' Conference, March 1, 1987, p. 5.
5. Ibid., p. 65.
6. Ibid., p. 92.
7. Ibid., p. 94.
8. Frank Luther Mott, *American Journalism*, Third Edition (New York: Macmillan, 1962), p. 479.
9. "Greeting," *The Idaho Recorder*, July 19, 1888, p. 2.
10. "Kind Words," ibid., August 23, 1888, p. 2.
11. "Another Change," ibid., October 11, 1888, p. 2.
12. "Lemhi's Representatives, What Have They Done?" ibid., February 21, 1889, p. 2.
13. "Woman Suffrage," ibid., April 10, 1895, p. 2.
14. "An Idaho Journal's Folly," *The Salt Lake Tribune*, December 5, 1890, p. 2.
15. "Keeping Up His Record," *The Idaho Recorder*, January 7, 1891, p. 2.
16. "The Arrest of Walsen," quoted from *The Pocatello Advance* of May 7, 1902, in ibid., May 20, 1902, p. 2.
17. "Walsen Is Brought Back," *The Lemhi Herald*, May 14, 1902, p. 1; "Two Indictments Are Returned," May 21, 1902, p. 1; "Knowledge Is Power," August 13, 1902, p. 2; "Printery in Trouble," October 8, 1902, p. 1.
18. "Court Calendar for Spring Term," ibid., April 29, 1903, p. 1; "In the District Court," November 12, 1902, p. 2; "In the District Court," November 19, 1902, p. 1; "Local Chronology of the Past Year," December 31, 1902, p. 1.
19. "Decision by Judge Rich," *The Idaho Recorder*, December 19, 1902, p. 3.
20. "Full Proceedings in District Court," *The Lemhi Herald*, May 13, 1903, p. 1.
21. Untitled note, *The Idaho Recorder*, June 13, 1889, p. 2.
22. "Sorry to Disappoint You," ibid., December 12, 1889, p. 3.
23. Untitled note, ibid., December 13, 1893, p. 2.

24. "Observer," *The Salt Lake Tribune*, August 10, 1893, p. 7.

25. "Called to Beyond," *The Recorder-Herald*, November 22, 1933, p. 1.

26. Nora Beale Jacob, "Biography of Maude Hulbert Horn, Editor of the George-town (California) Gazette, 1891–1924," M.A. thesis, California State University, Fullerton, 1980.

27. *The Georgetown Gazette*, August 6, 1886, p. 2, quoted in ibid., p. 44.

28. *The Georgetown Gazette*, April 18, 1889, p. 2, quoted in ibid., p. 48.

29. *The Georgetown Gazette*, May 31, 1894, p. 1, quoted in ibid., p. 50.

30. *The Georgetown Gazette*, November 12, 1896, p. 3, quoted in ibid., p. 71.

31. Letter to J. C. Horn postmarked May 2, 1898, quoted in ibid., p. 78; also p. 76.

32. *Sacramento Bee*, August 3, 1898, quoted in ibid., p. 79.

33. Maude Hulbert Horn diary, June 1, 1899, quoted in ibid., p. 82.

34. Quoted in ibid., p. 84.

35. Quoted in ibid., pp. 105–6.

36. North, *History of the Press*, p. 131.

37. Gay Day Alcorn, *Tough Country, The History of the Saratoga and Encampment Valley, 1825–1895* (Saratoga: Legacy Press, 1984), p. 176.

38. Sylvia Beeler, "First Episcopal priest to serve the Platte Valley," *The Snake River Press*, November 27, 1985, p. 3.

39. Laura C. Heath, " 'Liar' Founded Lyre," *The Rawlins Daily Times*, April 4, 1952, p. 7.

40. Ibid.

41. Alcorn, *Tough Country*, p. 186.

42. Heath, " 'Liar' Founded Lyre."

43. Ibid.

44. "The Forty-fourth State," *Platte Valley Lyre*, July 10, 1890, p. 4.

45. "Death of Alfred Heath," *The Saratoga Sun*, August 27, 1903, p. 1.

46. Cora M. Beach, *Women of Wyoming* (Casper: S. E. Boyer, 1927), vol. II, p. 264; and "Mrs. Laura Heath Dies Here at 76; Services Wednesday," *The Daily Times* (Rawlins), October 16, 1962, pp. 1, 16. The *Times* seems to have miscalculated Laura's age at the time of her death. She must have been 94, not 76.

47. Beach, *Women of Wyoming*, vol. II, p. 262; and "Mrs. Gertrude Merrell Died Tuesday Morning," *The Rawlins Republican*, February 19, 1925, p. 1.

48. "Mrs. Gertrude Merrell Died Tuesday Morning," ibid.

49. North, *History of the Press*, p. 165.

Chapter 4: Causes Great and Small

1. Quoted in Mott, *History of Magazines*, vol. II, pp. 206–7.

2. Quoted in ibid., p. 209.

3. "The Mormon Female," *Woman's Exponent*, February 1, 1879, p. 187.

4. "Death Closes Active Career," *The Salt Lake Tribune*, February 8, 1930, p. 26.

5. Jennie Anderson Froiseth, ed., *The Women of Mormonism; or The Story of Polygamy as Told by the Victims Themselves* (Detroit: C. G. G. Paine, 1886).

6. Untitled note, "Salutatory," and "Our Policy," *Anti-Polygamy Standard*, April 1880, pp. 1, 4.

7. "How Wives are Coerced into Giving Consent for their Husbands to Enter Polygamy," *Anti-Polygamy Standard*, April 1880, p. 2; "A Letter From an Old Mormon Lady," May 1880, p. 11; "The Wail of a Mormon Wife," July 1880, p. 25. James B. Allen and Glen M. Leonard, in *The Story of the Latter-day Saints* (Salt Lake City: Deseret Book Co., 1976), p. 354, describe the dilemma presented by the Ann Eliza Young case.

8. Untitled editorial, *Anti-Polygamy Standard*, February and March 1883, p. 85.

9. Carl I. Wheat, *Mapping the Transmississippi West* (San Francisco: The Institute of Historical Cartography, 1963), vol. V, footnote, p. 279.

10. "Bronze Plaque Pays Honor to Originator of Proposal for Sarah Daft Home," *The Salt Lake Telegram*, November 21, 1935, p. 8.

11. Mott, *History of Magazines*, vol. III, p. 309.

12. Willard and Livermore, *American Women*, vol. I, pp. 131–32.

13. Dorcas James Spencer, *A History of the Woman's Christian Temperance Union of Northern and Central California* (Oakland: West Coast Printing Company, 1913), p. 23.

14. Washington Gladden, "The Only Way to Become a Capitalist," "Light Wines of France and the Country Women," and untitled filler, *The Pharos*, November 1889, p. 1.

15. "Report of 'Pharos' Committee," ibid., p. 8.

16. "The Editor En Route to the East," ibid., p. 7.

17. Willard and Livermore, *American Women*, vol. I, p. 132.

18. Lauren Kessler, *The Dissident Press* (Beverly Hills: Sage Publications, 1984), p. 48.

19. Charles LeWarne, *Utopias on Puget Sound 1885–1915* (Seattle: University of Washington Press, 1975).

20. Orange Jacobs, *Memoirs* (Seattle: Lowman & Hanford Co., 1908), pp. 225–27, quoted in Barbara Cloud, "Laura Hall Peters: At the Heart of 19th Century Washington Radicalism," unpublished paper, 1978, p. 4.

21. Cloud, "Laura Hall Peters," p. 6.

22. *Seattle Post-Intelligencer*, February 10, 1887, quoted in ibid., p. 9.

23. Susan B. Anthony and Ida Husted Harper, eds., *The History of Woman Suffrage* (Indianapolis: The Hollenbeck Press, 1902), vol. IV, p. 972.

24. Barbara Cloud, "Cooperation and Printer's Ink," *Rendezvous, Idaho State University Journal of Arts and Letters*, vol. 19, no. 1 (Fall 1983), pp. 37–38.

25. *The Model Commonwealth*, November 19, 1886, quoted in ibid., p. 37.

26. "Valedictory," *The Model Commonwealth*, October 7, 1887, p. 4.

27. *Seattle Post-Intelligencer*, August 15, 1896, quoted in Cloud, "Laura Hall Peters," pp. 18–19.

28. Typescript of obituary, probably from *The Port Angeles Times*, January 19, 1902.

Chapter 5: The Suffragists

1. Elizabeth Cady Stanton, Susan B. Anthony, and Matilda Joslyn Gage, eds., *History of Woman Suffrage* (1886; New York: Arno and *The New York Times*, 1969), vol. III, p. 769.

2. Kessler, *The Dissident Press*, p. 16.

3. "Salutatory," *Sunday Mercury*, January 24, 1869, p. 2.

4. "Our Cause and Ourselves," *The Pioneer*, October 15, 1870, p. 1.

5. "Various Notes," *San Francisco Chronicle*, May 29, 1872, p. 2. While Pitts-Stevens hyphenated her name when she used it in her paper, other sources sometimes omitted the hyphen. In another variation, some used Pitt rather than Pitts.

6. "Woman Suffrage," ibid., January 30, 1870, p. 5.

7. "WHAT A PITY," *The Pioneer*, February 12, 1870, p. 2.

8. "A Blow in the Dark," ibid., June 4, 1870, p. 1; and "Our Cause and Ourselves," October 15, 1870, p. 1.

9. "A Nest of Free Lovers," *San Francisco Chronicle*, June 2, 1872, p. 1.

10. "Cluck, Cluck, Cluck," ibid., June 19, 1872, p. 3.

11. "The Overskirt War," ibid., April 11, 1873, p. 3.

12. "The Suffrage Revolt," ibid., April 27, 1873, p. 5.

13. "To The Public," *The Pioneer*, May 8, 1873, p. 2.

14. "A Wolf in the Fold," *San Francisco Chronicle*, April 10, 1873, p. 3.

15. Willard and Livermore, *American Women*, vol. II, p. 686.

16. "Convention Proceedings," *The Pioneer*, June 27, 1872, p. 8.

17. "A Day with our Colleague," ibid., January 5, 1871, p. 1.

18. Willard and Livermore, *American Women*, vol. II, p. 686.

19. Untitled note, *The Queen Bee*, June 6, 1883, p. 1.

20. Reda Davis, *California Women* (San Francisco: California Scene, 1967), p. 176.

21. "M. E. Church," *Carson Daily Morning News*, May 15, 1892, p. 3.

22. Davis, *California Women*, p. 176.

23. "Record of a Year's Work," *The New Northwest*, December 16, 1886, p. 1.

24. "Feminine Men and Masculine Women," ibid., May 15, 1871, p. 2.

25. Abigail Scott Duniway, *Pathbreaking: An Autobiographical History of the Equal Suffrage Movement in the Pacific Coast States* (Portland: James, Kearns & Abbott Co., 1914), p. 62.

26. Ida Husted Harper, ed., *The History of Woman Suffrage* (New York: National American Woman Suffrage Association, 1922), vol. VI, p. 545.

27. Gayle R. Bandow, "'In Pursuit of a Purpose:' Abigail Scott Duniway and the *New Northwest*," M.A. thesis, University of Oregon, 1973, p. 11.

28. "Our Paper and Ourselves," *The Pioneer*, September 13, 1869, p. 1.

29. Harper, *History of Suffrage*, vol. VI, p. 11.

30. Harper, ibid., p. 677.

31. Announcement, *The Western Woman Voter*, January 1911, p. 6.

32. Harper, *History of Suffrage*, vol. VI, p. 366.

33. Aileen S. Kraditor, *The Ideas of the Woman Suffrage Movement, 1890–1920* (New York: Columbia University Press, 1965), p. viii.

34. Ronald Schaffer, "The Problem of Consciousness in the Woman Suffrage Movement: A California Perspective," *Pacific Historical Review*, vol. XLV (1976), pp. 469–93.

35. "Woman's State Suffrage Association," *Saturday Evening Mercury*, August 14, 1869, p. 1.

36. "The Same One," *Western Woman*, July 11, 1907, p. 5.

37. Quoted in Helen Krebs Smith, *The Presumptuous Dreamers* (Lake Oswego, Oregon: Smith, Smith and Smith Publishing Company, 1974), vol. I, p. xiv.

Chapter 6: For the Sake of Religion

1. Letter to her sister, Lissie, March 21, 1874, copy in Library-Archives, Historical Department, The Church of Jesus Christ of Latter-day Saints, Salt Lake City (hereafter referred to as L.D.S. Library-Archives).

2. Leonard Bacon in *Biblical Repository*, January 1840, quoted in Mott, *History of Magazines*, vol. I, p. 370.

3. Mott, ibid., vol. I, p. 370; vol. IV, p. 290.

4. This idea is explored at length in Ann Braude, *Radical Spirits: Spiritualism and Women's Rights in Nineteenth-Century America* (Boston: Beacon Press, 1989).

5. Letter to Rhoda Bullock, March 13, 1874, L.D.S. Library-Archives.

6. "Smithfield Sunday School Gazette," October 31, 1869, unpaged, L.D.S. Library-Archives.

7. Thomas C. Romney, "Louisa Lula Greene Richards," *The Instructor*, September 1950, p. 262.

8. Letter to Zina S. Whitney, January 20, 1893, L.D.S. Library-Archives.

9. Advertisement, *The Salt Lake Daily Herald*, April 9, 1872, p. 3.

10. Untitled note, *Woman's Exponent*, July 15, 1872, p. 29.

11. "Education of Women," ibid., April 1, 1873, p. 163.

12. "News and Views" and "Household Hints," ibid., July 1, 1872, pp. 17 and 19.

13. Letter to Brigham Young, June 16, 1877, L.D.S. Library-Archives.

14. "Valedictory," *Woman's Exponent*, August 1, 1877, p. 36.

15. "A Queer Conference Visitor," *The Juvenile Instructor*, May 1, 1904, pp. 280–81.

16. Letter to Joseph F. Smith, November 25, 1907, L.D.S. Library-Archives.

17. Letter to Lula Greene Richards, November 30, 1907, L.D.S. Library-Archives.

18. Lula Green Richards, *Branches That Run Over the Wall* (Salt Lake City: The Magazine Printing Co., 1904), p. v.

19. Susa Young Gates, "The Woman's Exponent," undated typescript, L.D.S. Library-Archives, p. 1.

20. She seemed to prefer the hyphenated last name, although sometimes the hyphen was omitted, even in her own magazine.

21. "Newspaper Extracts," *The True Life*, August 1905, p. 626, quoting the San Jose *News*.

22. Eugene T. Sawyer, *History of Santa Clara County* (Los Angeles: Historic Record Company, 1922), p. 334.

23. Ibid.

24. Ibid.

25. Mary Hayes-Chynoweth, "Personal Experiences," *The True Life*, December 1906, pp. 360–64.

26. Ellen Chynoweth Lyon, "A Tribute of Love to Mary Hayes Chynoweth," ibid., August 1905, p. 612.

27. E. A. Hayes, "Some Recollections of Mary Hayes-Chynoweth's Life and Work," ibid., May 1, 1891, p. 296.

28. "In Memoriam," ibid., March 15, 1891, p. 210.

29. "Questions and Answers," ibid., August 1902, pp. 254–55.

30. "Questions and Answers," ibid., March 1903, p. 481.

31. "A Talk to Patients," ibid., p. 479.
32. Untitled note, ibid., p. 478.
33. "Secretary's Report," ibid., December 1903, p. 741.
34. Sawyer, *History of Santa Clara County*, p. 338.

Chapter 7: The Queen Bee and Other Characters

1. Caroline Nichols Churchill, *Active Footsteps* (Colorado Springs: Mrs. C. N. Churchill, 1909), p. 81.
2. The 1880 census listed her as Catherine Churchill, and she sometimes referred to herself as Catherine in *The Queen Bee*, but never in her biographical writings. The census listed New York as her birthplace and an age—43—that would have made 1837 the year of her birth.
3. "A Trip on the St. Paul, Minneapolis & Manitoba Railway," *The Queen Bee*, November 7, 1888, p. 1.
4. "Funeral Services for Mrs. Churchill Sat.," *Colorado Springs Gazette*, January 15, 1926, p. 5.
5. Untitled note, *The Queen Bee*, August 13, 1884, p. 1.
6. "The Twelfth Year," ibid., June 18, 1890, p. 1.
7. Caroline N. Churchill, *Over the Purple Hills* (Chicago: Hazlitt & Reed, 1877), pp. 253–56.
8. Churchill, *Active Footsteps*, pp. 252–53.
9. Ibid., pp. 146–47.
10. Untitled note, *The Colorado Antelope*, November 1879, p. 2.
11. Untitled editorial, ibid., October 1879, p. 2.
12. "Advantages Which the Antelope Has Over Other Papers," ibid., January 1880, p. 4.
13. Untitled note, *The Queen Bee*, August 31, 1887, p. 1.
14. "The Way the Future Historian will write up Leadville," *The Colorado Antelope*, October 1879, p. 1.
15. Ibid., December 1879, p. 2.
16. "Editorial," ibid., February 1880, p. 4.
17. "What our Editor Encounters in Selling the Antelope," ibid., December 1879, p. 4.
18. Untitled note, *The Queen Bee*, August 1, 1894, p. 1.
19. Billie Barnes Jensen, "The Woman Suffrage Movement in Colorado," M.A. thesis, University of Colorado, 1959, p. 62.
20. Churchill, *Active Footsteps*, pp. 213–14.
21. Untitled note, *The Queen Bee*, May 19, 1886, p. 1.
22. Untitled note, ibid., October 18, 1882, p. 1.
23. Untitled note, ibid., May 2, 1883, p. 1.
24. Untitled notes, ibid., February 21, 1883.
25. "What Our Editor Encounters," *The Colorado Antelope*, August 1881, p. 69.
26. Churchill, *Active Footsteps*, pp. 100–101.
27. Untitled note, *The Queen Bee*, July 2, 1884, p. 1.
28. Untitled note, ibid., March 22, 1893, p. 1.
29. "Equal Suffrage," ibid., November 15, 1893, p. 1.

30. Untitled note, ibid., December 13, 1893.
31. Untitled note, ibid., December 20, 1893, p. 1.
32. Untitled note, ibid., August 7, 1895, p. 1.
33. Churchill, *Active Footsteps*, p. 3.
34. Ibid., p. 5.
35. Ibid., pp. 23–25.
36. "Caroline Churchill Dies at Age of 93," *The Rocky Mountain News*, January 15, 1926, p. 7.
37. R. Dean Galloway, "Rowena Granice," *The Pacific Historian*, vol. 24, no. 1 (Spring 1980), pp. 105–6.
38. *History of Merced County, California* (San Francisco: Elliott & Moore, 1881), p. 119.
39. "Union Theatre," *Daily Alta California*, April 8, 1856, p. 2.
40. T. S. Kenderdine, *A California Tramp and Later Footprints* (Newtown, Pa.: Globe Printing House, 1888), pp. 273–74.
41. "Singular Theatrical Marriage," *Daily Alta California*, March 15, 1858, p. 1.
42. "The Gaieties," ibid., August 11, 1859, p. 2.
43. The editorial matter of first number of the *Banner* is reproduced in the *History of Merced County*, pp. 123–30.
44. Ibid., p. 162.
45. "A Tragedy at Merced," *Daily Alta California*, December 8, 1874, p. 1.
46. Galloway, "Rowena Granice," pp. 119–20.
47. "A Happy New Year to All," *San Joaquin Valley Argus*, January 1, 1881, p. 2.
48. "The Girls of Merced," ibid., November 15, 1879, p. 4.
49. Willard and Livermore, *American Women*, vol. II, p. 683.
50. *History of Merced County*, p. 119.
51. "Death Claims Mrs. Stow," *San Francisco Chronicle*, December 30, 1902, p. 5.
52. "Marietta L. Stow," *Frolic*, February 1890, pp. 8–9.
53. "Funeral of the Founder of the Birdie Bell Republic," *Oakland Times*, December 29, 1902, p. 1.
54. Newspaper clippings in the Marietta Stow scrapbook, University of San Francisco Special Collections, provide details about the lecture tours.
55. "Second President of the California Woman Suffrage Association," *Woman's Herald of Industry*, January 1882, p. 5; and Reda Davis, *Woman's Republic* (Pt. Pinos Editions, 1980), pp. 164–66.
56. "Mrs. Stow's Trinity of Calamities," *Woman's Herald of Industry*, September 1881, p. 1.
57. Advertisement, ibid., September 1881, p. 7.
58. "Mrs. J. W. Stow's Circular," dated San Francisco, January 7, 1877.
59. "The Stow Bill" was included as an appendix in *Probate Chaff* (San Francisco: Published by the author, 1879), pp. 287–88.
60. "Objects of the Association," *Woman's Herald of Industry*, September 1881, p. 1.
61. "Mrs. J. W. Stow," ibid., July 1882, p. 1.
62. "Mrs. Stow's Ambition," *San Francisco Chronicle*, July 4, 1882, p. 4.
63. "Troublous Times," *Daily Alta California*, October 26, 1884, p. 4.
64. "Comments of the Press," *Woman's Herald of Industry*, September 1882, p. 4.

65. Belva A. Lockwood, "Women Rulers," ibid., October 1884, p. 4.

66. "Woman's Presidential Campaign," ibid., November 1884, p. 1.

67. This and other comments on the campaign are quoted in Davis, *Woman's Republic*, pp. 173–87.

68. "Notes from Washington," *The New York Times*, January 13, 1885, p. 3.

69. Masthead note, *Frolic*, February 1890, p. 1.

70. "Editorial," ibid., May 1889, p. 13.

71. "Turned Sixty," ibid., February 1890, p. 8.

72. Untitled note, ibid., p. 1.

73. "Good-Bye!" ibid., p. 7.

74. "Funeral of the Founder of the Birdie Bell Republic," *Oakland Times*.

Chapter 8: Doctors and Editors

1. "Woman's Pacific Coast Journal," *Woman's Pacific Coast Journal*, March 1871, p. 176.

2. John S. Haller, Jr., *American Medicine in Transition, 1840–1910* (Urbana: University of Illinois Press, 1981), p. 100.

3. James Bordley III and A. McGehee Harvey, *Two Centuries of American Medicine, 1776–1976* (Philadelphia: W. B. Saunders Co., 1976), p. 187.

4. Mott, *History of Magazines*, vol. I, p. 440.

5. Ibid., vol. IV, pp. 312–13. Mott quotes Morris Fishbein, *A History of the American Medical Association*.

6. "Salutation," *Woman's Pacific Coast Journal*, May 1870, p. 8.

7. Letter, ibid., October 1870, p. 88.

8. "Mrs. Young in Oregon," ibid., September 1871, p. 75.

9. Untitled note, ibid., May 1870, pp. 3, 7; and "How the Junior Class All Signed the Pledge," June 1870, p. 20.

10. Untitled note, ibid., May 1870, p. 14.

11. "Answer to Correspondents," ibid., May 1871, p. 8.

12. "From Idaho to California," ibid., June 1870, p. 23.

13. "From Idaho to California," ibid., March 1871, p. 172.

14. Untitled note, ibid., December 1870, p. 125; and "Professional Courtesy," November 1870, p. 106.

15. "Personal," ibid., February 1871, p. 152.

16. "Fashionable Women," ibid., January 1871, p. 134.

17. "Letters to Irena," ibid., p. 141.

18. "The Nicasio Water-Cure," advertisement, ibid., August 1872, p. 115.

19. Harriet N. Austin, M.D., "Baths and How to Take Them," ibid., September 1872, p. 131.

20. "Personal," ibid., p. 136.

21. "Dr. Carrie Young, Early Advocate of Suffrage, Is Dead," *San Francisco Call*, November 4, 1911, p. 13.

22. Arthur Meier Schlesinger, *The Rise of the City, 1878–1898* (New York: Macmillan, 1933), p. 246.

23. Ellis R. Shipp, *The Early Autobiography and Diary of Ellis Reynolds Shipp, M.D.* (Salt Lake City: Deseret News Press, 1962), pp. 30, 292.

24. Bardella Shipp Curtis, "Dr. Milford Bard Shipp, Highlights," typescript in Ellis Reynolds Shipp Collection, Utah State Historical Society, p. 3.

25. "Introduction," *Salt Lake Sanitarian*, April 1888, p. 14.

26. "Physical Training in Women," ibid., June 1888, p. 60.

27. "A Scientific Attack on the Corset," ibid., April 1889, pp. 12–14.

28. "Our First Year's Work," ibid., p. 17.

29. "Editorial," ibid., October 1890, p. 14.

30. Gail Farr Casterline, "Ellis R. Shipp," in Vicky Burgess-Olson, ed., *Sister Saints* (Provo, Utah: Brigham Young University Press, 1978), p. 374.

31. "Our First Year's Work," *Salt Lake Sanitarian*, April 1889, p. 18.

32. Casterline, "Ellis R. Shipp," p. 376.

Chapter 9: Literary Ladies

1. Charles S. Greene, "Memories of an Editor," *The Overland Monthly*, September 1902, p. 268.

2. *The New-York Mirror*, March 1830, quoted in Mott, *History of Magazines*, vol. I, p. 354.

3. Mott, ibid., vol. II, pp. 113–14.

4. Caroline Ticknor, *Hawthorne and His Publisher* (Boston, 1913), p. 141, quoted in Mott, ibid., vol. II, p. 173.

5. Quoted in Grant Teasdale Skelley, "The *Overland Monthly* under Milicent Washburn Shinn, 1883–1894: A Study in Regional Publishing," Ph.D. dissertation, University of California, Berkeley, 1968, p. 19.

6. Charles S. Greene, "Magazine Publishing in California," *Publications of Library Association of California*, no. 2 (May 1898), p. 7.

7. Ibid., pp. 17, 18.

8. *The Golden Era*, March 10, 1883, p. 8, quoted in ibid., p. 25.

9. *The Argonaut*, March 25, 1877, quoted in Mott, *History of Magazines*, vol. III, p. 57.

10. Skelley, "The *Overland Monthly*," pp. 22, 62, 63.

11. "Current Comment," *The Overland Monthly*, January 1883, p. 97.

12. Mott, *History of Magazines*, vol. IV, p. 105.

13. Skelley, "The *Overland Monthly*," pp. 334–35.

14. Ella Sterling Cummins Mighels, *The Story of the Files* (San Francisco: World's Fair Commission of California, 1893), pp. 269–70.

15. "Five Years of Fiction and Verse," *The Overland Monthly*, December 1887, p. 663.

16. "Native Daughters of the West," *The Golden Era*, November 1885, p. 420, quoted in Skelley, "The *Overland Monthly*," p. 289.

17. Skelley, "The *Overland Monthly*," p. 111.

18. Milicent W. Shinn, "Mrs. Johnson," *The Overland Monthly*, February 1882, pp. 123–28; "Women as School-Directors," December 1886, pp. 628–33; "Poverty and Charity in San Francisco," November and December 1889, pp. 535–47 and 586–92.

19. Quoted in Skelley, "The *Overland Monthly*," p. 12.

20. "Etc.," *The Overland Monthly*, January 1884, p. 104.

21. "'A Fifth Shall Close the Drama with the Day,'" ibid., June 1890, p. 629.

22. Edgar J. Hinkel and William E. McCann, *Biographies of California Authors and Indexes of California Literature* (Oakland: The Alameda County Library, 1942), vol. I, p. 195.

23. Ibid., p. 272.

24. Mighels, *The Story of the Files*, p. 281, and "Her Pen Is Stilled," *Overland Monthly and Out West Magazine*, May 1924, p. 206.

25. Morris Wagner, "Harr Wagner: Biographical Notes," *The Western Journal of Education*, October 1936, p. 5.

26. Carrie Stevens Walter, "Madge Morris Wagner," *The Santa Clara*, July 1893, p. 23.

27. Greene, "Magazine Publishing in California," pp. 6–7.

28. J. Macdonough Foard, quoted in Doris Bepler, "History of California Periodicals to about 1880," *The Grizzly Bear*, March 1918, p. 10.

29. Madge Morris Wagner, "Liberty's Bell," *The Santa Clara*, July 1893, p. 21.

30. "Madge Morris Wagner," *The Morning Call*, September 20, 1893, p. 4.

31. Quoted in Frona Eunice Wait Colburn, "A California Poetess—As I Knew Her," *Overland Monthly and Out West Magazine*, May 1924, p. 205.

32. "Pen Is Stilled," *San Francisco Chronicle*, February 29, 1924, p. 4.

33. Colburn, "A California Poetess."

34. "Pen Is Stilled," *San Francisco Chronicle*.

Chapter 10: A Miscellany

1. "Salutatory," *Carson Daily Morning News*, May 15, 1892, p. 2.

2. Hubert Howe Bancroft, in *History of Washington, Idaho, and Montana, 1845–1889*, vol. XXXI of *The Works of Hubert Howe Bancroft*, p. 379, wrote that the railroad owned the paper. Barbara Lee Cloud quoted Charles Prosch to the effect that the property was heavily mortgaged to the railroad in her Ph.D. dissertation, "Start the Presses: The Birth of Journalism in Washington Territory," School of Communications, University of Washington, 1979, chap. 4, p. 4.

3. "To Our Patrons," *Kalama Semi-weekly Beacon*, May 19, 1871, p. 1.

4. "Ourselves," ibid., May 19, 1871, p. 1.

5. Ibid. The quotation that included this compliment, reprinted from the *Herald* of Grand Haven, Michigan, concluded, "We congratulate our friend Money on having such a newspaper and such a wife."

6. Herbert Hunt, *Tacoma, Its History and Its Builders* (Chicago: The S. J. Clarke Publishing Company, 1916), pp. 242–43.

7. Ibid., p. 242.

8. Unless otherwise noted, biographical information about Legh Freeman and his wives is taken from Thomas H. Heuterman, *Movable Type, Biography of Legh R. Freeman* (Ames: The Iowa State University Press, 1979).

9. "City Jottings," *The Salt Lake Tribune*, July 24, 1875, p. 4.

10. Quoted in Heuterman, *Movable Type*, p. 63.

11. Quoted in ibid., p. 82.

12. Ibid., p. 111.

13. Ibid., p. 133.

192 / Notes to Pages 137–147

14. Ibid., pp. 133–34.

15. C. Louise Boehringer, "Josephine Brawley Hughes—Crusader, State Builder," *Arizona Historical Review*, vol. 2, no. 4 (January 1930), pp. 98–99.

16. Information about Hughes was obtained, unless otherwise noted, from Boehringer, ibid., and from an unpublished paper, dated 1979, by Robert E. Lance, "First Lady of Arizona Journalism."

17. "Star Fought Against Gambling and Saloons Even in Wildest Frontier Days, Thanks to Mrs. L. C. Hughes," *Arizona Daily Star*, June 14, 1925, quoted in Lance, "First Lady."

18. "It Must Not Be a Democrat," *Arizona Daily Star*, February 16, 1895, p. 2.

19. "Our Associate Editor," *The New Northwest*, May 22, 1874, p. 2.

20. "A Forenoon with Contributors," ibid., September 7, 1877, p. 2.

21. Mary Osborn Douthit, ed., *The Souvenir of Western Women* (Portland: Anderson and Duniway Co., 1905), p. 173.

22. George S. Turnbull, *History of Oregon Newspapers* (Portland: Binfords & Mort, 1939), pp. 179–80.

23. "Mrs. C. A. Coburn Is Dead at 73 Years," *The Morning Oregonian*, May 28, 1913, p. 4.

24. Fred Lockley, "The Oregon Country in Early Days," *Oregon Journal*, January 11, 1915, p. 6.

25. Willard and Livermore, *American Women*, vol. II, p. 491.

26. Lockley, "The Oregon Country."

27. Willard and Livermore, *American Women*, vol. II, p. 491.

28. "Mrs. Mallory Is Dead," *The Oregonian*, September 4, 1920, p. 9.

29. "Mrs. Mallory Is Injured in Wreck," *Oregon Daily Journal*, April 7, 1919, p. 1.

30. "Essential Principles," *The World's Advance-Thought* and *The Universal Republic*, July 1892, p. 145.

31. "The Fourth Anniversary," ibid., part xi, 1890, p. 163.

32. Willard and Livermore, *American Women*, vol. II, p. 491.

33. "Mrs. L. A. Mallory Is Struck by Train," *The Morning Oregonian*, April 8, 1919, p. 6.

34. "Death Takes Annie Martin," *Nevada State Journal*, February 21, 1928.

35. "Valedictory" and "Salutatory," *Carson Daily Morning News*, May 15, 1892, p. 2.

36. "No Longer a New(s) Woman," ibid., October 31, 1895, p. 2.

37. "Once for All," ibid., June 10, 1892, p. 3.

38. "Amende Honorable," ibid., March 1, 1894, p. 2.

39. "Jottings," ibid., July 22, 1893, p. 3.

40. "Woman Suffrage," ibid., July 29, 1894, p. 3.

41. "Why This Fuss?" ibid., March 10, 1893, p. 2.

42. "The New Woman in Nevada," ibid., September 8, 1895, p. 3.

43. "Good Words from the East," ibid., March 24, 1893, p. 3.

44. "Miss Annie H. Martin, Beloved Resident of Carson, Passes Away," *The Carson City News*, February 21, 1928, p. 1; and "Annie Martin Laid at Rest," *Nevada State Journal*, February 23, 1928, p. 3.

45. The middle name is sometimes spelled Espy, sometimes Espe. *The Tourney* used Espy.

46. "The Tourney," *The Tourney*, March 1894, p. 2.

47. Maude Bell, "Women's Brains," *The Colorado Woman*, March 1895, pp. 193–94. This article typified opinion in the magazine under both names, *The Tourney* and *The Colorado Woman*.

48. "Announcement," *The Colorado Woman*, January 1895, p. 2.

49. "The World's Illness," ibid., February 1895, p. 92.

50. James E. Hansen II, *Democracy's College in the Centennial State* (Fort Collins: Colorado State University, 1977), p. 113.

51. Marvin Puakea Nogelmeier, *The Biography of Joseph K. Nawahi* (Honolulu: The Hawaiian Historical Society, 1988), p. vi. This work is a translation of J. G. M. Sheldon, *Ka Buke Moolelo O Hon. Joseph K. Nawahi* (Honolulu: E. L. Like and J. K. Prendergast, 1908).

52. George F. Nellist, ed., *Women of Hawaii* (Honolulu: E. A. Langston-Boyle, 1929), vol. I, p. 205.

53. Ibid.

54. Charlotte Perkins Gilman, *The Living of Charlotte Perkins Gilman* (New York: Arno Press, 1972, reprinted from 1935 edition), p. 111.

55. "Women in Literature," *The Morning Call*, March 15, 1891, p. 3.

56. Untitled note, *The Bulletin*, May 1894, p. 4.

57. "As Others See Us," *The Impress*, January 12, 1895, p. 15.

58. Gary Scharnhorst, *Charlotte Perkins Gilman* (Boston: Twayne Publishers, 1985), p. 58.

59. Gilman, *The Living*, p. 333.

60. "The Lincoln Independent," *The Lincoln Independent*, January 14, 1892, p. 2.

61. "Reply to the O.A.E.," *The Lincoln Republican*, August 5, 1892, p. 4.

Chapter 11: Group Portrait

1. "Women as Journalists," *The Queen Bee*, May 1, 1889, p. 1.

2. Statistics in this and the following paragraph are drawn from Jean Gaddy Wilson, "Women make up 13 percent of directing editors at dailies," *ASNE Bulletin*, January 1988, pp. 15, 16.

3. Patricia Nelson Limerick, *The Legacy of Conquest* (New York, London: W. W. Norton & Company, 1987), p. 323.

4. "Greeting," *The Idaho Recorder*, July 19, 1888, p. 2.

5. Richard E. Lingenfelter and Karen Rix Gash, *The Newspapers of Nevada* (Reno: University of Nevada Press, 1984).

6. Quoted in ibid., p. 156.

7. Quoted in ibid., p. 9.

8. "Dead," *Daily Appeal*, May 29, 1879, p. 2.

9. Lucy David Crowell, "One Hundred Years at Nevada's Capital," typed transcript of interview conducted by Mary Ellen Glass, University of Nevada, Reno, 1965, pp. 7–8.

10. Telephone interview with Henry R. Mighels, Nellie's grandson, April 27, 1989.

11. "Object," *The Nevada Citizen*, June 1897, p. 2.

12. Anthony and Harper, *History of Suffrage*, vol. IV, p. 811.

13. "The Old, Old Habit," *Eureka Weekly Sentinel*, April 24, 1897, p. 1.

14. Glenda Riley, *The Female Frontier* (Lawrence: University Press of Kansas, 1988), pp. 200–201.

15. "A Bright Girl," *Carson Daily Morning News*, March 3, 1893, p. 3.

Selected Bibliography

Directories

American Newspapers 1821–1936. New York: The H. W. Wilson Co., 1937.

Geo. P. Rowell & Co.'s American Newspaper Directory. New York: George P. Rowell & Co., 1869–1900.

N. W. Ayer & Son's American Newspaper Annual. Philadelphia: N. W. Ayer & Son, 1880–1900.

Newspapers in Microform, United States, 1948–1972. Washington, D.C.: Library of Congress, 1973.

Union List of Serials in Libraries of the United States and Canada. 3d ed. New York: The H. W. Wilson Co., 1965.

Bibliographies

Bepler, Doris West. "Descriptive Catalogue of Materials for Western History in California Magazines, 1854–1890." M.A. thesis, University of California, 1917.

Danky, James P., ed. *Women's Periodicals and Newspapers from the 18th Century to 1981: A Union List of the Holdings of Madison, Wisconsin Libraries.* Boston: G. K. Hall & Co., 1982.

Folkes, John Gregg. *Nevada's Newspapers: A Bibliography.* Reno: University of Nevada Press, 1964.

Lingenfelter, Richard E., and Karen Rix Gash. *The Newspapers of Nevada.* Reno: University of Nevada Press, 1984.

Mitchell, Marlene. "Washington Newspapers: Territorial and State." M.A. thesis, University of Washington, 1964.

Rex, Wallace Hayden. *Colorado Newspapers Bibliography, 1859–1935*. Denver: Center for Bibliographic Studies, 1939.

Stratton, Porter A. *The Territorial Press of New Mexico*. Albuquerque: University of New Mexico Press, 1969.

Journalism Histories

Alter, J. Cecil. *Early Utah Journalism*. Salt Lake City: Utah Historical Society, 1938.

Bancroft, Hubert Howe. *The Works of Hubert Howe Bancroft*. Vol. XXXVIII, *Essays and Miscellany*. San Francisco: The History Company, 1890.

Cloud, Barbara. "Establishing the Frontier Newspaper: A Study of Eight Western Territories." *Journalism Quarterly*, vol. 61, no. 4 (Winter 1984), pp. 805–11.

———. "Start the Presses: The Birth of Journalism in Washington Territory." Ph.D. dissertation, University of Washington, 1979.

Emery, Michael and Edwin. *The Press and America*. 6th ed. Englewood Cliffs, New Jersey: Prentice-Hall, Inc., 1988.

Giffen, Helen S. *California Mining Town Newspapers*. Van Nuys, California: Westernlore Press, 1954.

Halaas, David Fridtjof. *Boom Town Newspapers: Journalism on the Rocky Mountain Mining Frontier, 1859–1881*. Albuquerque: University of New Mexico Press, 1981.

Jordan, Myron K. "The Golden Age of the Press Revisited." Paper presented at West Coast Journalism Historians' Conference, March 1, 1987.

Karolevitz, Robert F. *Newspapering in the Old West*. New York: Bonanza Books, 1965.

Keen, Elizabeth. "Wyoming's Frontier Newspapers." M.A. thesis, University of Wyoming, 1956.

Kemble, Edward C. *A History of California Newspapers, 1846–1858*. Los Gatos, California: The Talisman Press, 1962. Reprinted from an 1858 supplement to the Sacramento *Union*, edited and with a foreword by Helen Harding Bretnor.

Kessler, Lauren. *The Dissident Press*. Beverly Hills, California: Sage Publications, 1984.

Lutrell, Estelle. *Newspapers and Periodicals of Arizona, 1859–1911*. Tucson: University of Arizona, 1949.

Mighels, Ella Sterling Cummins. *The Story of the Files*. San Francisco: World's Fair Commission of California, 1893.

Mookini, Esther K. *The Hawaiian Newspapers*. Honolulu: Topgallant Publishing Company, 1974.

Mott, Frank Luther. *A History of American Magazines*. 4 vols. Cambridge: Harvard University Press, 1957.
———. *American Journalism*. 3d ed. New York: Macmillan, 1962.
Myers, John Myers. *Print in a Wild Land*. Garden City, New York: Doubleday & Co., Inc., 1967.
North, S. N. D. *History and Present Condition of the Newspaper and Periodical Press of the United States*. Vol. 8 of Tenth Census, 1880. Washington, D.C.: Government Printing Office, 1884.
Schmitt, Jo Ann. *Fighting Editors*. San Antonio: The Naylor Co., 1958.
Turnbull, George S. *History of Oregon Newspapers*. Portland: Binfords & Mort, 1939.

Works on Women in the West

Anthony, Susan B., Ida Husted Harper, Elizabeth Cady Stanton, Matilda Joslyn Gage, eds. *The History of Woman Suffrage*. 6 vols. New York: Arno and *The New York Times*, 1969. Reprinted from earlier editions.
Armitage, Susan, and Elizabeth Jameson, eds. *The Women's West*. Norman and London: University of Oklahoma Press, 1987.
Brown, Dee. *The Gentle Tamers*. Lincoln: University of Nebraska Press, 1958.
Faragher, Johnny, and Christine Stansell. "Women and Their Families on the Overland Trail to California and Oregon." *Feminist Studies*, vol. 2, no. 2/3 (1975), pp. 150–56.
Fischer, Christiane, ed. *Let Them Speak for Themselves, Women in the American West, 1849–1900*. Hamden, Conn.: Archon Books, 1977.
Fowler, William W. *Woman on the American Frontier*. Hartford: S. C. Scranton & Co., 1876.
Fox-Genovese, Elizabeth. "Placing Women's History in History." *New Left Review*, no. 133 (May–June 1982).
Jeffrey, Julie Roy. *Frontier Women, The Trans-Mississippi West 1840–1880*. New York: Hill and Wang, 1979.
Jensen, Joan M., and Darlis A. Miller. "The Gentle Tamers Revisited: New Approaches to the History of Women in the American West." *Pacific Historical Review*, vol. XLIX, no. 2 (May 1980), pp. 173–213.
Kolodny, Annette. *The Land Before Her, Fantasy and Experience of the American Frontiers, 1630–1860*. Chapel Hill and London: The University of North Carolina Press, 1984.
Larson, T. A. "Dolls, Vassals, and Drudges—Pioneer Women in the West." *The Western Historical Quarterly*, vol. III, no. 1 (January 1972), pp. 5–16.

Luchetti, Cathy, in collaboration with Carol Olwell. *Women of the West*. St. George, Utah: Antelope Island Press, 1982.

Myres, Sandra L. *Westering Women and the Frontier Experience, 1800–1915*. Albuquerque: University of New Mexico Press, 1982.

Riley, Glenda. *The Female Frontier*. Lawrence: University Press of Kansas, 1988.

Schaffer, Ronald. "The Problem of Consciousness in the Woman Suffrage Movement: A California Perspective." *Pacific Historical Review*, vol. XLV (1976), pp. 469–93.

Schlissel, Lillian. *Women's Diaries of the Westward Journey*. New York: Schocken Books, 1982.

Sprague, William Forrest. *Women and the West*. New York: Arno Press, 1972. Originally published by The Christopher Publishing House, Boston, 1940.

Stratton, Joanna L. *Pioneer Women*. New York: Simon and Schuster, 1981.

Yamane, Nancy. "The Working Role of Women in the American West, 1880–1910." *Passports*, San Jose State University Studies in History, 1979.

Works with Biographical Information on Women Editors

Alcorn, Gay Day. *Tough Country, The History of the Saratoga and Encampment Valley, 1825–1895*. Saratoga, Wyoming: Legacy Press, 1984.

Bandow, Gayle R. "'In Pursuit of a Purpose:' Abigail Scott Duniway and the *New Northwest*." M.A. thesis, University of Oregon, 1973.

Beach, Cora M. *Women of Wyoming*, vol. II. Casper, Wyoming: S. E. Boyer, 1927.

Bennion, Sherilyn Cox. "Ada Chase Merritt and *The Recorder*: A Pioneer Idaho Editor and Her Newspaper." *Idaho Yesterdays*, vol. 25, no. 4 (Winter 1982), pp. 22–30.

———. "Enterprising Ladies: Utah's Nineteenth-Century Women Editors." *Utah Historical Quarterly*, vol. 49, no. 3 (Summer 1981), pp. 291–304.

———. "Lula Greene Richards: Utah's First Woman Editor." *Brigham Young University Studies*, vol. 21, no. 2 (Spring 1981), pp. 155–74.

———. "*The New Northwest* and *Woman's Exponent*: Early Voices for Suffrage." *Journalism Quarterly*, vol. 54, no. 2 (Summer 1977), pp. 286–92.

———. "*The Pioneer*: The First Voice for Women's Suffrage in the West." *The Pacific Historian*, vol. 25, no. 4 (Winter 1981), pp. 15–21.

———. "Woman Suffrage Papers of the West, 1869–1904." *American Journalism*, vol. III, no. 3 (1986), pp. 125–41.

———. "The *Woman's Exponent*: Forty-two Years of Speaking for Women." *Utah Historical Quarterly*, vol. 44, no. 3 (Summer 1976), pp. 222–39.

————. "Women Editors of California, 1854–1900." *The Pacific Historian*, vol. XXVIII, no. 3 (Fall 1984), pp. 30–43.

Bepler, Doris. "History of California Periodicals to about 1880." *The Grizzly Bear*, March 1918, pp. 10, 30–31.

Boehringer, C. Louise. "Josephine Brawley Hughes—Crusader, State Builder." *Arizona Historical Review*, vol. 2, no. 4 (January 1930), pp. 98–107.

Bruce, John. *Gaudy Century*. New York: Random House, 1948.

Casterline, Gail Farr. "Ellis R. Shipp." In *Sister Saints*, ed. Vicky Burgess-Olsen. Provo, Utah: Brigham Young University Press, 1978.

Cloud, Barbara. "Laura Hall Peters: At the Heart of 19th Century Washington Radicalism." Unpublished paper, 1978.

————. "Cooperation and Printer's Ink." *Rendezvous, Idaho State University Journal of Arts and Letters*, vol. 19, no. 1 (Fall 1983), pp. 33–42.

Cummins, Ella Sterling. "The Women Writers of California." In *The Congress of Women*, Mary Kavanaugh Oldham Eagle, vol. I. Chicago: W. B. Conkey Co., 1894.

Curtis, Bardella Shipp. "Dr. Milford Bard Shipp, Highlights." Typescript in Ellis Reynolds Shipp Collection, Utah State Historical Society.

Davis, Reda. *California Women*. San Francisco: California Scene, 1967.

————. *Woman's Republic*. Pt. Pinos Editions, 1980.

Day, Franklin Henry. *Autobiography*. San Francisco: Eastman & Co., 1903.

Douthit, Mary Osborn, ed. *The Souvenir of Western Women*. Portland: Anderson and Duniway Co., 1905.

Ferlinghetti, Lawrence, and Nancy J. Peters. *Literary San Francisco*. San Francisco: City Light Books and Harper and Row, 1980.

Galloway, R. Dean. "Rowena Granice." *The Pacific Historian*, vol. 24, no. 1 (Spring 1980), pp. 105–24.

Gates, Susa Young. "The Woman's Exponent." Undated typescript in Historical Department Archives, Church of Jesus Christ of Latter-day Saints, Salt Lake City, Utah.

Greene, Charles S. "Memories of an Editor." *The Overland Monthly*, September 1902.

————. "Magazine Publishing in California." *Publications of Library Association of California*, no. 2 (May 1898).

Hall, Frank. *History of the State of Colorado*, vol. 4. Chicago: Blakely Printing Co., 1895.

Hansen, James E., II. *Democracy's College in the Centennial State*. Fort Collins: Colorado State University, 1977.

Heuterman, Thomas H. *Movable Type, Biography of Legh R. Freeman*. Ames, Iowa: The Iowa State University Press, 1979.

Hill, Mary A. *Charlotte Perkins Gilman, The Making of a Radical Feminist, 1860–1896*. Philadelphia: Temple University Press, 1980.

Hinkel, Edgar J., and William E. McCann. *Biographies of California Authors and Indexes of California Literature*. Oakland, California: The Alameda County Library, 1942.

History of Merced County, California. San Francisco: Elliott & Moore, 1881.

Hunt, Herbert. *Tacoma, Its History and Its Builders*. Chicago: The S. J. Clarke Publishing Company, 1916.

Jacob, Nora Beale. "Biography of Maude Hulbert Horn, Editor of the *Georgetown* (California) *Gazette*, 1891–1924." M.A. thesis, California State University, Fullerton, 1980.

Jensen, Billie Barnes. "The Woman Suffrage Movement in Colorado." M.A. thesis, University of Colorado, 1959.

Kenderdine, T. S. *A California Tramp and Later Footprints*. Newtown, Pennsylvania: Globe Printing House, 1888.

Lance, Robert E. "First Lady of Arizona Journalism." Unpublished paper, 1979.

LeWarne, Charles. *Utopias on Puget Sound 1885–1915*. Seattle: University of Washington Press, 1975.

Mighels, Ella Sterling. "Her Pen Is Stilled." *Overland Monthly and Out West Magazine*, May 1924, p. 206. Additional articles on pp. 204 and 205.

Moynihan, Ruth Barnes. *Rebel for Rights*. New Haven, Connecticut: Yale University Press, 1983.

"Mrs. Agnes Leonard Hill." *The Journalist*, January 26, 1889, p. 11.

Nellist, George F., ed. *Women of Hawaii*, vol. I. Honolulu: E. A. Langston-Boyle, 1929.

Parsons, Eugene. "Colorado Literature." Chapter 42 in *History of Colorado*, Wilbur Fisk Stone, ed., vol. I. Chicago: The S. J. Clarke Publishing Co., 1918.

Romney, Thomas C. "Louisa Lula Greene Richards." *The Instructor*, September 1950, pp. 262–63.

Sawyer, Eugene T. *History of Santa Clara County*. Los Angeles: Historic Record Company, 1922.

Scharnhorst, Gary. *Charlotte Perkins Gilman*. Boston: Twayne Publishers, 1985.

———. "Making Her Fame, Charlotte Perkins Gilman in California." *California History*, vol. LXIV, no. 3 (Summer 1985), pp. 192–201.

Sheldon, J. G. M. *Ka Buke Moolelo O Hon. Joseph K. Nawahi*. Honolulu: E. L. Like and J. K. Prendergast, 1908. Translated into English by Marvin Puakea Nogelmeier as *The Biography of Hon. Joseph K. Nawahi*. Honolulu: The Hawaiian Historical Society, 1988.

Skelley, Grant Teasdale. "The *Overland Monthly* under Milicent Washburn Shinn, 1883–1894: A Study in Regional Publishing." Ph.D. dissertation, University of California, Berkeley, 1968.

Small, Daniel Edward. "Sam Davis of 'The Morning Appeal.'" M.A. thesis, University of Nevada, Reno, 1978.

Smith, Helen Krebs. *The Presumptuous Dreamers.* Lake Oswego, Oregon: Smith, Smith and Smith Publishing Company, 1974.

Spencer, Dorcas James. *A History of the Woman's Christian Temperance Union of Northern and Central California.* Oakland: West Coast Printing Company, 1913.

Tinling, Marion. "Hermione Day and the Hesperian." *California History,* vol. LIX, no. 4 (Winter 1980/81), pp. 282–89.

Wagner, Morris. "Harr Wagner: Biographical Notes." *The Western Journal of Education,* October 1936, pp. 3–6.

Walter, Carrie Stevens. "Madge Morris Wagner." *The Santa Clara,* July 1893, p. 23.

Willard, Frances E., and Mary A. Livermore, eds. *American Women.* New York: Mast, Crowell and Kirkpatrick, 1897.

Periodicals Edited by Women

Note: The list contains only publications examined in the course of research for this book. A more complete list appears in the appendix.

The Alki, Puyallup, Washington.
Anti-Polygamy Standard, Salt Lake City, Utah.
Arizona Daily Star, Tucson, Arizona.
The Bulletin/The Impress, San Francisco, California.
The Bulletin/The Pharos, Oakland, California.
Carson Daily Morning News, Carson City, Nevada.
The Colorado Antelope, Denver, Colorado.
The Contra Costa, Oakland, California.
Frolic, Oakland, California.
The Georgetown Gazette, Georgetown, California.
The Golden Era, San Francisco, California.
Golden Nine, San Pedro, New Mexico.
The Hesperian, San Francisco, California.
The Idaho Recorder, Salmon City, Idaho.
Kalama Semi-weekly Beacon, Kalama, Washington.
Ke Aloha Aina, Honolulu, Hawaii.
The Lincoln Independent, Lincoln, New Mexico.
The Model Commonwealth, Seattle and Port Angeles, Washington.
The Nevada Citizen, Reno, Nevada.
The Nevada Prohibitionist, Genoa, Nevada.

The New Mexico Interpreter, White Oaks, New Mexico.
The New Northwest, Portland, Oregon.
Ogden Freeman, Ogden, Utah.
The Overland Monthly, San Francisco, California.
The Pacific Monthly, San Francisco, California.
Platte Valley Lyre, Saratoga, Wyoming.
The Tourney/The Colorado Woman, Fort Collins and Denver, Colorado.
The Queen Bee, Denver, Colorado.
Salt Lake Sanitarian, Salt Lake City, Utah.
San Joaquin Valley Argus, Merced, California.
Saturday Evening Mercury/The Pioneer, San Francisco, California.
"Smithfield Sunday School Gazette," Smithfield, Utah.
The True Life, Eden Vale, California.
Weekly Bulletin of the Nevada Equal Franchise Society, Reno, Nevada.
The Western Woman Voter, Seattle, Washington.
White Pine Suffragist, Ely, Nevada.
Woman's Exponent, Salt Lake City, Utah.
Woman's Herald of Industry/National Equal Rights, San Francisco, California.
Woman's Pacific Coast Journal/Pacific Journal of Health, San Francisco, California.
The Woman's Tribune, Portland, Oregon.
The World's Advance-Thought and *The Universal Republic*, Portland, Oregon.
The Yellow Ribbon/Western Woman, San Francisco, California.
The Yerington Rustler, Yerington, Nevada.

Works by Women Editors

Note: The list contains only works examined in the course of research for this book. It is not a complete bibliography of works by the editors.

Churchill, Caroline Nichols. *Active Footsteps*. Colorado Springs, Colorado: Mrs. C. N. Churchill, 1909.
——— . *Little Sheaves*. San Francisco: Woman's Publishing Co., 1875.
——— . *Over the Purple Hills*. Chicago: Hazlitt & Reed, 1877.
Duniway, Abigail Scott. *Pathbreaking: An Autobiographical History of the Equal Suffrage Movement in the Pacific Coast States*. Portland: James, Kearns & Abbott Co., 1914.
Gilman, Charlotte Perkins. *The Living of Charlotte Perkins Gilman*. New York: Arno Press, 1972. Reprinted from 1935 edition.
Hill, Agnes Leonard. *The Colorado Blue Book*. Denver: James R. Ives & Co., 1892.

————. *Hints on How to Talk*. Chicago: R. R. Donnelley & Sons, 1891.

————. *"Said Confidentially."* Denver: The Smith-Brooks Printing Company, 1902.

————. "Social Questions." Denver: The Chain & Hardy Company, 1893.

Froiseth, Jennie Anderson, ed. *The Women of Mormonism; or The Story of Polygamy as Told by the Victims Themselves*. Detroit: C. G. G. Paine, 1886.

Richards, Lula Greene. *Branches That Run Over the Wall*. Salt Lake City, Utah: The Magazine Printing Company, 1904.

Shipp, Ellis R. *The Early Autobiography and Diary of Ellis Reynolds Shipp, M.D.* Salt Lake City, Utah: Deseret News Press, 1962.

Stow, Marietta L. B. *Probate Chaff*. San Francisco: Published by the author, 1879.

Newspapers

Note: Article citations may be found in endnotes.

The Carson City News, Carson City, Nevada.
Colorado Springs Gazette, Colorado Springs, Colorado.
Daily Alta California, San Francisco, California.
The Daily News, Denver, Colorado.
The Denver Daily Times, Denver, Colorado.
The Denver Republican, Denver, Colorado.
The Lemhi Herald, Salmon City, Idaho.
The Morning Oregonian, Portland, Oregon.
Nevada State Journal, Reno, Nevada.
The New York Times, New York City, New York.
Oakland Times, Oakland, California.
Oregon Daily Journal, Portland, Oregon.
The Oregonian, Portland, Oregon.
The Rawlins Daily Times, Rawlins, Wyoming.
The Rocky Mountain News, Denver, Colorado.
The Salt Lake Daily Herald, Salt Lake City, Utah.
The Salt Lake Telegram, Salt Lake City, Utah.
The Salt Lake Tribune, Salt Lake City, Utah.
San Francisco Call, San Francisco, California.
San Francisco Chronicle, San Francisco, California.
The Snake River Press, Baggs, Wyoming.

Additional Sources

Compendia and population reports from U.S. Census volumes for 1870, 1880, 1890, and 1900. Washington, D.C.: Government Printing Office and U. S. Census Office.

Crowell, Lucy David. "One Hundred Years at Nevada's Capital." Typescript of interview conducted by Mary Ellen Glass, University of Nevada, Reno, 1965.

Mighels, Henry R. Telephone interview, April 27, 1989.

Richards, Lula Greene. Letters, 1874–1907. In Historical Department Archives, The Church of Jesus Christ of Latter-day Saints, Salt Lake City, Utah.

Smith, Joseph F. Letter to Lula Greene Richards, November 30, 1907. In Historical Department Archives, The Church of Jesus Christ of Latter-day Saints, Salt Lake City, Utah.

Index

Underlined entries indicate that photographs are included in the photo section of this book.

Sloan, Edward L., 75
"Smithfield Sunday School Gazette," 74
Smith, George Venable, 51
Smyth, S. Gertrude, 101, 104
Snow, Eliza R., 75
Society, 24
Spark of Genius, 159
Specialized periodicals, 5–6. *See also Bug-Hunter*; *Indian Advance*; *Insurance Sun*; *Ladies' Mite*; *Music Life*; *Out of Doors for Women*; *Pacific Boys and Girls*; *Political Age*; *Revista Hispano-Americana*; *Spark of Genius*; *Washington Farmer*; *Western Society*
Specter of Grey Gulch, 24
Spiritualism, 43, 54, 73, 80, 144. *See also Carrier Dove*; *World's Advance-Thought and Universal Republic*
Sprecher, C. S., 128
Stanton, Elizabeth Cady, 57, 60, 102
Steele, Lee R., 97
Steele, Robert Johnson, 94–97
Steele, Rowena Granice, 93–97, 84, 105, 157
Stetson, Charles Walter, 150, 151
Stetson, Charlotte Perkins. *See* Gilman, Charlotte Perkins Stetson
Stevens, August K., 58, 61
Stone, Lucy, 57, 60, 66
Stow, Joseph W., 98, 99
Stow, Marietta Lizzie Beers, 84–85, 97, 98–105, 156, 157
Strong, J. D., 20
Strong, Mary L., 14
Suffrage. *See* Woman suffrage
Suffrage periodicals: characteristics, 57; difficulty of funding, 70; ideologies, 68–71; influence of, 70–71; number of, 6, 57. *See also Alki*; *Coming Century*; *Equal Rights Champion*; *Nevada Citizen*; *New Northwest*; *Pacific Empire*; *Pioneer*; *Queen Bee*; *Votes for Women*; *Weekly Bulletin of the Nevada Equal Franchise Society*; *White Pine Suffragist*; *Woman's Tribune*; *Yellow Ribbon*
Swisshelm, Jane Grey, 85

Temperance: editors' views on, 43, 46–49, 50, 61, 64, 88, 96, 101, 108, 109, 139, 163; number of periodicals, 6. *See also Nevada Prohibitionist*; *Pharos*; *Temperance Star*
Temperance Star, 4
Titled Plebian, 129

Tourney, 148
Train, George Francis, 59
True Life, 3, 81–83
True Life church, 82
Tucke, Mercie A., 73
Tucson Citizen, 139

Universal Republic. See World's Advance-Thought and Universal Republic
Utah Association for the Advancement of Women, 44

Vanquished, 22
Victims of Fate, 94
Village Mystery, 97
Votes for Women, 67–68

Wagner, Harr, 127–28
Wagner, Madge Hilyard Morris, 126–30, 131, 157
Walsen, George W., 32–33
Walter, Carrie Stevens, 126
Washington Farmer, 136–37
Weak or wicked?, 97
Weekes, Cora Anna, 17
Weekly Bulletin of the Nevada Equal Franchise Society, 68
Weekly Merced Herald, 95, 97
Weekly newspapers: conditions of founding and operating, 27; content, 28–29; edited by women, 5, 29; number of, 27; short lives of, 27. *See also Arizona Star*; *Durango Record*; *Georgetown Gazette*; *Golden Nine*; *Idaho Recorder*; *Kalama Beacon*; *Ke Aloha Aina*; *Lincoln Independent*; *Lodi Budget*; *Merced Banner*; *Mottsville Star*; *New Mexico Interpreter*; *North Pacific Times*; *Ogden Freeman*; *Piute Pioneer*; *Platte Valley Lyre*; *San Joaquin Valley Argus*; *Yerington Rustler*
Wells, Emmeline B., 4, 77, 157
West: defined, vii
Western Journal of Education, 128–29
Western Society, 4, 23
Western Woman. See Yellow Ribbon
Western Woman Voter, 68
White Pine Suffragist, 68
Why He Never Married, 97
Willard, Frances E., 158
Williamson, Frances A., 66, 161
Williamson, Mary Laura, 66, 161
Woman's Christian Temperance Union, 47, 48, 54, 61, 88, 139, 140, 158